REAL LIVES IN THE SIXTEENTH CENTURY

Real Lives in the Sixteenth Century presents a global history using four pairs of biographies to illustrate similar situations in different geographical regions. The vibrant narratives span four continents and include the following pairs: Henry IV of France and Hideyoshi of Japan, Hürrem Sultan (Roxelana) of the Ottoman Empire and Lady Zheng of the Ming dynasty, Afonso I of Kongo and Elizabeth I of England, and Pope Clement VII and Moctezuma II of Mexico.

Through exploring the lives of eight individuals from a variety of cultural settings, this book encourages students to think about the "big questions" surrounding human interactions and the dynamics of power. It introduces them to a number of key historical concepts such as feudalism, dynasticism, religious syncretism and slavery, and is a springboard into the history of the wider world, blending together aspects of political, cultural, intellectual and material history.

Accessibly written and containing timelines, genealogical tables and a number of illustrations for each biography, *Real Lives in the Sixteenth Century* is the ideal introductory text for undergraduates of pre-modern world history and of the sixteenth century in particular.

Rebecca Ard Boone is Professor of History at Lamar University, USA. Her previous publications include *War, Domination, and the Monarchy of France* (2007) and *Mercurino di Gattinara and the Creation of the Spanish Empire* (2014).

REAL LIVES IN THE SIXTEENTH CENTURY

A Global Perspective

Rebecca Ard Boone

LONDON AND NEW YORK

First published 2018
by Routledge
2 Park Square, Milton Park, Abingdon, Oxon OX14 4RN

and by Routledge
711 Third Avenue, New York, NY 10017

Routledge is an imprint of the Taylor & Francis Group, an informa business

© 2018 Rebecca Ard Boone

The right of Rebecca Ard Boone to be identified as author of this work has been asserted by her in accordance with sections 77 and 78 of the Copyright, Designs and Patents Act 1988.

British Library Cataloguing-in-Publication Data
A catalogue record for this book is available from the British Library

Library of Congress Cataloging-in-Publication Data
Names: Boone, Rebecca Ard, author.
Title: Real lives in the Sixteenth Century : a global perspective / Rebecca Ard Boone.
Description: First edition. | London ; New York, NY : Routledge/ Taylor & Francis Group, 2018. | Includes bibliographical references and index.
Identifiers: LCCN 2017048144 | Subjects: LCSH: Biography—16th century. | History, Modern—16th century.
Classification: LCC CT116 .B66 2018. | DDC 920.009/031—dc23
LC record available at https://lccn.loc.gov/2017048144

ISBN: 978-1-138-65638-3 (hbk)
ISBN: 978-1-138-65639-0 (pbk)
ISBN: 978-1-351-13535-1 (ebk)

Typeset in Bembo
by Apex CoVantage, LLC

Printed in the United Kingdom
by Henry Ling Limited

To Lucy and Helen Boone

CONTENTS

FIGURES

ACKNOWLEDGEMENTS

The wide expanse of global history covered in this book required research in a number of libraries. I would like to thank the staff of Schomburg Center for Research in Black Culture, New York Public Library, Columbia University Library, Biblioteca Nazionale Firenze, Biblioteca Medicea Laurenziana, Library of Congress, especially in the Hispanic Reading Room, and the Bibliothèque Nationale de Paris. For the past three years, I have also kept the interlibrary loan staff at Lamar University very busy, and I thank them for their help.

A number of individuals graciously looked over the manuscript and provided useful comments. Steven Zani, William Harn and Jim LaBove read the entire work and offered much support of this project. In the History Department at Lamar, Jimmy Bryan and Yasuko Sato devoted a great deal of time, energy, and expertise to the manuscript, and I especially thank Yasuko for her help with the Oda genealogy. I would also like to express gratitude to Gwinyai Muzorewa for his help on Afonso, Creighton Chandler and Miguel Chavez on Moctezuma, and Mark Mengerink and Jeff Forret for reading the early drafts of Chapters 1 and 4. Several Lamar students also provided input, including Adam Gorrell and John Rutherford, who provided helpful research. Two world history students, Alexandra Brooks and Paris Clark, read early drafts and gave useful suggestions. Ashley Thibodeaux read the entire manuscript and provided me with copious notes and observations from a student's perspective. I am also grateful to experts in many fields. Julie Landweber provided support on Hürrem, while Marcello Simonetta and Kenneth Gouwens provided plentiful and direly needed help on Clement VII. Kairn Klieman's insight was indispensable in configuring Afonso and Kongo.

I would also like to thank Patty Renfro in the history department at Lamar for an abundance of administrative help and support. Lamar University graciously provided me with a research grant and a developmental leave, which was essential to the project. To Eve Marie Rouillère and Rene Blank for providing lodging and support during the research stage of the book. Finally, I would like to thank my husband, Christopher Boone, for reading the whole manuscript many times over and supplying me with the best verbs anyone could ask for. My daughters, Lucy and Helen Boone, contributed to the project with their love and sound advice. This book is dedicated to them.

INTRODUCTION

Real Lives in the Sixteenth Century presents an introduction to world history using four pairs of biographies to illustrate similar situations in different geographical regions. Loosely based on Plutarch's *Parallel Lives*, the eight biographies focus on the consolidation of state power in the first global age. The vibrant narratives that span four continents include the following pairs: Henry IV of France and Hideyoshi of Japan, Hürrem Sultan (Roxelana) of the Ottoman Empire and Lady Zheng of the Ming dynasty, Afonso I of Kongo and Elizabeth I of England, and Pope Clement VII and Moctezuma II of Mexico. Using biography as a framework, the book provides an easy pathway for survey students to think about global cultures and key historical concepts such as feudalism, dynasticism, religious syncretism, and slavery in a variety of regions. This approach encourages students to tackle the 'big questions' relating to human interactions and the dynamics of power throughout the world.

Having enthralled generations for five hundred years, these stories have played an enormous role in the construction of national identities, and even today, the eight figures wield a great deal of symbolic power. A cursory glance on YouTube reveals them thriving as icons of contemporary popular culture, from Japanese video games to Turkish soap operas. *Real Lives in the Sixteenth Century* provides readers with a blend of recognizable and unfamiliar subjects as a comfortable starting point from which to explore world history.

To lead is human, and power, whether institutional or personal, contested or legitimate, religious or secular, provides the major theme of this book. What makes people obey? What makes people surrender to larger regimes? How do leaders persuade? In addition to providing concrete examples of effective (and ineffective) leadership, the book encourages the student to ask about what Fernand Braudel called the "limits of the possible." What was the potential sphere of action at a given place and time? What was imaginable within the confines of a particular historical moment? Are people in control of their own destiny?

Real Lives weaves elements of cultural, intellectual, and material history into the framework of a political narrative. It covers the cosmologies, philosophical traditions, and religious beliefs that underlay each society, while asking how cultural norms supported certain political actions and the extent to which political actors used ideologies as "instruments of empire." At the same time, the chapters introduce central key proverbs, metaphors, and cultural symbols, from the feather art of the Aztecs to the cherry blossoms of Japan. While providing the reader with a basic cultural literacy, this comparative approach to history also compels students to note distinguishing features among regional traditions and encourages them to think critically about the experiences, emotions, and ethical questions inherent in a shared humanity.

This introductory text is cogent and concise, intended to be relevant to the general student rather than those who plan to continue in the field of history. The simple prose is accessible for first generation university students and advanced high school students who have no prior knowledge of the covered regions and eras. Containing dramatic elements that appeal to all audiences such as romance, political intrigue, epic battles, sieges, witchcraft, and magic, the enduring stories will fascinate students and encourage them to learn more about history.

Selecting facts from an unimaginably wide pool is invariably a philosophical exercise and a book tackling the nature of politics in the sixteenth century crashes up against the inevitable wall of secrecy that surrounded the institution of the court. Chapter 2 deals specifically with the private nature of state power, but the problem permeates each history. Because many states did not keep public records of deliberations at court, where the most important decisions were made, contemporaries often guessed about what happened. Sometimes resident ambassadors relied on court gossip for their reports, at other times, chronicles and histories described events in order to place certain leaders in the best light possible. Accounts of events distorted by emotions and belief systems have never offered perfect reliability. Despite the limitations of source material, however, a study of the sixteenth century has much to offer students of history.

The sixteenth century was an age of terrifying, destructive violence in many parts of the world. Conditions conducive to an underlying instability originated centuries earlier. As the climate began a cooling trend around 1200 CE, nomadic peoples on several continents invaded settled, agricultural societies. Poor harvests and famine left populations susceptible to disease, and the death and disruption caused by the Bubonic Plague of the fourteenth century toppled social hierarchies and political regimes from Europe to Asia. Societies responded by adopting new technology and commercial structures to adapt to losing thirty percent of the labor force. But these adaptations, such as gunpowder and the printing press, encouraged more instability, most notably the Reformation and its attendant civil wars, while commercial interests led to global exploration. This movement of peoples in turn led to more epidemic disease (in America) and disruption in Africa and Eurasia.

This book does not specifically focus on global interaction. In the two encounter narratives (Mexico and Spain, Kongo and Portugal), the biographies focus on how the rulers dealt with external pressures in the context of their own state. The spread of global commerce created the modern world, but this book attempts to provide a snapshot of a world before our own age. All of the regions covered in this book have similarities. They are all settled, agricultural societies with intense social stratification and well established cultural traditions. Each defined themselves as "civilized" in their own way against outsiders. At the same time, they all had a sense that they, too, had been "uncivilized" at some point in their past. Some even believed that they had been more civilized themselves in some "golden age" of the past that gave them a sense of nostalgia. Others knew that they indeed had been the nomadic outsiders who had conquered and destroyed a more sophisticated civilization. Thus, all were in the process of having a conversation with their own past, in the way that we in the modern world are now having similar conversations. Then as now, self-criticism and self-reflection arose from a situation of instability.

At the same time, the book strives to present recognizable predicaments that are applicable at both the individual and political level. While addressing truly disturbing themes, it serves as a cautionary tale about a variety of frightening realities. It attempts to address the question of what, if anything, an individual can do to alleviate the sufferings of others.

The genre of biography distorts the accurate presentation of historical material in several significant ways. Focusing on individuals often gives them more importance and agency in determining the course of history. The "great man" theory of history of the nineteenth century proposed that heroic individuals have the ability to single-handedly change the world. In reality, a variety of social, economic, technological, and environmental factors have had just as much impact on the course of history as great leaders. Moreover, every powerful individual profiled in this book had a staff of professional advisors who did the hard work of directing policy, but these have been largely excluded from the narrative for the sake of simplicity. In an effort to create short, compelling biographies, many important historical figures have been left out of the story.

Nevertheless, students easily relate to individuals. Human beings more readily take an interest in people than in abstract concepts. As this is an introduction intended to entice a reader into the study of history, it has chosen the lives of eight extraordinary figures. They do not represent what life was like for the vast majority of people who lived at that time, but their grandeur is part of their charm. They really existed, and their lives had a lasting impact on their societies. The character, motivation, and decisions of these rulers mattered a great deal in an age of personal power, when abstract definitions of the state had barely emerged. Subjects had an interest in evaluating the motives of their leaders, and subsequently left a record for posterity. Although character and the decision-making abilities of high-ranking officials might mean less in the contemporary world, citizens today still need tools to evaluate their leaders, as well as examples against which to compare their own character, motivation, and decisions.

I have crafted narratives to provide pleasant and appealing reading, including an abundance of anecdotes, traditions, and side stories. Fanciful details, although apocryphal, have been included either because they influenced real events or contributed to building political identities. Aiming for effective communication, I intended these stories as a framework for larger ideas, not a complete history of each subject. Although the information presented in this book is based on historical sources, the facts have been forced into a rather artificial narrative. Each biography has been presented in the form of a story, with a narrative arc in order to build character and sometimes suspense. This approach has a classical heritage. To paraphrase one sixteenth-century historian who explained its value: stories are the flower of history, while lessons are their fruit.

My greatest wish is to convey a love for history and share the sense of adventure I felt while writing these biographies. Plutarch remarked that he wrote his *Lives* as much for himself as for his readers, as he imagined his subjects as his companions: "The experience is like nothing so much as spending time in their company and living with them: I receive and welcome each of them in turn as my guest." He added, "And oh, what greater delight could one find than this?" (*Aemilius* I.1–3).

A handbook of leadership, a mirror for self-reflection, an imaginary journey around the world, *Real Lives in the Sixteenth Century* aims to be something more to the reader than a required text in world history class.

1

HIDEYOSHI AND HENRY IV OF FRANCE

Legends about the heroic deeds of Hideyoshi and Henry IV have been told for centuries in Japan and France. Emerging as successful warlords in times of chaos and civil war, they seemed to spend half of their lives fighting endless sieges and battles and the other half in routine bouts of heavy drinking and debauchery. They began their lives as outsiders, but rose to the pinnacle of power in their respective states. Born a peasant, Hideyoshi distinguished himself as a samurai vassal of a ruthless and cruel lord, eventually placing every province in Japan under his military control. Henry IV, although born a prince, faced challenges as a religious dissident. Considered a heretic by the French royal family and a majority of French people, he had to conquer his enemies to claim his title as king. Once in power, both warriors put down their weapons and helped establish lasting eras of peace in their realms. Through military prowess and persuasive ability, Hideyoshi and Henry IV encouraged their subjects to surrender their private interests for the sake of the common good.

Toyotomi Hideyoshi (1536–1598)

In the chaos of sixteenth-century Japan three men united the fractured lands ruled by violent warlords into a single, powerful state. The tale of the unification of Japan is reflected in a story known even today by Japanese school children. In this story, a cuckoo bird illustrates how the three unifiers, Oda Nobunaga (1534–1582), Toyotomi Hideyoshi (1537–1598), and Tokugawa Ieyasu (1543–1616), established their authority. As they try to make the bird sing for them, each uses a different strategy. Nobunaga threatens, "Little bird, if you will not sing, I will kill you," while

FIGURE 1.1 Portrait of Toyotomi Hideyoshi as Imperial Regent, c. 1598. The original is in Kōdai-ji, a Buddhist temple established by Nene, his widow, to honor his memory.

Source: Paul Fearn/Alamy Stock Photo

Hideyoshi promises, "Little bird, if you will not sing, I will make you," and Ieyasu states, "Little bird, if you will not sing, I will wait." The story reflects the historical record; the brutal Nobunaga terrorized his enemies and left a trail of destruction. Hideyoshi persuaded the Japanese to think of higher goals and envision a united Japan, and Ieyasu decided not to fight against these two, but to simply wait until their death to take control of the state. The last of the three unifiers established a regime, the Tokugawa Shogunate, which would endure almost three hundred years. This chapter presents the history of Hideyoshi, the second unifier, who remains one of the most celebrated figures in Japanese history. From humble origins, he used a combination of wit, charm, and military genius to usher in a new era of peace for the Japanese people.

Historians do not know very much about the early life of Hideyoshi beyond his upbringing as a poor peasant. Born in 1536, his small frame and ugly face encouraged others to nickname him "Monkey." According to legend, his father died when he was a small child. As he grew into a restless youth, his mother and stepfather sent him away to a Buddhist monastery. He left soon afterward to sell needles from a cart, and perhaps even joined a roving gang of bandits. Although much of his early life remains clouded in mythology, historians are certain that at a young age, he entered the service of a powerful warlord, Oda Nobunaga.

The Sengoku era (1437–1603)

An emperor had ruled Japan from the capital city of Kyoto since the eighth century. Claiming to be descended from the goddess of the sun, he served as a religious figure for the Japanese. While emperors held symbolic authority within the state, they did not always govern it directly. More often, powerful generals, or *shogun*, held political and military control. Because the office of shogun passed from father to son, Japanese history is divided into dynasties of shogun families, or shogunates. In the middle of the fifteenth century, local warlords rebelled against a weak shogun. As the Ashikaga shogunate collapsed and the central government in Kyoto lost control over the country, Japan suffered over a hundred years of mass chaos and warfare. Japanese historians term this era *Sengoku Jidai* (Era of Warring States).

Japan, a country of islands and rugged mountains, developed a decentralized political tradition best described as feudalism. In a feudal system, powerful warlords gave land to vassals in exchange for military service. Anyone controlling a large amount of land could hire a personal army, so lords fought constant battles and lived in fortified castles. In these years, vassal warriors, or *samurai* (those who serve), pledged loyalty to *daimyō* (regional lords). Samurai lived under a code of conduct that encouraged them to consider honor more important than life. Losing one's honor required the performance of ritual suicide, *seppuku*, to regain it. In this ceremony, a samurai wearing a white kimono sat peacefully as he composed a death poem. He then took a short knife, kept on hand exclusively for this purpose, and plunged it into the side of his abdomen, slicing a deep tear across his belly that allowed his intestines to spill out. Ideally, the victim had a loyal supporter nearby to skillfully sever his head so that the agony of death would be momentary. A skillful swordsman could leave only a flap of skin connected to the body, so that the severed head might fall forward in a distinguished fashion. The code of the warrior demanded that a warrior commit *seppuku* in case of defeat, betrayal, or upon losing a lord, but this unwritten code had often served more as an ideal than a reflection of reality. In the chaotic Sengoku era, samurai often acted as free agents, loyal only to themselves in their quest for personal power. This lack of loyalty led to political disorder, which intensified as rival warlords enlisted poor peasants to fight for them as foot soldiers. Peasants who showed exceptional skill and military valor had the opportunity to rise in the social hierarchy. In Hideyoshi's case, which was completely unprecedented, a peasant rose to command members of the old samurai nobility. For this reason, the Sengoku era is also called the time of *genkokujō* (mastery of the high by the low).

The rise of Nobunaga

According to early biographers, Hideyoshi began his service with Nobunaga as a sandal-bearer in 1558. It was said that the eager 22-year-old not only held his lord's sandals, but even kept them in his kimono to keep them warm. Within a short time, Nobunaga promoted the young man to the position of the castle's kitchen supervisor and overseer of charcoal and firewood for the castle. Although the lord ridiculed his new servant for his small stature and wrinkly face, he also recognized his talent. Cheerful and energetic, the young castle administrator seemed to have a magical way of encouraging others to give their best effort. Nobunaga continued to trust him with more responsibilities, and soon put him to work organizing the building of castles and fortifications. One legend says that he rebuilt the walls of Nobunaga's castle in three days, a major accomplishment, as he knew nothing of masonry or construction. Instead, he relied on the expertise of the workers. At first the masons did not trust the young upstart and refused to work for him. However, Hideyoshi won the workers to his side by providing them with food and *sake*, a wine made from rice. As he mingled with the men over food and drink, he explained how they were not doing their jobs for him alone, or even for their lord, Nobunaga. Rather, they were building the fortifications for the protection of their own homes and families. His emotional appeal moved them, and he amazed the workers when he ultimately took up a shovel himself and joined the work effort. Hideyoshi had a talent for inspiring people to see their own work as part of a larger, more important, effort. Under his direction, people did their best to contribute to a common cause.

While Nobunaga saw something exceptional in Hideyoshi, the young retainer also recognized the ambition and potential of his lord. Oda Nobunaga was only one of hundreds of daimyō of the Sengoku era who wreaked havoc fighting rival warlords and destroying villages throughout the realm. The game had changed, however, in 1543, when Portuguese explorers arrived in Japan with firearms. They brought a primitive musket known as the arquebus, which proved more lethal than anything anyone had seen before that time. The Japanese quickly learned how to manufacture the firearms themselves, and the number of guns quickly multiplied across Japan. Recognizing the destructive force of these weapons, and realizing that they would soon determine victory on the battlefield, Nobunaga amassed an army of several thousand soldiers. He was also the first to understand that artillery and firearms required more complicated approaches to logistics and fortifications. Up to that time in the sixteenth century, samurai still fought on horseback with swords, just as in the medieval era. Increasingly, however, warlords like Nobunaga needed specialists who could coordinate all aspects of the war effort, especially experts in the fields of engineering, management, and economics. Hideyoshi served all of these purposes. So varied were his abilities that his fellow samurai at the court of Nobunaga nicknamed him "cotton" because he proved himself useful in everything.

In 1560, Oda Nobunaga distinguished himself among the other warlords in the battle of Okehazama, one of the most important turning points in the history of Japan. For the first time in nearly a century, one of the warlords, Imagawa Yoshimoto, marched his army to the capital city of Kyoto in a bid to seize control of the government. His march was the first move toward unification. Yoshimoto had allied with the second most powerful lord in Japan, Tokugawa Ieyasu, and together they fielded an army of 40,000 men. As they moved their massive army through the domains of Oda Nobunaga, a much less powerful lord at the time, they encamped and rested in Okehazama. Here Yoshimoto's army, over-confident from its recent victories, started some celebratory feasting and drinking. On the afternoon of June 21, 1560, Nobunaga's much smaller army of 2,000 soldiers took advantage of a fierce thunderstorm to secretly march toward Yoshimoto's army. As the skies suddenly cleared, Nobunaga's men surprised their drunken enemies with a sneak attack. In the fierce battle that followed, Nobunaga's army routed the enemy, claiming a decisive victory and taking Yoshimoto's severed head as a trophy. After the battle of Okehazama, Nobunaga positioned himself in the lead of rival warlords seeking to unify the state under their own military rule.

Hideyoshi urged Nobunaga to make the most of his victory at Okehazama by enticing the defeated samurai to his side. To conciliate the losing army, he had Yoshimoto's head and the corpses of his main supporters properly buried with appropriate funeral rites. He also constructed an honorable tomb and appointed priests to say prayers at their memorial. Appreciating the nobility of this act, thousands of samurai who had suddenly found themselves without a lord switched their allegiance to Nobunaga. The victory of Okehazama enabled Nobunaga to secure his most important ally: Tokugawa Ieyasu. From 1561, three men of exceptional talent worked together to unite Japan: Nobunaga, Hideyoshi, and Ieyasu.

Hideyoshi and Nene

By 1560, Nobunaga had promoted Hideyoshi to the rank of samurai, an unusual honor for the son of a peasant. The next year the young man fell in love with Nene, the daughter of a minor samurai at Nobunaga's court. Although her parents had preferred to marry her to a man of higher status, Nene saw something remarkable in the young samurai and persuaded her father to approve the marriage. She would remain his confidante and advisor until his death. Despite his love and respect for her, however, Hideyoshi did not remain faithful to their marriage. From his service at the court of Nobunaga until his death, he had a difficult time controlling an unusually high sex drive. When Nene complained to his lord about her husband's infidelity, Nobunaga sent her a letter of consolation. He told her how much he admired her beauty and assured her of Hideyoshi's love for her. He added, "However far he searches, this bald rat will never find anyone like you."

Despite his indiscretions, Hideyoshi's love for Nene never waned. Frequently away from the castle on military campaigns, he wrote her constantly to inquire about her health. Even decades later, after he had become the most powerful man in Japan, Hideyoshi faithfully wrote his wife tender letters. In one nostalgic letter to her he advised her not to forget the old days when they had coarse straw-mats as a carpet and cups made of the cheapest clay. Nene fulfilled her duties as a good wife according to the values of her time. She managed his household, provided companionship, took care of his mother, and gave prudent political advice. Throughout their long marriage, however, she remained childless.

Hideyoshi becomes a general

After twelve years of service, Nobunaga granted Hideyoshi a substantial fief, or feudal estate, which raised him to the status of daimyō. Now a lord in his own right, he had a castle, domains, and numerous samurai vassals who pledged loyalty to him. He also belonged to Nobunaga's inner circle of powerful generals. Although all pledged loyalty to the same lord, rivalries and resentments pitted them against each other. The general Akechi Mitsuhide, like Hideyoshi, rose from humble origins to distinguish himself through bravery on the battlefield and talent in architecture. Some suspected that he held secret ambitions for his own advancement. Hideyoshi's primary rival, however, was Shibata Katsuie. Thirteen years older, and from an old and distinguished samurai family, Katsuie never accepted Hideyoshi as his social equal. Nobunaga, for his part, treated all of his generals in a similar fashion—with extreme disrespect. He continued to call Hideyoshi "Monkey" even as he promoted him for his proven abilities as a general and administrator. Nobunaga frequently humiliated his short and unattractive vassal by making him dance for the entertainment of the others at court. On at least one occasion, he ordered Hideyoshi to shampoo the hair of the other generals. The powerful lord could also be rude to his samurai at court. For his own amusement, Nobunaga once pounded Mitsuhide's head with sticks, pretending to beat a drum. Such examples of poor treatment never damaged Hideyoshi's unwavering loyalty. On the other hand, Mitsuhide's resentments against his lord simmered under the surface and continued to grow.

Nobunaga, a tall and thin man who rarely smiled and never drank alcohol, had a reputation for cruelty. To contemporaries, he seemed completely lacking in compassion. As a young man he had killed his own brother, and as an adult he consistently refused to spare the lives of men, women, and even children who stood in the way of his path toward domination. In his quest to control Japan, he viewed any rival power as a threat.

In 1576, Nobunaga built Azuchi Castle, an enormous structure surrounded by a moat and stone walls over six meters thick. Above the solid stone foundation rose the keep of the castle: a five-story wooden structure painted in brilliant colors with images of tigers and dragons. The inside walls contained paintings of birds, flowers, scholars, religious figures, and landscapes, while pillars of lacquer and gold rose leaf rose majestically from floors covered in *tatami* (rectangular straw mats). The arrangement of the *tatami* mats made patterns, adding not only beauty but, as many believed, good fortune. The interior of the castle had a five-story atrium, with a walkway on the fourth floor. With such opulence he intended to show visitors his wealth and authority.

Nobunaga attacks religion and the state

Nobunaga showed little interest in religion. The traditional faith of Japan was Shinto, a belief system focused on ritual purity and the veneration of many gods who represent the forces of nature. However, another religion, Buddhism, had been practiced in Japan from at least the sixth century CE. Buddhism originated in ancient India. In the sixth century BCE, a young prince named Siddhartha Gautama meditated on the nature of suffering in the world. One day, while sitting under a tree, he came up with a solution to the problem of human suffering. He said that since the ultimate cause of suffering is desire, people might end their suffering by eliminating it. Instead, people should appreciate and be mindful of what they have without wanting more and try to distance themselves from emotional drama. If people realized that death and heartbreak were inevitable troubles that have no solution, they might learn to accept them, living in peace with themselves and others. Such insights gained Siddhartha Gautama the title of Buddha, or "Enlightened One." Followers wrote down his sermons, which eventually became the basic scriptures for the religion of Buddhism.

Over time, Buddhist philosophy developed into an organized religion that spread throughout Asia and as far as Japan. People devoted to the worship of the Buddha became priests and monks who carried out the rituals of the religion in temples and monasteries. Dedicated to maintaining the religion, the clergy gained respect, authority, and income. By the time of Oda Nobunaga, some powerful Buddhist monasteries even had their own towns and armies. Nobunaga regarded militant Buddhist monks as political rivals, and targeted them for destruction. He shocked many when he laid siege to the powerful Buddhist monasteries at Mount Hiei and destroyed them in 1571. Over three hundred monasteries had speckled the mountain and its valleys for over seven hundred years, serving as the spiritual center of Buddhism in Japan. In his brutal assault, Nobunaga burned the entire complex to the ground. His soldiers spared no one—including the tens of thousands of men, women, and children who also lived on the mountain. It was an act of brutality and sacrilege meant to send a message that he would not tolerate religion meddling in political and military affairs.

While lords and samurai battled endlessly for dominance, the emperor and shogun still resided in the city of Kyoto. By 1573, weeds had overgrown the imperial palace, which had become indistinguishable from the other houses in Kyoto. Politically weak and in need of money, some emperors resorted to selling their own calligraphy for income. The shogun at the time, Ashikaga Yoshiaki, proved to be an ineffective leader. The fifteenth shogun of the Ashikaga dynasty, Yoshiaki seemed to care more about luxuries and pleasures than military affairs. At first, Nobunaga supported him by building him a new palace and allowing the shogun to rule as his puppet. Within a few years, however, Nobunaga burned much of Kyoto to the ground and sent Yoshiaki into exile and obscurity. As a final blow to religious authority in the city, he destroyed many temples. The people of Kyoto watched in disbelief as he crushed their stone idols and used them for building material and stripped off their ornamentation to adorn his own private palace. As Nobunaga committed these acts of sacrilege, no one had the power to stop him.

Hideyoshi builds a reputation

In the service of his brutal master, Hideyoshi sometimes showed his own potential for cruelty. Two famous castle sieges illustrate a darker side to his character. During these sieges, the talented general put his insight into psychology and engineering expertise to use in defeating his enemies. In the siege of Tottori, 1580, he prepared months ahead of time by ordering his merchants to buy rice from the surrounding areas at several times the market price. The inflated prices encouraged those in the castle to sell their precious stores of rice. Hideyoshi then blockaded the castle, posting towers every 500 meters around the circumference. For two hundred days, the general and his soldiers kept watch outside as the enemy within succumbed to starvation and even cannibalism. In the end, Hideyoshi agreed to spare the lives of the survivors in exchange for the head of the commander in charge. The official's suicide finally ended the terrible siege.

In another brilliant siege, Hideyoshi diverted a river to flood Bitchu-Takamatsu Castle. In 1582, he employed thousands of workers to build a dyke almost three kilometers in length. In twelve days, they packed bags of sand into wooden frames to form a wall that was 7 meters high and 22 meters wide at the base. When the seasonal rains caused the river to overflow its banks, the dyke directed the water into a flat plain surrounded by hills. Hideyoshi's artificial lake completely submerged the castle, which lay in the middle of the plain. As at Tottori, the siege ended with the *seppuku* of the enemy commander.

Hideyoshi's success at siegecraft was accompanied by his equally remarkable efforts to reconstruct the castle towns he had destroyed. He made it clear that his ultimate aim was not destruction but improvement. The biography he commissioned, the *Tensho-ki*, begins with the fall of a castle at Miki in 1582. After the battle, he reconstructed the fortress, dredged the moat, rebuilt the surrounding houses, and enticed the townspeople back to the castle grounds. The inhabitants watched with amazement as their former enemy established a temple and marketplace. Hideyoshi's rebuilding efforts gave hope to people who had suffered long years of war and destruction. Soon his reputation distinguished him from Nobunaga and the other warlords of the Sengoku era.

Hideyoshi's skills as a warrior complemented his feats of engineering. In terms of swordplay and bravery, he proved the equal of the finest samurai of his time. The sight of Hideyoshi's golden gourd battle standard struck terror into his enemies, as did his elaborate suit of armor that included a magnificent black helmet crested with long iron spikes in the form of a sunburst. Nevertheless, Nobunaga's most famous general often preferred negotiation to battle. He did not shy away from bribery in order to win an enemy to his side. His best tools, however, were his charm and intelligence. With these he persuaded warriors to betray their own lords and enter the service of Nobunaga. He argued that personal loyalty mattered less than the all-important goal of creating peace for the common good. In contrast to Nobunaga's brutal treatment of rivals, Hideyoshi often showed mercy by sparing the life of his conquered enemies. Whereas others might have considered this a sign of weakness, he believed that it showed his courage. He feared no one and viewed every enemy as a potential ally. His confidence and trust in people encouraged the same in those who pledged their loyalty to him.

Contemporaries noted Hideyoshi's remarkable ability to stay calm under the most stressful situations. To regain focus and tranquility, Hideyoshi devoted himself to the ritual of the tea ceremony. The "way of tea" and its regimented steps encouraged mindfulness and self-discipline. In Medieval Japan, the tea ceremony had long been used by samurai to cope with the trauma of war. Hideyoshi also found relaxation in the *onsen* (mineral baths) that dotted the mountain areas of Japan. Volcanic activity pushed hot springs to the surface, creating opportunities to purify the body and mind. Concerned to the point of obsession with physical health, he frequently underwent a treatment known as moxibustion that involved burning the skin with mugwort at acupuncture points to increase circulation. His letters often contained detailed medical advice for his loved ones advising similar treatments. In one letter to his wife, Nene, he ended his affectionate note with an intimate suggestion: "And I think that it would be better if you were less constipated, so why don't you take an enema?" In the post script to the same letter, he continued, "I repeat: I would like you to take an enema to get the bowels moving. So I shall wait for a better report concerning your health and telling me how long it takes the enema to have its effect. I end here." Evidently, his urge to control political and military events seeped into the most intimate aspects of his private life.

Marriages and hostages under Nobunaga

In a system of feudalism, in which power is personal, loyalty proves all important and leaders often used the emotional ties between family members to build their power base. For this reason, Japanese warlords frequently married off female relatives to rival lords in order to secure alliances. Thus Nobunaga treated Oichi, his alluring younger sister, as a political pawn. At court, Hideyoshi's infatuation with the elegant and graceful noblewoman was widely known, but his desire for her remained hopelessly frustrated. Nobunaga considered his young general, a former peasant, unworthy of his sister. Instead, he married Oichi off to solidify an alliance with his former rival, Asai Nagamasa in 1564. She had one son and three daughters with him, but their marriage ended unhappily when her husband betrayed her brother. In retaliation, Nobunaga sent Tokugawa Ieyasu to destroy Nagamasa's castle. The defeated lord Nagamasa and his son committed *seppuku*, but Oichi and her three daughters escaped and returned to Nobunaga's castle. A few days after the battle, Nobunaga received a gift: the head of Nagamasa, his former brother-in-law, gilded in gold.

In addition to strategic marriages, the wives, children, and parents of samurai sometimes served as hostages to insure the loyalty of an ally. If an ally went back on his word, or failed to fulfill the obligations of a treaty, the hostages might be tortured and even killed. Nobunaga, like many other ruthless daimyō, engaged in the torture and humiliation of hostages. In one memorable case, Akechi Mitsuhide, one of Nobunaga's top generals, besieged the castle of an enemy who held his own mother as a hostage. As he himself held the enemy's two brothers captive, he promised to spare their lives if the commander of the castle surrendered. The commander surrendered the castle, but Nobunaga ordered Mitsuhide to execute the two brothers anyway, by burning them alive. In retaliation for this brutal act, the enemy tortured Mitsuhide's mother who perished in the flames. Not surprisingly, the cruel treatment of his mother caused Mitsuhide to hold a long-standing grudge against Nobunaga.

Betrayal and death of Nobunaga

By 1582 Nobunaga had control over 32 of Japan's 68 provinces. In that year, an act of betrayal by one of his own generals caused his downfall. In one account, Nobunaga had thrown an enormous party for Tokugawa Ieyasu, his most powerful ally and placed one of his generals, Akechi Mitsuhide in charge of the festivities. Known for his exquisite taste, Mitsuhide planned an elaborate banquet with entertainment and carefully chosen porcelain and lacquer dishes. During the party, an altercation broke out when Nobunaga commanded Mitsuhide to lead an expedition in support of Hideyoshi's army in the west. In a rage, Mitsuhide threw all of the fine dishes in a lake and set off on his horse.

Angry but seemingly obedient to his lord, Mitsuhide marched west with an army of 13,000 men. Not long after setting off, however, he directed his army to return to Kyoto. He told his soldiers that Nobunaga, who was lodging there, needed to inspect the army before its departure. It was a ruse invented to hide his true intention of mounting an armed insurrection against his lord. Mitsuhide found Nobunaga in the temple of Honnōji. He had just awakened and washed his face and hands when an arrow struck him between the ribs. As he drew it out, a shot from an arquebus shattered his arm. Stunned, but realizing that the treacherous Mitsuhide had surrounded the temple with his army, Nobunaga escaped to a quiet part of the temple and committed *seppuku* as the temple burned to the ground.

Mitsuhide's motives for treason against his lord are unclear. Certainly he had personal scores to settle with him, especially as Nobunaga had caused the gruesome death of his own mother. In some accounts, Mitsuhide claimed he wanted to rid Japan of a tyrant, or to avenge the death of priests and monks on Mount Hiei. Perhaps, as one observer at court remarked, he wanted to control the state himself: "[He] became so puffed up with great favors, and scorning the obligations of fidelity and gratitude, he began to extend his impious hopes to the monarchy of Japan." In Hideyoshi's eyes, however, Mitsuhide had betrayed his master and therefore deserved to die. He resolved to chase him down and kill him to appease the spirit of his dead master. Hideyoshi was first to pursue him, declaring a truce in his other battles and rushing to the capital. Thirteen days after the assassination his daimyō, Hideyoshi's army routed the enemy and Mitsuhide fled north. In the village of Ogurusu, a peasant spotted Misuhide and killed him with a bamboo spear. They brought his head to Hideyoshi, who took it to Honnōji temple for the approval of Nobunaga's spirit. Afterward, Mitsuhide's head was sewn onto its lifeless body and attached to a cross where it was left to quietly rot at the edge of Kyoto.

Hideyoshi consolidates his power

Nobunaga's death created a political crisis. He left two adult sons, Nobutaka and Nobukatsu, but neither had shown any real talent for leadership. Hideyoshi proposed that Nobunaga's 3-year-old grandson, Sambōshi, assume power when he came of age. In the meantime, a council of four generals would rule in his name: Hideyoshi, Niwa Nagahide, Ikeda Tsuneoki, and Shibata Katsuie. At first, a balance of power prevailed among them, but soon factions developed around Nobunaga's two sons. As Hideyoshi gained authority in the council, Shibata Katsuie, his older rival, began to mount a resistance against him. According to one colorful story, the old general attempted to undermine Hideyoshi's authority by reminding the others of Hideyoshi's humble origins. One day Katsuie addressed Hideyoshi in council, "Remember when you were a lowly servant in the house of Nobunaga and used to wash my hair? You were so good at it, I wonder if you would wash my hair right now." To everyone's surprise, Hideyoshi, even though he ruled as a powerful daimyō over many domains, agreed. With a calm expression on his face, he replied, "Not having practiced shampooing for a long time, I am not sure that I can do it to your satisfaction. Moreover, today I have been drinking, and my hands are somewhat out of gear. But as the request comes from one so great, I will try my best." As the younger man proceeded to wash the old general's hair, the other generals watched with astonishment. While Katsuie's stunt made him seem rude and mean-spirited, Hideyoshi's humble response impressed them with its humility and sincerity.

By 1583, Katsuie formed a strategic alliance with of one of Nobunaga's sons, Nobutaka, and led an armed resistance against Hideyoshi. He claimed to be supporting the legacy of Oda Nobunaga against an illegitimate power grab. To solidify the alliance, Nobutaka arranged a marriage between Katsuie and Nobunaga's younger sister, the widowed Oichi. She and her daughters moved into his main castle at Kita-no-shō. Within a few months, however, Hideyoshi had defeated his opponent's army, forcing a retreat of his rival's 3,000 soldiers into the castle keep. Katsuie and his loyal troops bravely fought through seven ferocious battles, but the old general eventually realized that his cause was lost. He climbed to the ninth floor of the castle with Oichi and eighty of his supporters. They brought up food and sake for a feast as well as straw to cover all of the floors. What began as a party turned into a funeral, as Katsuie gave his last speech, composed his death poem, and committed *seppuku*. Afterward, his loyal supporters killed their family members and then themselves as they set the straw on fire.

Oichi had a difficult decision to make. If she fled the castle, she would fall into the hands of Hideyoshi, a man who had pursued her for years. Staying in the castle meant an honorable death by the side of her husband, a man for whom she may have had tender feelings. Having served as a marriage pawn with little say over the direction of her life, Oichi decided her own fate in the end. She chose to die with Katsuie and commit suicide in the form of *jigai*, the female version of seppuku. Nevertheless, she allowed her three daughters to escape the burning castle, trusting that Hideyoshi would protect the young sisters, aged 10–14. Her faith in him was not in vain, as the victorious general rescued the girls and raised them as princesses in his own castle. Many years later, the youngest sister, Go, would become the mother of a shogun, while the oldest sister who most resembled her mother, Chacha, would soon become Hideyoshi's favorite mistress. Later taking the name Lady Yodo, she would give birth to his only two sons.

The wars of unification continued until every daimyō throughout the entire archipelago of Japan submitted to his authority. After the death of Katsuie, Hideyoshi eliminated all active resistance to his rule. Nobutaka committed suicide, Nobukatsu became an ally, and Sambōshi, feeble and weak, stayed loyal to Hideyoshi. Having converted to Christianity, Sambōshi died at the early age of 25. Only one impediment stood between him and absolute rule: Tokugawa Ieyasu. Previously allied with Hideyoshi under Nobunaga, Ieyasu now openly challenged him on the battlefield. The meeting of their armies in 1584 resulted in a stalemate that lasted for three weeks. Eventually, they negotiated a settlement in which Iayasu agreed to marry Hideyoshi's sister and accept his mother as a hostage. Hideyoshi agreed to adopt Ieyasu's second son as his own. By pledging loyalty to Hideyoshi, Ieyasu secured control over his domains and castles in the eastern region of Japan. He built a castle in a little fishing village called Edo. Today, this village to the east (*tō*) is the capital city (*kyō*) of Japan, better known as Tokyo (Eastern Capital).

Firmly established as ruler of Japan, Hideyoshi never took the title of shogun. Instead, he claimed to rule in the name of the emperor as *Taikō* (Imperial Regent) and adopted the title Toyotomi (Bountiful Minister) as his last name. He built an enormous and ornate castle in Osaka and reconstructed the city of Kyoto. In 1590, the Taikō mounted one of his most famous sieges against Odawara Castle, the last holdout against him located southwest of Edo. In an effort to exhaust the defenders of the castle, Hideyoshi prepared for a long stand-off. He allowed all of his soldiers to bring their wives to the front and provided non-stop entertainment in the form of acrobats, musicians, and actors. There were tea ceremonies and plays to distract the army, and merchants set up markets hawking whatever goods the people might need or desire. He knew that drinking sake and enjoying great parties, the soldiers could last indefinitely. Not only did this gain the allegiance of his soldiers, it provided a psychological message to the besieged: take your time, we can wait. After a three-month siege, Odawara Castle surrendered with little bloodshed. Toyotomi awarded the enemy lands to his ally, Ieyasu. These domains made him the wealthiest daimyō in Japan, as his income even surpassed that of the Taikō himself. With this gift to his ally, Hideyoshi wanted to send a message to other lords that they had much more to gain from alliance with him than resistance to his authority.

With every rival warlord pacified, Toyotomi Hideyoshi remained unsatisfied. He looked abroad for new conquests and set his sights on the "three countries" (China, Korea, India). When Korean ambassadors arrived at the court of the Taikō to congratulate him on his unification of Japan, Hideyoshi treated them with astonishing disrespect. He sent them away with a message to take to their king demanding that Korea provide a path for the Japanese to invade China. Aiming to subdue the "four hundred provinces" of the Ming dynasty, the Taikō dispatched over 150,000 soldiers to invade Korea in 1592. Armed with muskets and using superior military tactics honed during the brutal wars of the Sengoku era, the Japanese caused a great deal of destruction in the Korean peninsula. In response to the unprovoked attack, the Koreans called upon China, to which Korea was a tributary state, for help to defeat the army of what they termed the "Flood Dragon." After several years of bloody warfare, China's army definitively crushed the Japanese invasion, although the effort weakened the reign of the Wanli Emperor (profiled in Chapter 2). One contemporary described the bloodbath: "Sunken ships and decapitated corpses fill the sea with stench." In Kyoto a memorial to the war still stands today. The Mimizuka Monument contains the ears and noses of 38,000 Koreans massacred by the Japanese.

Although unsuccessful, the invasion of Korea had served to occupy the restless samurai who wanted war. It also indicated that the Taikō, like his European and Ottoman contemporaries, had pretentions to World Empire. Hideyoshi was well aware of the imperial enterprises of Spain and Portugal in the sixteenth century. When survivors of a shipwreck of a boat intended for China landed on a small western island of Japan in 1542, they found a decentralized state of independent and powerful warlords, many of whom welcomed the benefits of foreign trade. The Portuguese also ultimately brought Jesuits, members of a religious society devoted to spreading the Catholic faith around the world. Many of the Japanese were open to learning about Christianity. Despite his lack of interest in their religious mission, Oda Nobunaga supported the Jesuits by granting them land and toleration. In his view, they provided an alliance against militant Buddhism, which he considered a main rival for power. By the time of Nobunaga's death, perhaps over one hundred thousand Japanese had converted to Christianity. Indeed, in the decades after 1543, Portuguese dress, language, and customs had become fashionable among well-to-do Japanese. Many well-dressed women wore crosses and rosaries completely unaware of their deeper spiritual meaning.

Portuguese Christians lost a valuable ally when Nobunaga died. By the end of his life, Hideyoshi increasingly considered the foreign religion a threat to the general peace. Although he kept Portuguese envoys at his court and continued to favor European trade, he made it clear that he opposed the Christianizing mission of the Jesuits in Japan. When a new order of Christians, the Franciscans, arrived in the 1590s, he shocked the Christian community and all of Europe when he subjected twenty-six missionaries to a gruesome death by torture and upside-down crucifixion in 1597. It marked the beginning of an anti-Christian policy that would continue under Tokugawa Ieyasu.

The regime of the Taikō

Hideyoshi's policies had a profound impact on Japanese history. His regime ended the Sengoku era and laid the foundation for the *Pax Tokugawa*, a general peace that would last until the mid-nineteenth century. He pacified a society whose social norms glorified honor through warfare. After him, the Japanese developed a national culture increasingly proud of its commercial and artistic heritage. In a letter to a Portuguese official in 1591, Hideyoshi explained his role in establishing peace and stability:

> My country, which is comprised of sixty-odd provinces, has known for many years more days of disorder than days of peace; rowdies have been given to fomenting intrigue, and bands of warriors have formed cliques to defy the court's orders. Ever since my youth, I have been constantly concerned over this deplorable situation. I studied the art of self-cultivation and the secret of governing the country. Through profound planning and forethought, and according to the three principles of benevolence, wisdom, and courage, I cared for the warriors on the one hand and looked after the common people on the other; while administering justice, I was able to establish security. Thus, before many years had passed, the unity of the nation was set on a firm foundation.[1]

One of Hideyoshi's first acts was to disarm the common people by establishing a "sword hunt" throughout the land. He collected all of the weapons from the common people and melted them down to build a giant statue of the Buddha. Only samurai could carry swords, and guns were severely restricted. He surveyed the land and established laws that all had to obey. A centralized bureaucracy, not the lords, guaranteed the collection of taxes from the villages.

FIGURE 1.2 Kano Naganobu, *Merrymaking under Aronia Blossoms*, c. 1610. The painting depicts elegant guests of the samurai aristocracy dancing at a party to celebrate the blooming of the trees.

Despite having come from humble origins, Hideyoshi made status distinctions more rigid by outlawing social mobility. Perhaps he feared that men of low status like himself might rise to threaten his regime or considered social mobility as a destabilizing influence in society. His policies insured that peasants, craftsmen, and merchants would never be able to enter into the samurai nobility as easily as they had in the Sengoku era. He gave the daimyō special privileges above the common people, and laws determined what clothes people could wear. Good silk was reserved for the nobility. The lords were also allowed to rule in their domains without too much interference from the central government. It was an arrangement that favored those at the top, who, for this reason, supported Hideyoshi. He protected them from unruly peasants and threats of social disorder. They also stood to gain from the general peace. Nobunaga's reign of terror had taught them to fear for their lives, and few wanted to go back to the rampant violence of the Sengoku era. They began to cultivate themselves with education and taste, seeking discipline in self-control rather than war.

The common people benefitted as well because they no longer had to fear the poverty and destruction of their villages due to war. Under peaceful circumstances, farmers produced more rice to feed a larger population. Craftsmen and merchants, although restricted in terms of social status, made money catering to the desire of the nobility for luxuries. Traditionally, the social status of merchants was considered lower than peasants and artisans. However, merchants became increasingly rich and some married into the old samurai nobility. This rising social group of urban commoners sought out entertainments like the theater and literature, and increasingly dined in the new restaurants and clubs that opened in the cities. Hideyoshi was the first to establish an entire "pleasure quarter" in Kyoto 1589, which provided venues offering a wide variety of entertainment. Patrons went to the pleasure quarter to seek relaxation by eating delicious food, drinking sake to excess, and engaging the services of *geisha*. These hostesses offered their clients lively conversation, music, dance, and sometimes sex. The most beautiful and talented of these *geisha*, with their faces powdered white and heart-shaped lips painted a brilliant red, became celebrities in their own right. Hideyoshi himself used to frequent the pleasure quarter of Kyoto in disguise.

The former servant of Nobunaga who used to entertain the generals with his dancing never lost his talents as a showman. The Taikō understood the importance of pageantry and glamour in gaining support for his government. Appealing to the people's sense of nostalgia, he revived many medieval traditions and built up the image of the emperor as a divine figure through theatrical state performances. One of the biggest spectacles involved the official visit by the emperor to Hideyoshi's Kyoto mansion in 1588. The *Juraku Gyōkō*, as it was called, included a procession with 6,000 guards. Wearing Chinese silks of five colors, depicting seasonal birds and flowers, the spring cherries of Yoshino, and the autumn maples of Takidagawa, participants enjoyed banquets, musical recitals, and a wine-fueled poetry party. Guests composed over a hundred verses on the subject of pine trees, traditionally associated with long life. All of the details of the pageant were published in pamphlet form for the common people to share and discuss like celebrity gossip.

Celebrations of Japanese culture encouraged people to take pride in the symbols of a "national" culture and support the regime. On one occasion, Hideyoshi ordered the construction of over 1,500 impromptu tea houses for a massive tea party. Personally serving tea to over 800 guests, he aimed to bring the ceremony to the common people. At another festival he transplanted 500 cherry trees. His planting of cherry blossom trees not only served the purpose of bringing beauty to the city of Kyoto, they also had a symbolic and even spiritual meaning. As the red and pink flowers blossomed and fell, they represented the impermanence of life. They provided a reminder of the sacrifice of warriors as they spilled their blood in the prime of youth, while also bringing attention to the fact that all must fall and die. Cherry blossoms reminded people that the only solution to the problem of death is to cherish life while one has it. These were principles associated with Buddhism, and by linking state ceremonies to religious principles, Hideyoshi was able to gain the allegiance of his people. He made his subjects feel a part of something larger than themselves: a community with shared values.

Like many rulers, Hideyoshi wanted to establish a dynasty by making his political authority hereditary. He had two sons by Lady Yodo, the young daughter of Oichi rescued with her sisters from Katsuie's castle. Although his first son, Tsurumatsu, died at the age of 2, the second, Hideyori, lived to reach adulthood. As the mother of Hideyoshi's heir, Lady Yodo gained increasing amounts of power at court. Contemporaries at the palace grew to resent her role as "gate keeper" to her lord, selecting which ambitious men would win an audience with him. Those who described her as ruthless and manipulative even inquired into the legitimacy of her sons. Hideyoshi had a wife and hundreds of concubines, yet throughout his life, none of these women had produced children for him. Why, they asked, was he able to father children in his late fifties with Lady Yodo after a lifetime of failing to produce offspring?

At the end of his life, many contemporaries suspected that Hideyoshi's character had been corrupted by absolute power. His savage treatment of the Koreans and Christian missionaries revealed an increasingly bloodthirsty side to his personality. Towards the end of his life, not even family and friends felt secure at court. Hideyoshi ordered the execution of his nephew along with his entire immediate family. Another scandal of his later years concerned a tea master, Sen no Rikyū, who had been the most celebrated designer of tea houses and vessels of his age, as well as a codifier of ceremonial practices. One temple of Zen Buddhism had even erected a statue of him. Although Rikyū had been his friend and advisor for years, Hideyoshi decided to have him arrested and forced him to commit suicide at the age of 69. Contemporaries speculated that the scandal involved the tea master's attractive daughter, but no real motive has ever been found for this savage act of betrayal.

Before Hideyoshi died in 1598, he urged Tokugawa Ieyasu to adopt Hideyori as his own son and heir. Tokugawa agreed, and finally united the country under his own rule in 1600. Nene, who survived Hideyoshi, made peace with the new Tokugawa regime and became a Buddhist nun. She had urged Lady Yodo to accept the new government, but Lady Yodo refused and incited her son Hideyori to mount a resistance against the house of Tokugawa. They were defeated after the siege of Osaka Castle in 1615, where both mother and son committed suicide as Hideyoshi's magnificent castle burned down in flames. Hideyori's 8-year-old son was then decapitated by order of Ieyasu. The Toyotomi blood line having been eradicated, Ieyasu took the title of shogun and established a new dynasty, the Tokugawa Shogunate. It established peace in Japan for over 250 years and it lasted until 1868, when the Meiji emperor opened Japan to the modern, industrial world.

Despite the unsettling nature of his later years, Hideyoshi has remained a popular figure in Japanese history. Traditional biographies of Hideyoshi attributed to him ten traditional virtues: fidelity, justice, bravery, compassion for the people, righteousness, honesty, wisdom, fortune within, authority without, intelligence, curiosity, and charity in perception. Contemporary Japan owes much to Hideyoshi's impressive work of centralization. The stories are told again and again of how the monkey-faced peasant helped to build a modern nation.

Before his death at the age of 63, Hideyoshi composed his death poem:

> My life
> Came like dew
> Disappears like dew.
> All of Osaka Castle
> Is dream after dream.[2]

Death poem of Hideyoshi (slightly adapted), originally published in Kuwata Tadachika, *Taikō no tegame* (Tokyo: Bungei Shunjū-sha, 1959), p. 76. Cited in Mary Elizabeth Berry, *Hideyoshi* (Cambridge, MA: Harvard University Press, 1982), p. 235. Courtesy of the Harvard University Asia Center.

Chronology

1453   Sengoku era begins.
1536   Birth of Hideyoshi.
1542   Portuguese land in Japan.
1558   Hideyoshi enters court of Oda Nobunaga.
1560   Battle of Okehazama. Hideyoshi marries Nene.
1571   Nobunaga destroys Buddhist monasteries of Mount Hiei.
1582   Sieges of Bitchu-Takamatsu and Miki. Nobunaga assassinated by Mitsuhide.
1583   Katsuie defeated at Kita-no-shō.
1590   Siege of Odawara Castle.
1592   Japanese invasion of Korea.
1598   Death of Hideyoshi.
1603   Tokugawa Ieyasu appointed shogun.
1615   Fall of Osaka Castle and death of Hideyori.

Sources for further reading on Hideyoshi

The best biography of Hideyoshi in English is Mary Elizabeth Berry, *Hideyoshi* (Cambridge: Harvard University Press, 1982), which covers all aspects of his life, concentrating on the political nature of his regime. For those interested in his military accomplishments, the short book Stephen Turnbull, *Toyotomi Hideyoshi: Leadership, Strategy, Conflict* (Oxford: Osprey, 2010) provides a detailed account and maps of his major campaigns. It also contains illustrations of his stunning military uniforms. Another biography based on contemporary biographies of Hideyoshi is Walter Dening, *The Life of Toyotomi Hideyoshi* (New York: AMS Press, 1971), originally published in Kobe, Japan in 1930. It contains many colorful, but possibly fanciful, stories tending to glorify the subject. Much of Hideyoshi's correspondence has been translated into English in Adriana Boscaro, ed. and trans., *101 Letters of Hideyoshi: The Private Correspondence of Toyotomi Hideyoshi* (Tokyo: Sophia University, 1975). Merry Wiesner-Hanks, *Religious Transformations in the Early Modern World: A Brief History with Documents* (Boston, MA: Bedford St. Martins, 2009) contains an important letter to the Portuguese Viceroy of the Indies quoted in the text. A great source of interesting anecdotes is James Murdoch and Isoh Yamagata, *A History of Japan, Volume II: During the Century of Early Foreign Intercourse 1542–1651* (Kobe, Japan: Office of the "Chronicle," 1903). It is largely based on reports provided by Portuguese envoys. Eiji Yoshikawa, *Taiko: An Epic Novel of War and Glory in Feudal Japan* (Tokyo: Kodansha International, 1992) is an English translation of a Japanese historical novel about Hideyoshi from the middle of the twentieth century. Over nine hundred pages, it is a fictionalization of the seventeenth-century chronicle, *Taikō ki*. Students wanting more information about the Sengoku era can find good summaries in George Sansom, *A History of Japan 1334–1615* (Stanford, CA: Stanford University Press, 1961) and John Whitney Hall, ed. *The Cambridge History of Japan, Volume 4: Early Modern Japan* (Cambridge: Cambridge University Press, 1991).

Henry IV (1553–1610)

Prince, heretic, warrior, and king: the romantic figure of Henry IV carved a legendary path through French history. When religious wars divided his kingdom, he emerged as the commander of a religious insurgency. He married a royal princess and then vigorously fought against her family and faith. In the end, a combination of good fortune and talent enabled him to unite a country after decades of bloody conflict. The course of his amazing life from rebellious warlord to beloved king has provided the nation of France with one of its most enduring cultural legacies.

Born in 1553, Henry began life as prince and heir of Navarre, a rugged kingdom in the southwest of France near Spain. After his older brother had died as an infant, Henry's mother took extreme precautions to protect her second son. For the first year of his life, they wrapped the infant in cloth they rarely changed in the belief that urine and feces would protect his body from infection. As the boy grew into a

FIGURE 1.3 Frans Pourbus the Younger, *Bust of Henry IV wearing the cross of the Holy Spirit*, c. 1611.

Source: Chateau de Versailles, France/Bridgeman Images

man, Henry's personal hygiene continued to suffer. Contemporaries noted that he smelled like the flesh of rotten animals.

On his mother's side, three generations of illustrious French women had dominated the Navarre family. These included his great grandmother, Louise de Savoy, a political mastermind who ruled France for a time in the name of her son, Francis I; his grandmother, Marguerite of Navarre, a brilliant poet; and his mother, Jeanne D'Albret, who led the Protestant movement in France with devotion and strength. The king and queen of Navarre sought to toughen the boy by allowing him to spend his childhood playing rough games with the local boys of the nearby village. At the same time, they encouraged the prince to read the classic works of ancient Greece and Rome, the Italian Renaissance, and the Bible. It proved to be an effective education for a soldier and statesman.

The era of religious wars

Henry of Navarre came of age in an era of religious warfare when Catholics and Protestants fought for control of France. In the centuries that followed the collapse of the Roman Empire, the countries of Western Europe had been united under one interpretation of Christianity, Catholicism. The institution of the Roman Catholic Church arose in late antiquity and survived through the middle ages with its structure intact. The Church was a hierarchical system of offices, including priests, bishops, cardinals, and popes, which supervised the spiritual life of every Christian from Ireland and the German lands to Italy and Portugal. However, in 1517 the German monk Martin Luther (1483–1546) questioned the necessity of this institutional structure to the faith, asking why Christians needed priests, bishops and popes to direct their religion. Couldn't Christians simply read the Bible? Interestingly, few people had asked this question before Luther, because so few Christians could read Latin, the only language authorized by the Catholic Church. In addition, the enormous cost of a Bible transcribed by hand limited access to the scriptures. The invention of the printing press in the German city of Mainz in 1453 had a revolutionary impact on the religion. Using this new technology, Luther published a Bible in the language of the common people of his region, German, that was accessible to those outside of the clergy. Protesting many tenets of the Catholic faith and dogma, Luther and his followers came to be known as Protestants.

An increasing number of people began to read and interpret the Bible in the sixteenth century. A Frenchman named Jean Calvin (1509–1564) adopted the Protestant faith and simplified it. Like Luther, Calvin did not think Christians should pray to the Virgin Mary, the mother of Jesus. However, he went further to say that his church would have no saints, no priests, nor any images of Mary or Jesus. A Calvinist church would be simple and pure, with no ornamentation and only a cross at the altar. Calvin also preached "predestination," the idea that some individuals had been chosen by divine providence to go to heaven and others to hell. In this view, people could do nothing to change the fate God had determined for them; nor could they choose whether or not to believe, for everything had been planned out and divinely ordained before the beginning of time. Calvin's faith emphasized the need for Christians to submit to the will of God. In England, some of Calvin's followers became known as Puritans, while in France Calvinist reformers took the name Huguenots.

Unlike Protestant reformers, Catholics believed that an individual could improve the chances of going to heaven through prayer, good works, and the performance of certain rituals. For Catholics, the most important ritual was the Mass, or Eucharist, which reenacted Jesus' last supper before his death by crucifixion. At a crucial moment in the ceremony, bread and wine actually transformed into the body and blood of Jesus through a process called "transubstantiation." Protestants didn't believe in transubstantiation. Nor did they believe that priests had the ability to make anything sacred or holy with a ritual or blessing. Although both Protestants and Catholics worshipped Jesus as a personal savior who granted his believers salvation and eternal life after death, they viewed each other as earthly enemies who polluted the community of the faithful. Throughout sixteenth-century Europe, many people believed that simply allowing heretics to live would bring down the anger of God on all believers. Both sides looked to men of status and prestige to protect them. When the two sides took up arms against each other, the tensions unleashed in the Reformation turned violent.

John Calvin had sent letters to Antoine de Bourbon, Henry's father, asking for his support for the Protestant cause. Calvin, a reformer trained as a lawyer, extended Martin Luther's religious ideas into a political ideology with an agenda. Having been exiled from France as a subversive, Calvin set up a theocratic state in Geneva where he wrote and enforced the laws according to his religious vision. From this base, he had agents operating throughout Europe spreading the Calvinist religion and fighting to overthrow Catholic governments. They had underground councils and chains of command that planned military strikes against their Catholic enemies.

Antoine de Bourbon wavered in his support of the more extreme reform movement and ultimately stayed loyal to the Catholic faith. Jeanne, Henry's mother, became a devout Protestant. Eventually these religious differences destroyed the marriage, leaving Henry shuffled between them. Antoine took the boy with him to the royal court in Paris, and from the age of 8 to 13 he played with the young king Charles IX and his brothers, the future kings Francis II and Henry III. Henry of Navarre studied a variety of academic subjects in these years, but did not distinguish himself as a scholar. His favorite book was Plutarch's *Parallel Lives*, which included accounts of famous men and women of Greece and Rome. Although rambunctious, he eventually learned to behave at court like a gentleman and a prince. Contemporaries described the youth as short and wiry of frame with reddish hair, lively facial expressions, and a quick wit. After the death of his father, Henry went to live with his mother in her domains in the southwest of France. She raised her son in accordance with strict Biblical principles by encouraging him in daily prayer, reading the Scriptures, and avoiding the sins of the flesh. Having taken up the leadership of the Protestant movement in France, Jeanne actively groomed her son to fight for the reformed religion. After Henry turned 16, Jeanne wrote that she could no longer bear to see her son growing weak in the company of womenfolk. It was time for him to take up arms "for the glory of God, the service of the king, and the duty of his [royal] blood."

The monarchy of France

In the sixteenth century, the kingdom of France included a patchwork of feudal domains. Traditionally, the lords of these domains served as armed warriors, or knights, for more powerful lords. Although France had a king whom all regarded as superior, sometimes the lords of the largest domains challenged his authority. As in all feudal societies, the noble elite operated under a code of honor, or chivalry, that glorified service and personal loyalty. Antoine de Bourbon's dying words about his son perfectly illustrate these values, "May he serve the king well." On the other hand, since feudal warriors glorified service through war, the emerging religious divisions gave them many opportunities to show their honor through violence in a new crusade against the enemies of their faith. Despite the wishes of his father, Henry of Navarre would battle with the armies of several French kings.

The ruler of France at the time was Catherine de Medici (1519–1589). Born into a Florentine banking family, she suffered a tumultuous childhood as the niece of Pope Clement VII (profiled in Chapter 4). At the age of 14, Catherine married the second son of the French king who inherited the throne in 1547 as Henry II, the tenth king of the Valois dynasty. She bore him ten children, including four sons. When Henry II died at a jousting tournament in 1559, his eldest son became King Francis II. As a youth of 15, the new monarch relied on trusted advisors to guide him. Catherine, as queen mother, made sure that he listened to her advice above all others. Who better than the mother of the king to look after his best interests? However, many people in France disliked the queen mother, whom they viewed as a scheming and manipulative power behind the throne. It did not help that Catherine de Medici was foreign, or that she came from Florence, the home of Niccolò Machiavelli. In his famous book *The Prince*, this political thinker seemed to encourage rulers to use cruelty if the ends justified the means. Indeed, Machiavelli had dedicated his controversial book to Catherine's father, Lorenzo de' Medici. Although Catherine was a devoted mother who sought the best for her children under difficult circumstances, popular opinion portrayed her as a ruthless and power-hungry woman who used any means necessary, including violence, to get her way.

As a prince, Francis II had married the adolescent Mary Stuart, Queen of Scotland (1542–1587). Her French uncles were members of the Guise family who led a coalition of militant Catholic extremists. Under the head of the family, Henry, the Duke of Guise, they encouraged the king to call for the total extermination of the Protestant "heresy" in France. Under their leadership, zealous Catholics had killed several hundred Huguenots. After eighteen months, however, Francis II died of an ear abscess. The crown passed to his younger brother, Charles IX, who became king of France at the age of 11. Once again, the balance of power shifted to Catherine de Medici, who as regent made decisions in the name of her son.

Above all, Catherine sought peace between the Catholics and Protestants, but divisions within the royal family itself made this difficult. The Guise family fought for the Catholic faith, while the Bourbons, Henry's family, fought for the Protestants. Catherine tried to attract princes from both families to court, where they could settle their differences without waging war. To entice them, she hosted lavish balls and masquerades for their entertainment, nor was she above using the promise of sex to bring the young warriors to her palace. She kept dozens of attractive young ladies on hand as her "flying squadron," an army of female spies who reported on potential troublemakers. Not surprisingly, Jeanne d'Albret viewed the royal court as a den of moral corruption and tried to keep her son Henry as far from it as possible.

Catherine de Medici cared little about the theological differences between Catholics and Protestants. She tried calling a council in 1561 to establish a compromise between the two interpretations of the religion but neither side could agree on the critical issue of transubstantiation, the question of whether the bread and wine of the Mass actually became the body and blood of Jesus. When the council failed, she declared partial toleration for the Protestants as a compromise. This angered the Catholics, who made up almost ninety percent of the population in France. The law courts of the state, the *Parlements*, protested the edict in the strongest terms, but eventually they had to yield to royal power.

When the queen mother offered toleration to the Huguenots, her Catholic subjects took matters into their own hands by physically attacking Protestants who dared to worship openly. In 1562 the Duke of Guise and his Catholic soldiers came upon a Protestant church service and opened fire. The unprovoked massacre killed at least thirty people and injured a hundred. Both sides used the attack as an excuse to muster more troops. As Guise gathered an army of 20,000 men, Protestant churches began to arm themselves. Many Catholics dreaded the Huguenots as a shadow conspiracy and proposed that even allowing a Protestant to live was an abomination against God. Neither side called for peaceful toleration of the other. Given the difference between these views, any ruler aiming for peace would have been in a difficult situation.

Having originally supported toleration for the Huguenots, Catherine changed her mind and drew closer to the side of the Catholics. For the next several years, the royal house, now influenced by the Catholic faction led by the Guise family, carried out a policy of brutal oppression against the Protestants. One government official, Blaise de Monluc, boasted of personally executing 400 Huguenots. It was said that one could chart his path through France by following the bodies he left hanging from trees. "One man hanged," he said, "was worth one hundred killed in battle." The violence bubbled up from the bottom of society as well. The peasants, most of them loyal Catholics, often initiated the massacres against Protestants. Neither side had respect for the young king. Monluc reported that he had overheard a commoner call Charles IX a "kinglet of shit."

Marriage and massacre

As the violence intensified, Catherine devised a new solution to the problem of religious warfare. She would establish peace by marrying her 19-year-old daughter,

Marguerite of Valois, a Catholic, to Henry of Navarre, a Protestant. When Henry's mother, Jeanne d'Albret, opposed the match, Catherine sent her gifts and letters pleading for her approval. With great reluctance Jeanne agreed to the wedding, only to die three weeks later. Although her doctors pointed to a lung infection as the cause of death, a rumor circulated that she had been poisoned. According to an unfounded but widely believed story, Catherine had sent Jeanne a pair of poisoned gloves just before she died. The queen mother's enemies claimed that she kept an Italian skilled in making lethal potions in her service, as poison was her weapon of choice against political adversaries.

Despite the royal family's adherence to the Catholic faith, they continued to keep high-ranking Protestants close to them at court. Indeed, the young king formed a strong emotional bond with Gaspard de Coligny, a Huguenot, who served as Admiral of France. The young king looked to the admiral as a father figure. When Coligny began to take Catherine's place as main advisor to the king, however, the queen mother looked toward the admiral with growing mistrust.

The wedding between Henry and Marguerite, the "Pearl of the Valois," took place in Paris on 21 August, 1572. Chronicles related that the princess, remarkable for her beauty and intelligence, had little interest in marrying a Protestant from the south of France, who reportedly smelled like garlic and rot. One story claims that during the ceremony, when the priest asked if she agreed to take Henry as her husband, she said nothing. Her brother, the king, forced her to nod with a smack to the back of her head, and the priest pronounced the couple married. The city celebrated the royal wedding with several nights of feasting and games.

Tragically, however, the carnival atmosphere of Paris turned somber on 22 August, when a bullet from a would-be assassin hit Coligny in the arm. That night, as the admiral took to his chamber to recover, Charles IX and his mother stayed by his bedside. A mood of pervasive fear enveloped the royal court. While Protestants worried that Catholics might make another assassination attempt, Catholics feared retaliation. The next day, Catherine called a meeting of her council to decide the king's next move. No one knows for certain who proposed a preemptive strike against the Huguenots, but the entire council, including the king and his mother approved the plan. Fearing a counter attack, the royal family called for the immediate execution of Admiral Coligny and several dozen Protestant leaders who had gathered for the royal wedding.

On 24 August, St. Bartholomew's Day, supporters of the Guise family found Coligny in his palace chamber and pierced him through the side with a spear. They then threw him out of the window, where another man finally ended his life by chopping off his head. Rumors circulated that the head was presented to the king and queen mother, who had it embalmed and sent to the pope in Rome. Soon after Coligny fell, the Guises and their agents embarked upon a brutal hunt for the leaders of the Protestant movement.

For years afterward, Henry of Navarre would say that thinking about the horrible events of that fateful day made his hair stand on end. Having been summoned to the king's bed chamber with his cousin, the prince of Condé, he and his entourage of Huguenot supporters anxiously made their way through the corridors of the palace. At the threshold of the king's apartments, doors opened to allow Henry and Condé to enter and quickly shut behind them, leaving his companions and supporters in the hall. A massacre followed. While Henry and Condé remained safe inside the king's chamber, they could hear the screams of their closest friends and allies, many of whom had been childhood friends, butchered by the Guises and their supporters in the halls and courtyard of the palace. It was a blow to the movement as well as a personal and emotional loss for Henry.

Outside the palace, the common people followed the lead of the court and slaughtered Protestants wherever and however they wanted. According to one account, enraged Catholics murdered a Protestant couple, stripped their little daughter naked, and dipped her in the blood of her parents. Her tormentors warned that if she did not become a Catholic, she would suffer the same fate as her parents. Mobs dehumanized their victims as they speared and mutilated their bodies. It was said that the Seine river ran red with the blood of nearly three thousand victims. Some used the mayhem to settle personal scores, as debtors killed their creditors, servants killed their masters, and sons killed their fathers. The poor stripped the dead bodies of clothing, a precious commodity in the sixteenth century, leaving heaps of bloody and naked corpses along the streets of Paris. At the same time, however, some Catholics hid and protected their Huguenot friends. Even the Catholic Duke of Guise spared the lives of three small children, intending to baptize them into the Catholic faith.

FIGURE 1.4 François Dubois, *An Eyewitness Account of the St. Bartholomew's Day Massacre,* c. 1572. Historians are not certain that the artist, a protestant, actually witnessed the massacre.

Source: Niday Picture Library/Alamy Stock Photo

Both sides engaged in ritual violence as they tortured and killed their enemies in the name of their religion, but they went about it differently. Protestants targeted priests, bishops, monks, and nuns, while Catholics did not distinguish between heretics. Whereas Protestants tended to deface and vandalize the symbols of the Catholic faith, smashing statues of Mary, throwing communion wafers to dogs, and smearing feces on the water basins used to baptize the faithful, Catholics sought to destroy the Protestant bodies. For this reason, they often mutilated corpses, dragging them through the streets, cutting out their intestines, and slicing off their genitals. Both sides dehumanized the other, referring to their religious enemies as parasites or vermin. Regarding their enemies as inhuman devils rather than people, many considered it their moral duty to rid the Earth of unbelievers. The printing presses spewed out anonymous pamphlets that stoked the flames of religious hatred by publicizing the atrocities committed by the other side and depicting their enemies as agents of Satan.

In 1574, the troubled and sickly King Charles IX suddenly died at the age of 24. His younger brother acceded to the throne as Henry III. The new king proved as ineffective as the previous two in dealing with the religious turmoil. Remarkably unconcerned with politics or military strategy, he directed his energy toward elegant and fashionable attire, perfume, and his three hundred lap dogs. At court he surrounded himself with *mignons*, attractive young men who curled their long hair and wore make up. The king and his courtiers closely followed outrageous fashion trends, such as wearing doublets, or quilted jackets, with four sleeves—two for their arms, and two remaining in back of their outfit for no apparent reason. To many of his contemporaries, the king seemed to care more about his *mignons* than his subjects.

The St. Bartholomew's Day massacres left the Huguenots without a leader. Jeanne d'Albret and Coligny had died, while Henry of Navarre and his cousin, Condé, had been taken captive by the court. What remained of the Protestant cause, however, only strengthened its resolve. Protestant armies conquered and fortified a number of towns in the south of France in the Languedoc region. From this base, they created a political agenda calling for the overthrow of the French monarchy and the establishment of a republic in France. Several influential writers looked to the Estates General, a traditional assembly, which included representatives from the French clergy, nobility, and common people, to depose the French king. Having read about the democracies of ancient Greece and Rome, they maintained that the people had the duty to resist a tyrant. Protestants aimed at nothing short of full revolution.

The vast majority of French Catholics, however, believed that their kings ruled as sacred monarchs. Beginning with Clovis, the first king of the Franks who converted to Christianity in the sixth century CE, kings were anointed by bishops with a sacred oil that made them holy in the sight of God. The special status gave French kings the "royal touch," a magical ability to cure disease by placing their hands on the sick. For French Catholics, kings represented divine will on earth, and an attack on the monarchy itself was a crime against the entire natural order as established by

God. The Huguenot call to revolution, which threatened traditional beliefs about the religious, political, and social order, incited in Catholics an even greater urgency to destroy their enemies.

Henry in command

Henry survived the massacre by quickly converting to Catholicism. He remained at the palace as a captive of the royal family under heavy surveillance. Despite the horrifying loss of many family and friends, Henry acted as though nothing had happened. He played the charming courtier, joking, carousing, and hunting with the royal family and the Guise brothers who had carried out the murder of his companions. His carefree superficiality was a ruse to hide his considerable intelligence, however, as Henry only pretended to be shallow and dim to gain the trust of his captors. Slowly they gave him more privileges until one day, 5 February, 1576, he rode his horse into the royal woods to hunt and never returned to the royal palace. Instead, he galloped off to the south of France where he joined the Protestant army.

After the death of Jeanne D'Albret, Henry inherited the throne of Navarre and took control of the Protestant army. In command of tens of thousands of soldiers, Henry now had an opportunity to show his talent for leadership. He employed state of the art military tactics on the field such as the *pistolade*, in which soldiers on horseback charged ahead while firing their guns and switching to hand-to-hand combat as they moved in closer. Most important, the king of Navarre impressed his soldiers with displays of exceptional bravery and courage. His troops could see the white feather he wore in his cap as it moved up and down the front of lines of the battlefield, and he often left the combat zone covered in blood and gunpowder. In one engagement, Henry found himself completely surrounded by enemy soldiers. Considering himself lost, he shouted out to his troops, "Are there fifty gentlemen with courage enough to die with their prince?" A company of horsemen rallied to his service and saved his life. On another occasion, a messenger from the German lands handed a piece paper to Henry as a bullet went straight through his head. The poor messenger was killed instantly, but Henry did not flinch. His valor often seemed excessive and foolhardy to his main advisors, but it undoubtedly boosted the morale of his army.

When not engaged on the battlefield, Henry of Navarre spent evenings with the local country gentlemen, gambling, feasting, swigging wine, and chasing women with the local country gentlemen. His behavior sometimes scandalized the local communities where he set up court. In the town of Agen, Henry purportedly organized a magnificent ball and invited a number of ladies from the families of the region. As the dancing reached its liveliest point late in the night, Henry ordered all of the lights put out, leaving the ballroom in total darkness. His aim was to give his guests (and himself) the opportunity to engage freely in anonymous sex, but his plan backfired. Concerned about their honor, and undoubtedly fearing sexual assault, several young women panicked. One leaped out of a window and broke her leg, becoming the subject of an old folk song that memorialized the event for centuries. Such lecherous behavior had little impact on Henry's marriage. Marguerite, whose numerous sexual escapades had scandalized the French court for years, did not expect marital fidelity from her husband, nor did Henry, for his part, mind his wife's affairs. On the surface, Henry's addiction to pleasure led opponents to discount his abilities. Those who underestimated him, however, were mistaken; behind his roguish charisma lay a reserve of serious military force.

Tensions between Protestants and Catholics intensified when the youngest of Catherine de Medici's four sons, the Duke of Anjou, died in 1584. He was a romantic figure who had once threatened to challenge his older brother, Henry III, for the throne of France. At times he seemed to ally with Navarre and the Protestants, and at one point appeared to be engaged to marry the Protestant Elizabeth I of England (profiled in Chapter 3). However, his death at a young age complicated the political situation, as it left only Henry III as the last of the Valois dynasty. In the event that Henry III died, the crown would then by law descend on his closest male relative, the senior member of the Bourbon family, who happened to be Henry of Navarre. The fact that only one man's life stood in the way of a Protestant heretic on the throne of France struck terror into the hearts of French Catholics. In response to this threat, the leaders of the Guise family formed what was known as the Catholic League. Organized into political cells in the cities, they allied with Spain, recruited soldiers to fight for a country united under the Catholic faith, and took the motto, *Un roi, une foi, un loi* (One king, one faith, one law).

Henry III did not take a strong position on either side of the religious debate. Like his mother, he repeatedly switched sides to favor one over the other. Although firm in his Catholic faith, the king of France had political reasons to support the Protestants who controlled the southern half of the country. Wanting peace above all else, Henry III and the queen mother, Catherine, appeased the Protestants at first by granting them more freedom than they had previously enjoyed. In response, the Catholic League declared open rebellion against the monarchy and refused to recognize the will of the king as law. In 1585, Henry III switched sides again, favoring the Catholics by revoking his earlier edicts that had granted rights to the Huguenots.

While the royal family wavered, Henry of Navarre continued to fight in the south. With his small army, he did not dare fight large, pitched battles, where his soldiers would be outnumbered. Instead, his army harassed the enemy in nearly constant skirmishes. The exceptional battle of Coutras, on 20 October 1587, however, proved his ability to win a more traditional battle. Fought outside a village near Bordeaux in southwest France, Henry's army faced a much larger royal army. Henry III sent one of his favorite *mignons*, the Duke of Joyeuse, a handsome man in his mid-twenties, to lead the Catholic forces. His army, formed into in two long lines, contained an impressive display of noblemen on horseback, adorned from head to toe in shining armor. One eyewitness claimed he had never seen an army in France so covered in gold leaf.

Compared to the colorful and majestic army of the royalists, Henry of Navarre's Protestant soldiers appeared dingy in their leather clothes and dull steel breastplates.

Nevertheless, this army made better use of the terrain, setting themselves beyond a deep ravine, and hiding infantry among marshes and thickets. Henry had arranged his army into effective squadrons of pikemen, arqubusiers, and light cavalry. As was his custom, his cavalry led the charge into battle singing Psalm 118: "This is the day that the Lord has made. I shall rejoice and be glad in it." Fighting shoulder to shoulder with his men on the frontline, Henry suddenly found himself facing the standard bearer of the enemy army. Amazed and overjoyed to recognize him as a childhood friend, Henry cheerfully charged ahead, grabbed him by the waist, and shouted, "Surrender, Philistine!" Even in the thick of battle, Henry could hardly hide the friendliness that defined his character.

With a combination of superior artillery and fierce hand-to hand combat, Navarre's army routed the royalists. As many as three thousand soldiers fell, among them hundreds of knights of the highest nobility, while the Protestants lost only fifty men. After the stunning victory at Coutras, Navarre's military advisors suggested he take advantage of his success by combining his forces with an army of Protestant troops arriving from the German lands. Instead, he split up his army and marched to a distant town where, in a striking act of romantic chivalry, he placed twenty-two captured flags at the feet of his mistress, Dianne d'Andouins.

The Catholic League

Following these defeats, the brothers who led the Catholic League, Henry of Guise and his brother, the cardinal of Guise, did not trust King Henry III and his royal army with enforcing the new anti-Huguenot policy, nor did their League supporters in Paris. On 12 May, 1588, they joined forces to lead an uprising in the city. Angry mobs rose in revolt against the king, building barricades in the streets and shouting, "Long live the Duke of Guise." Henry III, who had completely lost control of his kingdom, was forced to flee Paris. The Catholic League, now fully in control of the city, carried out a policy of terror, executing not only Protestants, but also moderate Catholics who showed any degree of support for the monarchy. The three-way fight between Henry of Navarre, Henry of Guise, and Henry III was called the "War of the Three Henrys" (1587–1589).

Henry III increasingly considered the Guise brothers and the Catholic league a dangerous threat to his royal authority. Seven months after the day of the barricades, Henry III invited the Guise brothers to his castle in the town of Blois on 23 December. As Henry welcomed the Duke into his chamber, the king ordered his guards to seize and slaughter him. His brother, the cardinal waiting in the next room, was quickly shackled and executed the following day. In order to avoid the possibility of supporters collecting relics of the two martyred brothers, the king had their bodies hacked into pieces and burned; the ashes were then scattered in the wind. That evening, Henry III calmly celebrated Christmas Mass. The queen mother, lying on her deathbed, had not approved of her son's ruthless actions, scolding, "What do you think you have done? You have killed two men who have left a lot of friends." Two weeks later, Catherine de Medici died at the age of 71.

The unexpected executions of the Guise brothers incited fanatical Catholic preachers to call for the death of the king as a tyrant. Angry mobs in Paris shouted, "Murder! Fire! Blood!" and "Vengeance!" Seven months later, on August 1, 1589, a young monk sought Henry III at his army's camp in St. Cloud, west of Paris as the king prepared for an attack on the city. Posing as a messenger, the monk drew closer to the king, pulled out a hidden dagger and drove it into the king's abdomen. The wound proved mortal. For the first time in history, a French king had been killed by one of his subjects. In the streets of Paris, Catholics feasted and danced to the news of his death.

Henry of Navarre becomes king

The Salic Law, one of the most ancient and fundamental laws of France, stipulated that the crown could only pass through the male line. The death of Catherine de Medici's four sons without heirs transferred the kingdom to the nearest male relative, Henry of Navarre. Although he now ruled France as King Henry IV, a majority of the French people considered him a Protestant heretic and therefore ineligible for the crown. Through sermons and pamphlets, the leaders of the Catholic League warned that Henry IV's true aim was to torture and kill French Catholics. Chaos and terror reigned throughout Paris and the kingdom, which suffered the ravages of famine, plague, and massive inflation. Peasants who grew tired of marauding armies burning their villages and fields rose in revolt throughout France. If Henry wanted to rule as king, he would have to conquer the land he had inherited by military force.

Making his motto "Victory or death," Henry IV laid siege to Paris in 1590. With the help of 5,000 English troops sent by Elizabeth I, Henry had been able to take the towns surrounding the capital. For four months, he blockaded the city. The inhabitants were forced to eat rats to survive. Finally the Catholic Parisians appealed to the Catholic Philip II, the King of Spain, to relieve them. He responded by diverting the Spanish army from the Netherlands to France in order to force Henry IV to protect his hard-won territory. However, instead of meeting the Huguenots in open battle, the Spanish troops forced their way into Paris to establish a garrison in the city. The Parisian Catholics welcomed the foreign army, shouting, "Long live Philip II."

Henry IV attempted to take advantage of the League's alliance with Spain to appeal to French patriotism against a foreign power. In the end, however, the overwhelming majority of French people remained firm in their demand for a Catholic king. In 1593, Henry IV relented and agreed to be "instructed" by a council of Catholic scholars. Shortly afterward, he officially converted in a public ceremony rich with pageantry and grandeur. Many of his subjects rejoiced, although some questioned his sincerity. A longstanding tradition has Henry IV justifying his decision to convert with the comment, "Paris is well worth a Mass." Whether he actually said this is uncertain, but the French still use the phrase today when confronted with a situation requiring a difficult compromise. With his conversion, Henry appeared to put loyalty to his country above his own religious beliefs. However, his devotion to the Catholic faith, once he accepted it, seemed genuine to those closest to him. His coronation took place in February, 1594.

Henry takes control of France

Not surprisingly, the members of the League did not accept Henry's conversion and continued to fight. They set up barricades in Paris and prepared for a revolution. After a long and painful siege, Henry IV took control of the city in 1594. One report says that he passed through the gates of Paris in good cheer, saying, "All I demand is your affection, good bread, good wine, and friendly faces." The weary but relieved people of Paris greeted him with shouts of *Vive le roi* (Long live the king). He did not punish his defeated adversaries, whether members of the League or foreign troops. Instead, he allowed them to leave in peace. As the 3,000 Spanish soldiers left the capital, Henry reportedly told them, "Give my regards to your king, but do not come back."

Once in power, Henry did not hold grudges against former enemies. Although he never forgot the murder of his companions in the St. Bartholomew's Day massacre, he forgave those responsible for it. When Charles of Guise, the son of Henry of Guise (executed by Henry III), offered his loyalty to Henry IV in a ceremony at the palace of the Louvre in 1595, the king embraced him. Referring to him as his nephew, as though his father had been his brother, the king paid tribute to the man who had been his bitter enemy for most of his life. Henry astonished the audience when he recalled how he and Henry of Guise had been close friends who admired each other in many ways. He added, "We are all capable of youthful follies . . . I'll forget about these."

The charitable opinion of Catherine de Medici he expressed in a letter written long after her death in 1599 illustrated his remarkable capacity to see the best in others:

> But I ask you, what could the poor woman do, left with five children to provide for after the death of her husband, and with two families, ourselves and the Guises, who thought about usurping the crown? Wasn't it necessary that she play many roles to fool both while protecting her children, who reigned one after the other, thanks to the guidance of so shrewd a woman? I am surprised she never did worse![3]

He refused to condemn Catherine for engaging in betrayal and deceit in order to protect her children. Such was her primary function as a mother of a family, and especially, the mother of kings. Nor did Henry deny his own guilt as one who fought against the monarchy. Rather than nursing resentments from the past, Henry looked forward to rebuilding the kingdom.

The king made it clear that former enemies had much to gain from supporting his reign. Flattery and the offer of friendship proved attractive to many who once swore to kill him by any means necessary. In the end, Henry often resorted to paying people for their loyalty, buying off many noblemen and making gifts to towns, either exempting them from taxation or simply providing cash payments. His minister, the Duke of Sully, estimated that he had spent millions of *livres* (French pounds) to win the loyalty of the people. Henry remarked that these expenses were a bargain in the long run, since a war would have cost ten times as much.

The Huguenots worried that Henry's conversion would leave them helpless against their Catholic enemies. However, Henry worked to make a place for them in the French kingdom. In 1598 Henry put forth a royal decree, the Edict of Nantes, which gave Huguenots the right to worship in designated places as well as access to equal justice and the right hold offices. The *parlement* defied the will of the king by refusing to register the edict. Henry IV met this challenge with an impassioned speech to the assembly. He claimed that his power rested on two foundations: tradition and force. As he stated, "I have established the state which is mine by inheritance and by conquest." Seeking to persuade rather than coerce his subjects, he spoke to them plainly: "You see me here in my study, and I am speaking to you, not in royal attire with cape and sword, but dressed like the father of a family, in a simple jacket, speaking frankly to his children." Reminding them of the pain and suffering caused by religious wars, he convinced his officials to accept the edict. At the same time, he vowed to be tough with those still offering resistance to his authority. He threatened to decapitate any person who preached religious violence or revolution, and added, "I have leaped onto city walls, I can leap over your barricades."

Once he secured his royal authority, Henry worked hard to win the hearts of all of the French people. He seemed to have something to offer people in all walks of life, and talked to subjects as though he sincerely loved them. Understanding that many had suffered starvation and loss during the wars, he promised that no peasant family would be so poor that they could not afford "a chicken in every pot on Sunday." It was a memorable phrase that evoked a sense of French identity, from the celebrated dish of *coq au vin* (chicken and wine), to the image of the rooster, a traditional symbol of France.

The succession question

Henry had pacified his kingdom, but problems remained in his relationship with the pope as well as the ongoing threat of Spanish invasion. As he put it, "I am attacked by so many burdens and problems that I hardly know which saint to pray to." The king understood that lasting peace would be impossible without a stable monarchy, and this required an heir to the throne. In 1594 a young student from a Jesuit college lunged out of a crowd with a dagger aimed at the king's throat. Fortunately, the knife only cut his upper lip and chipped a tooth, but Henry feared that his death would plunge the country into another civil war. His wife, Marguerite of Valois, had not given him any children; in 1582, she went back to her mother and never returned to his court. In 1599, Henry sought an annulment of their marriage from the pope. Although the Catholic Church prohibited divorce, it often granted annulments to marriages that were invalid or illegitimate. Often, couples seeking an annulment claimed that the marriage had never been consummated by intercourse. When the papal commissioner questioned Henry about whether the couple had "communicated together," the king reportedly answered, "On the night of our wedding we were both so young and randy that stopping us would have been impossible." Eventually the marriage was declared invalid on the grounds that Marguerite had been pressured against her will into matrimony by her mother, which had indeed been the case in 1572. The queen cooperated with her husband on the issue of the annulment, persuaded not a little by substantial cash payments.

The annulment of his marriage allowed Henry to select a new bride. He had wanted to marry his favorite mistress, Gabrielle d'Estrées, his lover of almost ten years. A natural beauty, she had long shared his camp tent during the years of endless warfare, where she washed his clothes and handled his correspondence. As a Catholic, she served as a diplomat for him with the League, and sat on the king's advisory council along with Henry's sister, Catherine. After giving birth to three of Henry's children, Gabrielle died after going into labor with his fourth, a stillborn baby. Her death caused him incredible grief, which he attempted to relieve with an unrestrained bout of womanizing. He confessed that for two weeks he had not slept twice in the same bed.

In 1600, Henry chose Marie de Medici, an Italian duchess, as his second queen. A very distant cousin of Catherine de Medici, Marie was the daughter of the Duke of Tuscany and the Archduchess of Austria. She brought with her an enormous dowry of 3.5 million *livres*. Although the marriage produced three children, it was not particularly happy. Henry had at least fifty named mistresses in addition to innumerable sexual encounters with unnamed partners. His exploits earned him the nickname *vert galant* (the green gallant), an old man with a youthful love of pleasure. A jealous queen, Marie showed resentment when Henry insisted that she raise their children together with those of Gabrielle and his other mistresses. Despite these tensions in the household, contemporaries described Henry as a doting and affectionate father to his nine children. French artists have often portrayed Henry IV playing with his children at court, crawling on his hands and knees with a child riding horsey on his back. Images such as these won the hearts of his people and reinforced his symbolic role as a father to his country.

The new regime

When Marie de Medici gave birth to a son in 1601, the future Louis XIII, France celebrated. With the succession secured for another generation, the years of bloodshed and civil war were over. As they breathed a collective sigh of relief, Henry and his main advisor, the Duke of Sully, went to work rebuilding the country. A Protestant until his death, Sully had served Henry faithfully for decades, waking every morning at 4 a.m. During the wars, Sully put his considerable talent for mathematics to use predicting the parabolas of cannon balls and bullets, a strategic skill of critical importance on the battlefield. With the kingdom at peace, Sully focused on finances and engineering. He balanced the budget and established a corps of royal engineers to build bridges, roads, and canals. Indeed, before him, France had to hire foreigners to complete engineering projects, because no one in the entire country had sufficient education or training. Sully changed this situation by making engineering a high status and well paid occupation, a policy that set France on a path to prosperity and technological innovation. At the same time, he valued agriculture as a foundation of the economy. As he colorfully explained, farming and livestock were the "two breasts" by which France was fed, "the true mines and treasures of Peru." With his love of order and stability, Sully provided a great balance to the fun-loving but emotionally volatile Henry IV. It is a great testament to Henry's leadership ability that he recognized the brilliance of his right hand man.

Central to Sully's plan was the reconstruction of Paris as a capital city. He envisioned grand spaces where the king could demonstrate his power by putting on shows of royal grandeur, whether spectacles or parades. These important and magnificent spaces are still used and enjoyed in Paris to this day. Such shows brought the public as spectators into a common space dominated by a central power. By watching the same performances and ceremonies, the French people increasingly believed they had something in common with each other, something that made them specifically French. Drawn to the capital, the nobility was less likely to raise armies on their own feudal domains. The glittering and seductive nightlife of Paris, combined with the luxuries provided by peace and prosperity compensated the nobility for the loss of their military campaigns. Moreover, these aristocrats developed increasingly ostentatious tastes and soon supported entire industries to clothe them in the latest fashions and to supply their growing desires for the finest things Paris could offer. Originally catering to noble tastes, these new industries resulted in a rapid rise of middle class merchants and craftsmen who also sought out marks of social distinction.

The peasants, by agreeing to lay down their arms, surrendered a great deal of military power to the central government. However, their lands became more productive with the arrival of peace and the end of warfare and chaos. They also grew to believe that King Henry IV cared about them personally. When a group of peasants known as the *croquants* ("clodhoppers") rose in revolt against the nobility in the south of France, Henry listened to their grievances and worked to appease them by lowering their taxes. He even commented that since the *croquants* were fighting government officials, he was tempted to become one himself. The king worked to keep local landowners and treasury officials from oppressing the peasantry. Despite their low position in society, French peasants rarely blamed their kings for their suffering. They looked to him to bring justice against the people they considered their real enemies, the local nobility. And in return, most French kings took seriously their role as protective father of all their subjects.

Henry's reputation as a womanizer did nothing to diminish his popularity with the French people, and his weakness for women continued into his old age. While in his fifties, he developed a passion for Charlotte de Montmorency, a young girl of 15. To bring her within reach, he arranged a marriage between the girl and one of his cousins, the prince of Condé. After the marriage, Condé took his young bride to Brussels specifically to avoid the advances of the king on his wife. Henry ordered the couple back to court, but Condé refused. Enraged at this defiance, Henry threatened to make his way toward Brussels, vowing to take an army of 50,000 men north to invade the Netherlands unless Charlotte returned to court. By May of 1610 he had an army of 30,000 prepared to march north. Nevertheless, the ill-advised French invasion of the Netherlands never happened.

On May 14, 1610, the king was riding in a carriage near the Louvre when it stopped in a traffic jam. As the windows were open to let in the fresh air of a sunny spring day, a fanatical Catholic named Ravaillac lunged into the carriage and plunged a carving knife deep into Henry's chest. His knife punctured Henry's lung and cut his aorta, killing the king within a few minutes. Ravaillac was captured and tortured in order to find his accomplices. Despite being burned with molten lead and having his flesh torn off with hot pincers, he ultimately revealed no co-conspirators. Ravaillac suffered the customary punishment for regicide, death by drawing and quartering. The executioners lashed his arms and legs to four horses, and when they spurred the horses to gallop in four directions, they tore his body into pieces.

Henry's son by Marie de Medici, Louis XIII, was only eight years old at the time of his death. Too young to preside as king, Marie de Medici ruled France as regent until he reached maturity. Despite the turmoil and intrigue of his early years, Louis XIII ruled France with an exceptionally competent minister, Cardinal Richelieu. His son and successor, Louis XIV, continued to strengthen and centralize the French monarchy. Traumatized by the anarchy and violence of the sixteenth century, the kings of the Bourbon dynasty ruled France as absolute monarchs for nearly two hundred years until Louis XVI and his wife, Marie Antoinette were deposed and decapitated by guillotine during the French Revolution of 1789. Henry IV's legacy was to tie the people of France to an idea of sacred kingship. Although the Revolution destroyed the institution of the monarchy, devotion to the unity of the state remains. Orderly, benevolent, and paternal, Henry's vision of state power remains influential today.

Chronology

1553 Birth of Henry of Navarre.
1559 Francis II becomes king of France.
1560 Charles IX becomes king of France.
1562 Massacre at Vassy. First civil war begins.
1572 St. Bartholomew's Day Massacre. Henry converts to Catholicism.
1574 Henry III becomes king of France.
1576 Henry of Navarre escapes captivity and renounces Catholicism.
1588 Day of the Barricades. Catholic League takes over Paris.

1589   Death of Catherine de Medici. Assassination of Henry III. Henry of Navarre inherits the throne of France.

1593   Henry IV converts to Catholicism.

1594   Coronation of Henry IV. He successfully takes the city of Paris.

1598   Edict of Nantes grants Huguenots limited rights.

1610   Assassination of Henry IV. His son, Louis XIII becomes king of France.

Sources for further reading about Henry IV of France

There are many lively biographies of Henry IV, but the most recent and authoritative in English is *Henri IV of France: His Reign and Age* by Vincent J. Pitts (Baltimore, MD: Johns Hopkins University Press, 2009). A good introduction for a general reader is David Buisseret, *Henry IV King of France* (Boston, MA: G. Allen & Unwin, 1984). A more critical perspective on the king is Roland Mousnier, *The Assassination of Henry IV: The Tyrannicide Problem and the Consolidation of the French Absolute Monarchy in the Early Seventeenth Century*, trans. Joan Spencer (New York: Charles Scribner's Sons, 1973). The era of the French wars of Religion is extremely complicated, but overviews may be found in R. J. Knecht, *The Rise and Fall of Renaissance France* 1483–1610 (Oxford: Blackwell, 2001) and *The French Wars of Religion 1559–1598* (London: Routledge, 2010). Mack Holt, *The French Wars of Religion 1562–1629* (Cambridge: Cambridge University Press, 1995) also provides a good overview, but concentrates less on the figure of Henry IV himself. A classic work on the era for scholars of history is J. H. M. Salmon, *Society in Crisis: France in the Sixteenth Century* (London: Routledge, 1979). An older, short, and extremely general overview of the era for a general reader may be found in J. E. Neale, *The Age of Catherine de Medici* (London: Jonathan Cape, 1943). A revisionary work on the Wars of Religion is Robert Kingdon, *Myths about the St. Bartholomew's Day Massacres 1572–1576* (Cambridge, MA: Harvard University Press, 1988). A social and economic perspective on the era is Henry Heller, *Iron and Blood: Civil Wars in Sixteenth-Century France* (Montreal: McGill-Queen's University Press, 1991). Lively treatments of battles and diplomacy in France, Spain, and England may be found in Garrett Mattingly's *The Armada* (Boston, MA: Houghton Mifflin, 1959). A good book on the general history of France is James B. Collins, *From Tribes to Nation. The Making of France 500–1799* (Toronto: Thompson, 2002). For a more in-depth discussion of the complex relationship between Church and state in seventeenth-century France, see Joseph Bergin, *The Politics of Religion in Early Modern France* (New Haven, CT: Yale University Press, 2014).

Comparison between Hideyoshi and Henry IV

As outsiders, Hideyoshi and Henry IV relied on their own energy and initiative to make their way in the world. Although born a prince, Henry IV suffered discrimination as the member of a hated religious minority. Hideyoshi began life as a strange-looking peasant. Both men inspired contempt, but found ways to win people to their side. Making the most of their humble qualities, one imagines them playing a performance throughout their careers. Henry IV was dirty, unkempt, and smelled like carrion and garlic. Hideyoshi, on occasion, danced like a monkey at the court of Nobunaga. Such qualities did not inspire ridicule, but rather admiration as displays of the courage that had their counterpart on the battlefield. They partied and got drunk, loved women, made funny jokes, and won the loyalty and admiration of the common folk. These characteristics, combined with bravery and a higher purpose, gave them a charisma that has lasted centuries.

Above all, Hideyoshi and Henry IV were men of words. Although they impressed their followers with military victories, they succeeded and conquered because they communicated a compelling vision. They convinced contemporaries that they had more to gain from friendship than enmity. Of course, had they not been brave or crafty, no one would have listened to them. Nevertheless, had they relied on cleverness and brute force alone, they would not have led their people out of chaos into lasting nation states.

The unending brutal wars that each man faced emerged out of the conditions inherent in feudal society. In the middle ages, wealth and status came from land that was granted to warriors by more powerful warlords as a reward for prowess on the battlefield. For centuries, Japan and France was dominated by an elite society of samurai and knights who engaged in endless conflicts concerning loyalty or betrayal. That world was bloody enough, but by the sixteenth century, a new element introduced complications to this world: the gun. The primitive hand-held firearm called the arquebus, a precursor of the musket, had changed the nature of the battles, as feudal lords began to enlist common people as foot soldiers to fight for them. This engaged the entire population in war. It also ensured that the people would begin to assert their own interests and demand concessions from their warlord leaders. There was a phenomenal upsurge in social mobility. Larger armies required more technical expertise and a better-defined rationale for putting lives on the line. This was fertile ground for new ideologies that arose as an effort to enlist the support of the populace for a particular cause. Was Nobunaga fighting for a united Japan, as Hideyoshi proclaimed? Or was he using that ideology to enlist soldiers to increase his personal power? Similarly, more than one historian has suggested that the religious conflict in France between Catholics and Protestants had more to do with rivalry than personal conviction. Historians can only guess at motives.

Despite the greater complexity of warfare—new weapons, better organization, larger armies, higher ideological stakes—some things did not change. The nature of power itself remained personal. One was expected to show loyalty to an individual, not to a legal code, state, or ideology. This system of personal loyalty required a code of honor. Whether chivalry or the way of the samurai (*bushido*), a vassal owed loyalty to a person. This code stressed self-discipline and respect for others of the same group. The shame of misconduct or betrayal had to be extinguished by death. In Japan, this was *seppuku*, or ritual suicide. In Europe, perhaps the best equivalent is the duel. Over 4,000 people lost their lives in duels in the reign of Henry IV. As in Japan, these ritual forms of death only applied to aristocrats, for both societies restricted honor to the nobility. Both *seppuku* and the duel represented the ultimate honor as self-annihilation. This connection only increased the instability that permeated both cultures.

In many ways, Hideyoshi and Henry IV broke free from the constraints of tradition to establish new regimes. They found a way to make their contemporaries put their weapons down and agree to peace. People of every social and economic status found something to like about the new orders they established.

These two leaders provided assurances to the aristocracy that they would remain at the top of the social hierarchy. In both societies, the divisions between social classes hardened. In Hideyoshi's case, this was the distinction between farmers and warriors—under him, no samurai was allowed to live in the village, nor could any village peasant take up arms. In this way, the warrior aristocracy lost access to the peasant armies they might use to take over the central government. But this also meant a greater stratification of society with less social mobility. In the case of Henry IV, France restricted the right to bear arms to the nobility.

The swords carried by the nobility increasingly served purely ceremonial functions. The aristocracy began to distinguish itself through taste, education and refinement rather than military valor. Both rulers established glittering and seductive courts that required the presence of courtiers, not soldiers. Here there participated in the rituals of royal pageantry that centered on the ruler as the primary source of honor.

A renaissance of learning accompanied this shift in noble function. The contemporaries of Hideyoshi and Henry IV self-consciously revived the literature, pastimes, and culture of the Middle Ages. In Europe, this meant jousting and the romances of Roland and King Arthur. In Japan, there was a renewed emphasis on the courtly romances of the Heian era. Speaking and writing with eloquence gained in importance. The self-discipline required for education replaced military discipline. Perhaps most strikingly, appreciation of beauty took on a new importance in each society. The aesthetics of Japan and France diverged enormously, as France preferred the look of Greco-Roman classicism, while the Japanese developed a theory of *wabi-sabi*. Classicism looked toward the balance and harmony of clean lines and mathematical proportions, especially privileging symmetry in design. On the other hand, *wabi-sabi*, as Rikyū pursued it through the way of tea, preferred objects with a rustic, natural, and asymmetrical appearance. Both admired the beauty of the old and antique for its own sake.

Perhaps the best illustration of these aesthetic ideals can be seen in layout of the formal garden. The European garden of this time was divided into geometric sections called parterres, with flowers forming the hedges, and a fountain providing a focus point right in the middle of the garden. In contrast, the ideal Japanese garden took the form of a natural world, but reduced into miniature forms, so that even small spaces would have rivers, hills, trees, rocks, and possibly waterfalls. The garden proclaimed the prestige of the nobility, for no one else could afford land, leisure, and the labor required to maintain a plot of earth which serves no other purpose than to provide a beautiful space for pleasure or meditation. Such status displays replaced violence as a means to convey honor.

Merchants, professionals, and skilled craftsmen also had much to gain with the new regime. Both Hideyoshi and Henry IV understood the importance of fostering trade and commerce. When the aristocracy settled in capitals such as Edo (present-day Tokyo) and Paris, they brought an influx of tradesmen and professionals to sustain them. They needed doctors, lawyers, merchants, tailors, teachers, entertainers, and any number of occupations. Soon these courts, with their entourages, blossomed into mega-cities. In Tokyo and Paris, some members of this middling group grew richer than the aristocracy. Freed from the need to maintain ceremonial functions, many found other ways to spend exorbitant amounts of money on books, journals, concerts, art, and theater. Popular culture flourished in the seventeenth century, For the first time, literature portrayed the lives of ordinary people without noble status. The subjects of these new books were not epic battles, court romances, or religious treatises, but dramas and comedies centering on the life of ordinary people. As those in the middle of the social order grew conscious of their own status, material consumption increased, providing more economic opportunities as well as anxiety about one's place in the world. In both Paris and Tokyo businessmen frequented entertainment districts where they could drink too much, frolic with the "ladies of the night," and briefly forget the never-ending struggle to get ahead in the world.

By and large, the peasantry on the bottom of society resigned itself to its position. Under Hideyoshi and Henry IV, at least, the peasants had faith in their leaders. Although the farmers of the village lost ground in terms of political independence, they gained much from the establishment of peace. They no longer had to fear the rape and pillage of marauding armies, nor suffer their houses being burned to the ground in war. As the land became more productive, the diet of French and Japanese peasants improved. Nevertheless, taxes and other indignities and injustices weighed heavily on the poorest and hardest working people in the centuries after Hideyoshi and Henry IV. These would eventually result in massive upheavals: the French Revolution in 1789, and the Meiji Restoration of 1868.

A variety of spectacles and shows of state power served to unify the various social groups within the realm. The royal fireworks and pageantry that accompanied the arrival of Marie de Medici found its counterpart in the Gyōkō festival of the emperor's arrival. These were political displays intended to awe spectators by their grandeur. They also made people feel a part of the national story. Seeing and experiencing the same things, or reading about these things in the papers and journals gave the subjects something in common. This was the bread and butter of an emerging national identity. Despite the differences in income, occupation, or social status, all participated in some way in the life of the state. Only fifty years after bitter internal conflicts, the average person living in 1640 was fairly content to work peacefully as a subject of the French king or Japanese emperor.

Historians have used the word "absolutism" to describe both regimes. This word implies the absolute rule of the monarch, free from the constraints of law. However, despite their success at centralizing their states, neither Henry nor Hideyoshi tried to rule outside of legal traditions that regulated political behavior. Both understood the importance of strong institutions in preserving the state. Nevertheless, the incredible amount of power they wielded did seem to go to their heads and lead to some irrational choices at the end of their regimes. But these transgressions, such as leading armies into Belgium or Korea for little strategic advantage, pale in comparison with the destructive forces of chaos they overcame. That is why even today they continue to hold a special place in the hearts of the people of Japan and France.

Questions to consider

1   Hideyoshi and Henry IV emerged after decades of instability and bloodshed. How much of their success was due to the times and how much was a result of their own leadership abilities?

2   Hideyoshi and Henry IV made claims about honor and loyalty, yet both fought against established authorities. How did they defend their actions as being honorable? In a society based on warrior values, which do you think matters more, strength or fidelity?

3   What was the effect of religious division on feudal conflicts? In what ways is religious warfare more destructive? Why do you think this is?

4   Do you think that Nobunaga and Hideyoshi were justified in using ruthless tactics for the sake of national unification? Were they necessary?

5   Once in power, Hideyoshi and Henry IV faced little resistance. Why? What made people want to obey their regime? Which do you think mattered more to their supporters, personal qualities or the promise of benefits?

Notes

1 Merry Wiesner-Hanks, *Religious Transformations in the Early Modern World: A Brief History with Documents* (Boston, MA: Bedford St. Martins, 2009), p. 156.
2 Mary Elizabeth Berry, *Hideyoshi* (Cambridge, MA: Harvard University Press, 1982), p. 235. Berry's translation substitutes "Naniwa" for Osaka Castle, which is used in the translation found in Boscaro's *101 Letters of Hideyoshi* (Tokyo: Sophia University, 1975), p. 78.
3 Vincent J. Pitts, *Henri IV of France: His Reign and Age* (Baltimore, MD: Johns Hopkins University Press, 2009), p. 31.

2

HÜRREM SULTAN AND LADY ZHENG

For centuries historians and writers have portrayed the stories of Hürrem Sultan and Lady Zheng as classic romances and tales of intrigue. At the age of 14, Hürrem was captured in a slave raid and placed in the harem of the Ottoman sultan, where Suleiman the Magnificent fell in love with her and made her his sultana. In imperial China, the young Lady Zheng endured a series of competitions to enter the inner palace of the Ming dynasty as a concubine, where she won the love of a lonely and misunderstood emperor. Both women faced harsh criticism from palace officials for the "hidden influence" they wielded over their lovers and for striving to place their sons on the throne. Despite a lack of evidence, critics accused the women of endless scheming, intrigue, murder, and contributing to the downfall of their respective dynasties. Described as fascinating and seductive, the women also served as scapegoats for men who saw influential women as a threat to the stability of the political and social order.

Hürrem Sultan, or Roxelana (c. 1505–1553)

The story of the astonishing rise of Hürrem Sultan from captured slave girl to empress of the Ottoman Empire has endured for centuries. Known as Roxelana in Europe, Hürrem inspired numerous plays, paintings, books, and even a symphony throughout the Middle East and Europe. As the beloved wife of Suleiman the Magnificent, she managed to wield an unprecedented amount of authority in the palace and leave her mark on the empire. Enemies at court accused her of witchcraft and murder, but modern admirers describe her as a political mastermind who fought for her people. Without a doubt, she emerged as a survivor from a harsh and brutal environment by the force of her personality. Her captivating story illustrates the power of love in one of history's most important dynasties.

FIGURE 2.1 Workshop of Titian, *La Sultana Rossa*, c. 1550. The Venetian painter, who had never visited Istanbul, had not seen Hürrem Sultan in person. While her costume is based on contemporary descriptions of Ottoman dress, the sultana's face is entirely imaginary.

Source: Collection of the John and Mable Ringling Museum of Art the State Art Museum of Florida, Florida State University

The slave from Ruthenia

As the daughter of a Greek Orthodox priest in Poland–Lithuania, Aleksandra Lisowska, as she was known as a child, could hardly have imagined her destiny as an Ottoman sultana. Her small town, Rohatyn, now within Ukraine, had once been part of Russia. These steppe lands on the eastern frontier of Christian Europe shared a border with states once founded by the Mongols and Turks, the nomadic peoples of Eurasia who were united into an empire under Genghis Khan (1162–1227). Called Tatars by the Europeans who feared and despised them, the Mongols and Turks raided the border towns for slaves to sell in the markets of the Ottoman Empire.

With his massive army of Mongolian and Turkish warriors, Genghis Khan had built the largest empire the world had ever seen. In the western part of that empire, *khans* (rulers) adopted the religion of Islam and broke into smaller *khanates* (states). One of these khanates, the Golden Horde, forced Russians to pay tribute for centuries, until in 1480, when Ivan III liberated his country from the "Tatar yoke." By Aleksandra's time, the Golden Horde had dissolved into smaller states, but the Tatars continued to threaten the towns and villages of Eastern Europe until as late as the eighteenth century. Aleksandra and her fellow villagers of Rohatyn lived in fear of the slaving raids for good reason, as such raids resulted in the enslavement of nearly 2.5 million Ukrainians between 1400–1700.

The course of Aleksandra's life changed forever at the age of 14, when a roving band of Tatar horsemen sacked her village in a quest for human cargo and livestock. Armed with swords and arrows, the Tatars slaughtered the elderly of the village and tied up the remaining men, women, children, and livestock. The survivors were forced to march hundreds of miles with hands and necks tied to a stick on their back to the city of Caffa, the main slave depot in Crimea. Once sold, many worked as slaves in the fields or as domestic servants. For men, the most frightening prospect was a brutal life spent as a galley slave, rowing endlessly beneath the deck of a large ship. Attractive young women feared the life of a slave concubine, bought exclusively to serve the sexual desires of a master.

Aleksandra's small frame, red hair, and delicate features convinced her captors that she would fetch a high price in the better slave markets of Istanbul, the capital city of the Ottoman Empire. In these markets, rich men and government officials bought attractive women to live in their *harem*, a secluded part of a household reserved for female relatives and concubines. At that time, Ottoman law allowed a man to marry up to four wives, but placed no legal limit on the amount of concubines, both slave and free, that he could keep in his harem. Only the very rich could afford to support a harem, however. The vast majority of farmers and craftsmen, not having the means to feed, clothe, and shelter multiple wives and concubines, lived in small houses with one wife.

Crossing the Black Sea on an overcrowded slave ship, Alexandra and the other slaves endured a terrifying passage. With no room to sit or lie down, the slaves ate and slept while standing. The many slaves who died along the journey were simply tossed into the sea. Aleksandra survived to reach the market in Istanbul, where a palace official bought her to serve as a concubine at Topkapı, the palace of the sultan. Forced to leave every aspect of her previous life behind, Aleksandra would never again see her homeland or family. A new life awaited her in the heart of the Ottoman Empire.

Islamic empires of Asia

In the sixteenth century, a number of empires dominated the middle of the Eurasian continent between Europe and China. The Ottomans controlled much of the western Mediterranean, Turkey, and Arabia. Farther east, the Safavid Empire ruled over Persia and Afghanistan, while the Mughal Empire encompassed most of northern India. These states shared an Islamic heritage as well as similar ideas about government. In all, authority was concentrated in the hands of one, all-powerful monarch who had the power of life and death over his subjects. This leader, whether sultan (Ottoman) or shah (Safavid or Mughal), ruled personally as the head of a dynastic family that was, in essence, the state itself. These rulers built enormous palaces to house their families and the central administration. The grand palace complexes inspired fear and awe in the subjects of the ruler. The tall, stone walls that surrounded them served to keep the ruler, his family, and the government completely hidden from view. At once secretive and sacred, the royal courts inherited a culture of divine kingship from the ancient empires of Persia and Byzantium.

The opulence of the palace interiors, for the few who entered them, reflected the extreme wealth of these empires. As the "middle men" of trade between Europe, Africa, and Asia, the Ottoman, Safavid, and Mughal empires became extraordinarily rich. By the middle of the sixteenth century, vast commercial networks brought luxury goods, slaves, intellectuals, and artists from all over the world. The domains of the kings and queens of Europe could not compare in terms of wealth, size, or military strength to the empires of Asia in the sixteenth century.

The Ottoman Empire had grown from humble origins as one of many bands of nomadic tribes in central Asia. The founder of the Ottoman Empire, Osman (died c. 1323), led his Turkish warriors in raids against the Byzantine Empire as a *gaza* (holy war) in the name of Islam. His conquest of Anatolia, now modern-day Turkey, laid the foundation for the empire that bore his name, Ottoman. For thirty-six generations, a descendant of Osman ruled the empire as sultan until the twentieth century.

Osman's successors gradually made the transition from the leaders of a band of frontier warriors to rulers of a centralized state. In 1453, Mehmed II "the Conqueror" captured the ancient city of Constantinople, the capital of the Byzantine Empire. He renamed the city Istanbul and made it the center of a rapidly expanding empire. By 1520, Suleiman the Magnificent, the great grandson of Mehmed II, ruled over lands that included hundreds of millions of subjects throughout Asia, Africa, and Europe.

The imperial palace of the Ottoman Empire, Topkapı, stood high on a hill overlooking the Bosphorus, the narrow body of water linking the two continents of

Europe and Asia. Arcades with colorful marble columns surrounded four courtyards resembling parks with elegant fountains. Approximately four thousand residents spent their entire lives within the walls of the Topkapı palace, which included a hospital, mosque, bakery, and apartments. In the largest and most lavish apartments of the palace, long velvet couches stretched along the sides of the rooms, fine oriental carpets covered the floors, and intricate tile work with Arabic designs graced the walls and ceilings. The palace reflected the opulence of an empire at the height of its power.

The Harem

The majority of the residents of Topkapı entered the palace, like Aleksandra, as slaves. Indeed, slavery lay at the heart of the Ottoman system of government. Almost all of the palace officials, soldiers in the army, and women who gave birth to future sultans, arrived as slaves from other lands. Since Islam prohibits the enslavement of free Muslims, the Ottomans imported slaves from the Christian lands they conquered. The slave system employed by the empire had several political advantages. Having no family, slaves who became government officials could offer absolute devotion to the sultan. Without nephews, cousins, or even siblings asking for money or favors, palace officials could make promotions based on merit, not family connections.

The young slave from Rohatyn lived her life in the most secluded and sacred part of the palace, the harem. Only the sultan, his immediate family, slaves, and eunuchs were permitted into this inner sanctuary. One side of the harem housed the female members of the sultan's family as well as hundreds of slave girls who served as concubines to the sultan, while the other side provided the residence for hundreds of slave boys trained for the military corps.

The female side of the harem contained around 150 palace women whose primary purpose was to continue the dynastic family. The majority of the women were kidnapped slaves from Christian lands. Some had been captured by Tatar slave raids, while others had been kidnapped by pirates on the high seas. Many girls had been given to the sultan as gifts from powerful men and foreign dignitaries.

Upon entering the palace as a slave girl, Aleksandra would have been thoroughly scrubbed to remove all dirt and the stench of urine, filth, and vomit that had permeated the horrifying sea voyage. In addition, she would have been forced to endure a gynecological exam verifying her virginity. Only in a state of cleanliness and purity were the imperial concubines allowed into the harem. Although their primary purpose was reproduction, the girls learned the Turkish language, the religion of Islam, and how to demonstrate absolute submission to the will of the sultan. In addition, the girls studied literature, music, art, or dance according to their individual talent. The Ottoman officials considered this education necessary to create elegant and refined companions for the sultan. Although slaves, the palace women were expected to have the dignity necessary to fill a variety of roles as mothers of future sultans, wives of government officials, or female administrators within the harem.

For centuries, the image of the harem has fascinated Europeans who have seen it as a highly erotic space. In the sixteenth century, Venetian ambassadors returning from Topkapı described the *seraglio* (harem) as including dozens of voluptuous *odalisques* (harem women) reclining in leisure or splashing around naked in the large marble pools of the harem. The idea of a man secretly peeking in from behind the lattice-work of arabesque walls on unsuspecting bathing women excited the western imagination. The reality as experienced from the perspective of the odalisques was quite different. Much of their life was extremely regimented, focused on education and training, and might have seemed very much like a life spent in a religious convent.

Despite the obligations of study, exercises, and expectations of obedience, the women of the harem found ways to enjoy their leisure time. Shut off from the rest of the world, they often entertained each other by playing games and telling stories. Some of the most popular tales came from the *Thousand and One Nights*, a collection of fairy tales, fables, and romances. Also known as the *Arabian Nights* in English, it recounted the story of a king who vowed revenge against all women after he caught his wife cheating on him. Every night he slept with a different woman and put her to death the next morning. He killed scores of young women until the chief minister's daughter, Shahrazad, volunteered to marry the king. After the king had taken her to bed, the beautiful and intelligent Shahrazad did something that none of his previous wives had done: she began to tell him a story. Refusing to reveal the end until the next evening, the king was forced by curiosity to keep her alive one more day. Shahrazad continued telling tales for a thousand and one nights, until finally the king fell in love with her and made her his queen. The central theme of the *Arabian Nights* is the power of love. Undoubtedly Aleksandra would have been familiar with this work; perhaps she had taken its message to heart.

Men in the harem

Supervising the female slaves were the palace eunuchs, the only grown men (with the unusual exception of dwarves and mutes) allowed in the harem besides the sultan. Because they underwent castration, they posed no threat to the sanctity of the forbidden spaces or the sexual purity of the harem women. Islam forbade the castration of Muslims, so eunuchs also came from the ranks of the slave boys abducted or bought from Europe and Africa. Why certain boys were selected for castration is not clear, but surgeons usually performed the procedure before the age of puberty, when it could be done more safely. By the sixteenth century, the Ottomans favored "root and branch" castration, which means removal of the testicles and the penis. Although as many as ten percent of patients died during the surgery, some endured the procedure willingly. The position of *aga*, chief supervisor of the harem, was one of the most powerful offices in the government, and the agas of both the male and female harem wielded a great deal of status, authority, and wealth. Some adult males underwent the operation to further their careers in government.

The male side of the harem included boys selected for military training and government service. For centuries, Ottoman power rested on battalions of slave warriors known as *Janissaries*, boys taken from Christian lands to serve as soldiers in the Ottoman army. When the Empire expanded into the Byzantine lands, it did not force the conversion of the inhabitants to Islam. Instead, Christian and Jewish residents continued to practice their religion while paying an additional tax to the government. In the lands of the Balkans, villagers paid tax in the form of children. Every three to seven years, during the *devşirme* (collecting), Ottoman commissioners rounded up male children between the ages of 8 and 20, and selected the strongest and most fit for Janissary service.

The boys selected as slaves moved to the palace, where, under a brutal, disciplinary regime, they learned to obey the sultan in everything. Willing to die at any moment for their ruler, the Janissaries made a particularly fearsome fighting force. In addition to discipline, palace officials also provide education and training that allowed officials to identify the boys' personal strengths and talents. Many Janissaries moved on from military service to hold high-ranking offices in the government. Indeed, with the exception of the sultan, almost all of the most powerful men in the imperial bureaucracy had entered Topkapı as slaves.

Although aspects of their life seem excessively harsh to modern readers, the Janissaries, concubines, and eunuchs of the palace enjoyed a standard of living well above what normal people endured in the sixteenth century. Despite an absolute lack of freedom, they did not have to worry about hunger or shelter. The residents of Topkapı had access to entertainment and extraordinary luxuries. Highly trained and educated, they learned to recognize their own privilege.

Despite the initial horror of captivity, incoming slaves like Aleksandra quickly realized that the palace system worked as a meritocracy. It offered misery and degradation, for sure, but also the possibility for advancement. Certainly she must have missed her family and resented the system that deprived her of every emotional comfort she had ever known. At some point, however, she, like the others, seems to have made peace with her circumstances and adapted to life in the harem. From that time on, Aleksandra, now known as Roxelana (the Russian or Ruthenian girl) decided not only to play by the rules of the system but also to win.

Roxelana realized that reproduction offered a concubine her best hope of advancement in the harem. The Ottoman court followed Islamic law, which gave slaves impregnated by their master important rights; she could not be sold away from her child, and she gained her freedom upon the death of her master. Among concubines in the royal harem, the highest honor achievable was the title of *haseki* (favorite), gained when a concubine gave birth to the sultan's son. Within a few years of arriving at the palace, Roxelana found her way to the sultan's bedchamber.

Suleiman the Magnificent

Under Suleiman I (1494–1566), the Ottoman Empire reached its greatest geographical extent and the height of its opulent splendor. As a young prince, he and his mother, Hafsa Sultan, had been sent to the province of Manisa in western Turkey. Ruling this province gave him valuable experience as a military commander and administrator. After the death of his father, Suleiman and his mother returned to Topkapı Palace at Istanbul where he acceded to the throne in 1520.

In keeping with the Ottoman tradition of the warrior king, Suleiman spent a great deal of time on military campaigns that extended all the way from Indus

River in India to the Danube in central Europe. Like many other rulers of his age, he found inspiration in the example of Alexander the Great and aimed for world domination. He conquered the island of Rhodes (1521) and the kingdom of Hungary (1525). Four years later, he laid siege to Vienna. The siege was unsuccessful, but having an Islamic army so far inside Western Europe struck fear into the heart Christian Europe. In terms of diplomacy, Suleiman considered himself the rival of Charles V, the Christian king of Spain and Holy Roman Emperor. Sworn enemies, both Charles V and Suleiman I believed that God had chosen them as divine agents to conquer the entire globe.

Ottoman historians have traditionally revered this sultan as Suleiman the Law-maker, because he provided law codes for the many provinces of the empire. It was not an easy task, as the empire contained a great variety of religions, languages, and customs. The Ottomans believed that their sultan had been charged by God to

FIGURE 2.2   Workshop of Titian, *Suleiman I*, c. 1550. Having never seen the sultan himself, Titian may have based the sultan's likeness on a coin.

Source: World History Archive/Alamy Stock Photo

administer justice to his subjects, and Suleiman took that obligation seriously. Aiming for peace within his lands, he followed the principle of religious toleration and allowed different ethnic groups to rule themselves at the local level.

Renowned for his courage and intelligence, Suleiman also appeared to have a more tender side to his character. In 1524, a Venetian ambassador described him as melancholy, or prone to depression. An avid writer of poetry and patron of the arts, Suleiman did not hide his sentimentality. He formed strong emotional attachments to loved ones at court. Many ambassadors noted his strong bond with his mother, Hafsa, whom he raised to the status of *valide sultan*, a rank of great prestige that allowed her to coordinate all aspects of the palace.

Suleiman also developed a close relationship to his grand vizier, or chief minister, Ibrahim. Originally from Venice, Ibrahim had been kidnapped as a child and brought to the palace as a slave. A bright student who excelled in his studies, he became a constant playmate of the young prince. Suleiman made him falconer when he acceded to the throne and soon after awarded him the highest office in the land. It was reported that Ibrahim and Suleiman were so close that they slept with their heads touching in the same bed. This story is unlikely, however, given that the grand vizier, as a grown man who had not been castrated, would not have been allowed in the sacred and forbidden inner rooms of the palace. However, Suleiman and Ibrahim made successful partners. Suleiman conquered and ruled, while Ibrahim conducted diplomacy, commanded the army, and employed artists and craftsmen to embellish the public image of the sultan, staging magnificent displays of imperial power. Suleiman found in Ibrahim a fellow warrior who also shared a love of poetry and music. According to one legend, it was Ibrahim who presented Aleksandra to the sultan as a gift.

Before Suleiman met Roxelana, he showed a great deal of affection for Mahidevran, the mother of his first son, Mustafa. A brunette from Circassia, a region renowned for beautiful women, Mahidevran had also come to harem as a slave. As *haseki* and the mother of the prince, she wielded a great deal of power within the harem. The sultan was very attached to Mahidevran and her son Mustafa, but custom and tradition required him to sleep with other concubines. Creating a surplus of royal heirs in order to ensure continuity of the dynasty was one of his duties as sultan. Mahidevran understood this, but still harbored jealousy against potential rivals in the harem.

Suleiman and Hürrem

In a report from 1524, a Venetian ambassador described Roxelana as "young, but not beautiful, graceful and petite." She was probably around 16 when she met Suleiman. There were no eyewitness accounts of their first meeting, but if it followed the longstanding tradition of the court, Hafsa, the sultan's mother, would have selected her as a lady-in-waiting for the female relatives of the sultan. On certain occasions these chosen ones entertained the sultan and his family with musical performances. Some danced, while others played instruments. Roxelana, known to have a beautiful singing voice, might have sung a song. At the end of the performance, Suleiman would have tossed his handkerchief to the girl indicating his desire to see her later in his bedchamber.

The Venetian ambassador recounted that when Mahidevran realized that the sultan had summoned Roxelana to his chamber, she went to her in the harem and jealously attacked her, saying, "Traitor. Sold meat. Do you want to compete with me?" She then tore the young girl's dress, scratched her face, and pulled out tufts of her hair. When a eunuch came to fetch Roxelana for the sultan, the battered girl refused to go, saying that her sorry condition was not worthy of his majesty. The eunuch reported this back to the sultan, but he insisted that she come to his chamber anyway. When Suleiman saw the girl crying in such distress, he asked who had committed the brutal attack. She told him everything that Mahidevran had done. He then summoned Mahidevran and asked if she had indeed attacked Roxelana. Replying yes, she went further to complain that the Russian girl deserved worse than she got, having refused to obey her as the *haseki*. Mahidevran's arrogance dampened the sultan's feelings for her. Eventually he ended their relationship and sent her with her son to the provinces.

With the departure of Mahidevran from court, Roxelana spent more time with the sultan. Despite Suleiman's reputation as a fearsome tyrant who had the power to execute any of his subjects at his will, Roxelana refused to fear him. She knew the peculiar capital punishment that awaited harem women who displeased the sultan; they were tied up in a large sack and drowned alive. Nevertheless, she had the courage to express her lively personality in his presence. That he appreciated her sense of humor is clear from the nickname he gave her, Hürrem. Turkish for "the laughing one," the new name replaced her given name, Aleksandra, and her nickname at court, Roxelana.

It is not clear when Hürrem converted to Islam, but some sources indicate that she studied the laws of the religion and used them to her advantage. For her conversion, Hürrem had only to say one sentence with conviction: "There is no god but God, and Muhammad is his messenger." This statement expresses a belief in monotheism and a willingness to see the Koran, a collection of scriptures recited by the seventh-century Arabian prophet, Muhammad, as the holy text of Islam. The Koran, written in Arabic, provides a view of Allah, the god of both the Jews and Christians, as compassionate and merciful. The faithful could expect to gain eternal life in heaven. The word "Islam" means submission to the will of Allah. Although the basic ideas of Islam are simple, throughout the years scholars had expanded the religion to include a system of laws, the *Sharia*. The Ottoman government tried to obey these laws whenever possible. According to the *Sharia*, a free Muslim woman who has sex with a man who is not her husband commits a sin in the eyes of God. Providing this as a justification, reports indicated that Hürrem, once free and Muslim, refused to have sex with the sultan unless he made her his lawful wife. Perhaps for this reason, around 1533 or 1534, Suleiman decided to break with hundreds of years of Ottoman tradition and marry his former slave.

The royal wedding was a magnificent spectacle. In the Hippodrome, the ancient chariot racetrack of Constantinople, festivities included tournaments between

Christian and Muslim knights and a parade of exotic animals. Hürrem and her ladies-in-waiting, who could not be seen by the public, enjoyed the games from behind screens made of golden latticework. Throughout the city, feasting and music filled streets that had been decorated with garlands of flowers and flickering lights at night. Everywhere in the city revelers took turns swinging back and forth on the temporary swings set up by palace officials for the occasion.

The marriage brought the new sultana a substantial dowry of 5,000 ducats in addition to her salary of 2,000 silver coins a day. Some of this money went to fund massive building projects, including the Haseki mosque complex. Built in the district of the women's market, the enormous building included a mosque, soup kitchen, religious college, elementary school, and a hospital. It was the third largest mosque in Istanbul, after those of Mehmed the Conqueror and Suleiman himself. In addition to the institutions in Istanbul, she also established charities in Mecca, Medina, and Jerusalem, some of which continued to feed the needy until the twentieth century. Such projects revealed her growing authority at court.

Hürrem's standing in the palace grew to unprecedented heights. According to the Venetian ambassador, she wore luxurious garments that contained jewels worth 100,000 ducats. To put this wealth in perspective, the ransom required by the Spanish to free the city of Rome in 1527 (as described in Chapter 7) would have paid for four of the sultana's gowns. She also took steps to increase her influence by moving the female side of the harem into the same building as the sultan's apartments. This would have long lasting effects on Ottoman history. Proximity gave the wives, mothers, and daughters of the ruler great influence over the sultan. Ottoman historians call the century and a half after Hürrem the "Sultanate of women," as powerful concubines and mothers directed policy for the dynasty.

Hürrem eventually gave birth to five of Suleiman's children in an astonishingly short amount of time. Mehmed, a son, in 1521, Mihrimah, a daughter, in 1522, Selim and Bayezid, both boys, in 1525. She gave birth to her last child in 1531: Jihangir, a boy born with a sharp mind, but a hunched back. With five sons, (including Mustafa, son of Mahavidran), the sultan did not need to worry about having an heir to succeed him, and Hürrem discouraged Suleiman from bringing other concubines into his bed. For the first time in Ottoman history, a concubine demanded fidelity from a sultan, and the sultan obeyed.

Enemies

Suleiman's love for Hürrem and the political influence and power it provided her aroused much suspicion within the court. Many accused her of witchcraft and said that she used magical potions to keep the sultan enthralled. One rumor claimed that she imported hyenas in order to use their body parts in her love-charms. In many cultures, hyenas represent sexual deviancy, as the female of the species has protruding genitals and dominates her male partners. Such rumors circulated among the palace officials and spread to European ambassadors and envoys, many of whom held their own misgivings about a woman with so much influence.

The reports of Europeans at the court contain a great deal of information about palace women, but such reports are often unreliable. Men outside of the sultan's immediate family could not see or talk to any woman within the palace. Instead, they relied on the hearsay and the gossip of government officials, who themselves had little access to women. As "unseen forces," women in positions of authority disturbed both Ottoman and European men. At the same time, stories and gossip about the royal family proved irresistible to readers. The intrigue documented by the reports of Venetian ambassadors probably entertained their original audience—the senators of the Venetian republic. Although they were considered classified information, many reports were leaked to the public and found their way into print for public consumption.

Reports from the envoys indicated that Hürrem had significant enemies in the palace. From the beginning of her relationship with Suleiman, Mahidevran had been her main rival. Increasingly however, Hürrem regarded Mahidevran's son Mustafa as a greater threat due to the tradition called "open succession" in the Ottoman Empire. According to this custom, the sons of a sultan had to fight each other to determine who would inherit the crown. It was believed that whoever won in the end would have done so according to the will of God. Once a prince had won the throne, he had the legal right to execute all of his brothers. For this reason, Hürrem knew Mustafa becoming sultan would mean the death of her own sons. Only Jihangar, the hunchback, who was prohibited from the sultanate due to his physical disability, did not fear Mustafa. Indeed, these half-brothers developed a strong relationship with each other. Although Mustafa and his mother had been sent to the provinces, the first son still posed a threat. As he grew, his courage, intelligence, and charisma made him a favorite with the public as well as the powerful Janissaries.

Ibrahim, the grand vizier and best friend of Suleiman, presented another threat to Hürrem. Since childhood, Ibrahim had been like a brother to Suleiman. When Ibrahim married Suleiman's sister, Hatice, he became his actual brother-in-law. Rivals for the attention of Suleiman, Hürrem and Ibrahim followed similar life paths and had many interests in common. They entered the palace as slaves, excelled in their studies, and loved art and music; he distinguished himself as a violin player, while she sang with a beautiful voice. Most important, both proved themselves talented political strategists. Because each sought an exclusive partnership with Suleiman, however, these two could not remain friends.

By the 1530s, Suleiman and Ibrahim had drifted apart. The grand vizier had built a luxurious palace near the Hippodrome with extensive gardens, and chose to spend more time there than at court. More frequently, he made political decisions without consulting the high council of state. His independence from the sultan grew as he led the army to victory in what is now modern Iraq. Without the approval of Suleiman, Ibrahim gave himself a new title, in which appeared the word "sultan."

Suleiman seemed to believe that Ibrahim had overstepped the bounds of appropriate behavior for a former slave. One night in the spring of 1536, just after returning from a successful military campaign, Ibrahim and Suleiman dined together. The next morning Ibrahim's body was found in the guest bedroom where he slept. Agents obeying the orders of Suleiman had cut his throat as he lay sleeping. As if to emphasize the grand vizier's fall from grace, the sultan had his old friend's naked body thrown outside the harem walls and then buried in an unmarked grave.

Contemporaries and historians have wondered what might have motivated Suleiman to kill his former best friend. Some believed that the sultan intended the execution as a brutal show of absolute power to serve as a warning to others. His action showed that anyone could be promoted or executed at the will of the sultan, regardless of position or status. Although no clear evidence tied Hürrem to the execution, many at court suggested that she used her influence to turn Suleiman against Ibrahim. Portrayed by her enemies as scheming and manipulative, the sultana served as a convenient target for the fear and resentment of the palace officials.

Court gossip also linked Hürrem to the murder of another rival, Suleiman's first son, Mustafa. He had been the sultan's favorite son early in his reign, but he soon lost this privileged position to Hürrem's first born, Mehmed. A charming and intelligent young man, Mehmed, the sultan's second son, died in 1543 of smallpox. After his death, many favored Mustafa as a successor. Ruling in the provinces as a governor, he had proven his abilities as a military leader.

Mustafa's popularity and success, however, did not guarantee his place in the line of succession, nor even his continued existence. When rumors circulated that certain soldiers were talking about replacing the "old man" on the throne with his youthful son, Suleiman started to suspect treason. Perhaps he kept in mind the history of his father, Selim I, who had indeed overthrown his own father. Selim I had forced the early retirement of Suleiman's grandfather, who died mysteriously soon after leaving court, most likely by poison. Once on the throne, Suleiman's ruthless father executed all of his brothers and nephews. For these reasons, Suleiman may have considered his own son a threat to his rule.

Knowing that Mustafa would likely kill Hürrem's sons upon seizing the throne, Mahidevran tried her best to protect her son from a preemptive strike from her rival. According to one rumor, the sultana had sent Mustafa a gift of clothes that she had laced with poison, but Mahidevran intercepted them before they could harm her son. His mother had also warned him to beware of his father, but to no avail. In 1553, while on a military campaign, Suleiman summoned his son to his military tent. Although warned by his mother not to go, Mustafa went anyway. Upon his arrival, two mute eunuchs strangled him to death with a bowstring. As a member of the dynasty, Mustafa had the right to a bloodless death. According to reports, Suleiman had watched the execution of his first son from behind a curtain in the tent.

Officially, Suleiman had ordered the execution of both his friend and his son, but many at court believed that Hürrem had plotted the murders for years. They continued to describe her as a malicious witch who poisoned Suleiman's mind with her diabolical charms. Psychologically, blaming Hürrem might have served another purpose, as those loyal to Suleiman and his dynasty did not want to think that a just and benevolent sultan could be capable of killing his best friend and son. For them, the sultana made a convenient scapegoat for any of the sultan's morally questionable actions.

Whether or not Hürrem actually caused the death of Ibrahim and Mustafa, she moved quickly to take advantage of their deaths to promote her interests in the palace. The grand vizier's death left his office open to others. When the sultan selected Rustem, one of the richest governors in the empire, Hürrem encouraged Rustem to marry her 17-year-old daughter, Mihrimah. As the wife of the sultan, and the mother-in-law of the grand vizier, Hürrem now had an even firmer hold on political affairs.

Hürrem's correspondence indicates that she took a lively interest in politics and served as an advisor to her husband. When military campaigns took Suleiman away from the city, she served as his eyes and ears within the palace. For example, in one letter, Hürrem advised her husband that strategic hostage taking would reassure his subjects of his strength. She wrote, "Now my fortune-favored, my sultan . . . neither the son of the heretic [the Shah of the Safavid Empire] nor his wife has been captured, nothing has been happening. Now if a messenger arrives saying, 'no progress here, nothing there,' no one is going to be happy." Although confined to the harem at Topkapı, the sultana had a wide network of informants who brought her important news.

Whether by training or inheritance, her daughter, Mihrimah, also took an active role political role. Mihrimah, whose name means "sun and moon," had, perhaps more than any of her siblings, captured the heart of her father. Suleiman took her on military campaigns with him, where she often rode on horseback at his side. Some stories claim that she even went into battle with her father. After the death of her mother, Mihrimah served as his most trusted political advisor at the court.

Hürrem's legacy

Hürrem's active political role had won her many enemies at court and in the public arena. Nevertheless, Suleiman stayed loyal to his sultana until the end. His devotion did not diminish even when her beauty faded with age. One envoy ventured to guess that her ability to understand the sultan's mind better than anyone else gave her so much power over him. When she died of disease in 1558 at the age of 53, Suleiman was inconsolable. What exactly had the sultana meant to Suleiman? Writing under his pen name, *Muhibbe* (the lover), the sultan expressed his affection for his wife:

> My very own queen, my everything,
>> My beloved, my bright moon;
> My intimate companion, my one and all,
>> Sovereign of all beauties, my sultan

My life, the gift I own, my be-all,
    my elixir of Paradise, my eden,
My spring, my joy, my glittering day,
    my exquisite one who smiles on and on. . .

My Istanbul, my Karaman, and all the
    Anatolian lands that are mine;
My Bedakhsan and my Kipchak territories,
    my Baghdad and my Khorasan.

My darling with that lovely hair, brows curved like a bow,
    eyes that ravish: I am ill.
If I die, yours is the guilt. Help I beg you,
    my love from a different religion . . .[1]

The verses are from a poetic letter written by Sultan Süleyman the Magnificent for Hürem Sultan translated by Talat S. Halman in *Rapture and Revolution. Essays on Turkish Literature,* translated by Talat S. Halman. Permission courtesy of Syracuse University Press.

Suleiman's dedication to Hürrem is very much in keeping with a long tradition of romantic love expressed in Arabic literature. In this tradition, a man consumed with passion and desire pines away for an absent love. Suleiman was on military campaigns throughout his reign, and rarely spent more than a few months at a time with Hürrem. For many years, he had to content himself with her image in his mind. Perhaps Sulieman was inspired by the Arabic poems of the seventh century that described the love of a man named Qays for Layla, a woman he could never have. Wandering through the desert for years in search for his love, Qays eventually goes insane. The theme of unfulfilled love served as a spiritual metaphor, as poets began to see the longing for the absent lover as a reflection of one's desire to find God. In this way, life itself was seen as a spiritual journey of desire that ends happily with the union of the human and divine in the afterlife. One could see the history of Suleiman and Hürrem as a simple romance or a tale of political intrigue, but perhaps it also contains a deeper spiritual meaning. Regardless, at its base it is a story of the power of love.

To be sure, Hürrem engaged in the unseemly and morally compromising side of power politics, showing no mercy to her enemies or those she considered the enemy of her husband or her children. For centuries, historians blamed her for the decline of the entire dynasty. When her son, Selim II, succeeded his father, he proved to be an ineffective leader. Nicknamed Selim the Sot for his love of wine, even though alcohol was forbidden to Muslims, the young sultan paid more attention to luxuries and entertainment than expanding the frontiers of the empire. Mustafa, some claimed, would have been a more worthy successor to Suleiman. In this view, Hürrem had sabotaged the fortunes of the dynasty by interfering in court politics. It is worthwhile to consider, however, that historians cannot be sure of her role in court intrigue, all of which had been kept extremely secret.

Evidence suggests another, more positive side to her character. Many of her actions indicated that she cared about others and the common good, such as funding projects that favored women and the poor. In addition, she served as a diplomat between the Ottoman court and Poland. Although incapable of stopping the Ottoman slave trade, she did at least try to hinder the influx of slaves from her homeland by negotiating privileged trade agreements with the king of Poland, who ruled over western Ukraine at the time. Perhaps due to her influence, diplomats from the two courts discussed the return of captives to their homes. For centuries, eastern Europeans have told folk tales about a Ukrainian girl kidnapped by Tatars who, once in the sultan's harem, tried to help the people of her native land. In modern times, Ukrainians have made Hürrem into a heroine and symbol of independence. Her statue stands today in the town square of her home village of Rohatyn, Ukraine, bearing the inscription, "Roxelana: First and Only Empress of the Ottoman Empire."

Chronology

1453	Mehmed II "The Conqueror" takes the city of Constantinople.
c. 1505	Birth of Hürrem.
c. 1520	Hürrem arrives at Topkapı palace.
1520	Suleiman I becomes sultan of the Ottoman Empire.
1529	Ottomans unsuccessfully lay siege to Vienna.
c. 1534	Marriage of Suleiman and Hürrem.
1536	Assassination of Ibrahim.
1553	Assassination of Mustafa.
1558	Death of Hürrem.
1566	Death of Suleiman I; Selim II, son of Hürrem, becomes sultan.

Sources for further reading about Hürrem

The most comprehensive source for information about Hurrem is Leslie Pierce, *The Imperial Harem: Women and Sovereignty in the Ottoman Empire* (Oxford: Oxford University Press, 1993). The introduction to Galina Yermolenko, *Roxolana in European Literature, History and Culture* (London: Routledge, 2010) contains the classic account of court intrigue. Information on the nature of slavery and concubinage can be found in Madeline Zilfi, *Women and Slavery in the Late Ottoman Empire: The Design of Difference* (Cambridge: Cambridge University Press, 2010). A colorful discussion of life in the harem for general readers can be found in Alev Lytle Croutier, *Harem: The World Behind the Veil* (New York: Abeville Press, 1989). For a comparative view of palace women in world history see Anne Walthall, ed. *Servants of the Dynasty: Palace Women in World History* (Berkeley, CA: University of California

Press, 2008). General information on the Ottoman Empire can be found in Halil Inalcik, *The Ottoman Empire: The Classical Age 1300–1600* (London: Phoenix Press, 1988; first published in 1973), and Suraiya N. Faroqhi and Kate Fleet, eds., *The Cambridge History of Turkey, Vol. II: The Ottoman Empire as a World Power 1453–1603* (Cambridge: Cambridge University Press, 2012). A good discussion of the origins of the dynasty can be found in Cemal Kafadar, *Between Two Worlds: The Construction of the Ottoman State* (Berkeley, CA: University of California Press, 1995). For information on Suleiman, see Metin Kunt and Christine Woodhead, eds., *Suleyman the Magnificent and His Age: The Ottoman Empire in the Early Modern World* (London: Longman, 1995). Reports from the imperial ambassador Ogier Busbecq have been translated by Edward Seymour Forster, ed., *The Turkish Letters of Ogier Ghiselin de Busbecq: Imperial Ambassador at Constantinople, 1554–1562* (Baton Rouge, LA: Louisiana State University Press, 2005). Unfortunately, there are no English translations of the reports of the Venetian ambassadors. Those who are willing to tackle sixteenth-century Italian with a Venetian accent can find abundant stories and information in Eugenio Alberi, ed., *Relazioni degli ambasciatori veneti al senato durante il XVI secolo, serie 3* (3 vols; Florence: Società editrice Fiorentina, 1842–1855). For a fun, pop culture take on Hürrem, students can find episodes of the Turkish soap opera, *Magnificent Century*, which offers a sumptuous and dramatic representation of the intrigues and romance at the court of Suleiman the Magnificent with English subtitles. While on YouTube, students may want to listen to Joseph Hayden's 63rd symphony, *La Roxelane*.

Lady Zheng (c. 1568–1630)

The biography of Lady Zheng offers an illustration of a traditional figure in Chinese history: the beautiful concubine who brings down a powerful dynasty. When the favored consort of the Wanli Emperor tried to place her son next in line for the imperial throne, she caused a political crisis that divided the court for decades. Although critics described her as crafty, wicked, and merciless, she provided love and emotional support for a lonely emperor faced by a hostile court. Set in one of the most glorious eras in Chinese history, the Ming dynasty, the story of Lady Zheng illustrates how an emperor's attachment to a woman created a moral crisis in a regime that required the ruler to sacrifice almost every aspect of his humanity for a rigid, bureaucratic system.

FIGURE 2.3   The official court portrait of Lady Wang, mother of Wanli's eldest son, provides an idea of court attire for imperial consorts in the Ming dynasty. No visual image of Lady Zheng has survived.

Source: History/Bridgeman Images

The Wanli Emperor

For over 3,000 years, the Chinese have divided their history into dynasties, or regimes ruled by the descendants of a specific family. In 1368 the Ming (or "brilliant") dynasty began when a peasant overthrew the government and established himself as the new emperor, Hongwu. He took power away from the rich aristocrats who ruled the central government and gave it back to the local villages. In his effort to establish a utopia of law and order throughout the land, he set the new dynasty on a firm foundation. As the empire gained strength, the third Ming emperor, Yongle, sent the great sea captain Zheng He to explore the world. In 1406 the celebrated navigator made the first of numerous expeditions as far as Africa. With almost 30,000 men in fleets of ships that could hold a thousand sailors each, he sailed the seas to establish trade routes and spread the word about the greatness of the Ming dynasty. Yongle also built the Forbidden City, the walled palace complex that served as the seat of government and the symbolic and ritual center of the Chinese empire until the twentieth century.

Strong emperors had brought stability and great wealth to China. After over two hundred years, however, peace and prosperity seemed to be weakening the emperors on the throne. Chinese historians who noticed the slow and steady decline of each dynasty referred to the phenomenon as the "dynastic cycle." Every dynasty seemed to begin with emperors who put the wellbeing of the people first. But after so many generations of the same family in power, the emperors, called the "sons of heaven," started to look after their own selfish interests. At the end of a dynastic cycle, the emperors tended to indulge in luxury and neglect their duties. When this happened, the Chinese believed that the dynasty began to lose its "mandate from heaven." When a ruler lost the mandate from heaven, natural disasters like floods and earthquakes ravaged the land, foreign invaders threatened the borders, and oppressed peasants started rebellions. These calamities eventually brought an outsider to the throne. The new emperor established his descendants in power and so began the next dynastic cycle. For many, the reign of Wanli (1563–1620) marked the moment when the Ming dynasty began to lose its mandate.

Wearing a yellow silk dragon robe that took over ten years to make, Wanli sat on the throne as the thirteenth emperor of the Ming dynasty. The belief in the mandate from heaven created a heavy moral burden for Wanli. Assuming the throne as a nine-year-old boy, he listened to the advice of trusted elders. His mother, Empress Dowager Li, entrusted the first grand secretary, Zhang Juzheng, with training the emperor and running the government during his childhood. Sporting a long beard and stiff creases in his robe, Tutor Zhang spoke to the young emperor with a voice of authority. He explained that the order of the universe itself depended on the emperor's good character. In order to rule with wisdom, the boy, as the son of heaven, needed to learn the classics of literature and history by heart. Wanli did his best to please his tutor.

Luckily, Wanli was a bright child and very advanced for his age. Able to read by age 4, he had a special talent for calligraphy, the art of writing with a brush and ink.

Around the age of 10, Wanli proudly showed Tutor Zhang some of the beautiful characters he had painted, almost one foot high. Instead of praising the boy, his tutor scolded him. He said that emperors should work on being virtuous, not making pretty pictures. Many an emperor had been led from the path of virtue by taking too much interest in hobbies, he warned, and then Zhang eliminated the art of calligraphy from his curriculum. From lessons such as these, Wanli learned that he was not supposed to have interests of his own.

Zhang Juzheng was notoriously strict and frugal. When Wanli, as an adolescent, wanted to present gifts to the palace women, Tutor Zhang advised him against it and encouraged him to think of the poor who suffered from cold and hunger. The First Grand Secretary's tight-fisted attitude toward expenditures and tough approach to ruling brought order to the palace and money into the treasury. As a young man, Wanli trusted and revered him.

The young emperor also respected and obeyed his mother, the Empress Dowager Li. Because filial piety, the respect that children show their parents, was so important in China, the emperor's stern mother seemed to have more power at court than her son. She never hesitated to scold or discipline the son of heaven, even as a teenager. According to one story, the 17-year-old emperor had been drinking one evening in the Forbidden City with two eunuch companions. At a certain point in the night, the drunken emperor ordered the eunuchs to sing a popular song. When they replied that they did not know the song, Wanli sentenced them to death on the spot. Making them kneel in front of him, he took out his sword and aimed at their heads. His companions pleaded for mercy, and in the end, his sword only cut off their hair, leaving their heads intact. In response to this poor behavior, Dowager Li forced her son to kneel while she scolded him and threatened to place his younger brother on the throne in his place. In the end, Wanli started to cry and beg for her forgiveness. Although she did not involve herself in matters of politics, she was a strong presence in the court and a symbol for the empire as "divine sage mother."

Dowager Li once claimed that she hoped Zhang Juzheng would direct the emperor until he turned 30, but the first grand secretary died in 1582. At that time, Wanli was 19 and old enough to rule without strong guidance, but the loss of his trusted advisor left an enormous power vacuum at court. Soon after Zhang's death, one faction of ministers started to denounce the deceased first grand secretary as having been corrupt. According to these officials, Zhang had accepted bribes, lived in ostentatious luxury, and kept a harem of women whom he showered with gifts. Some suggested that he aimed to take over the throne itself. The attacks made it seem as though his frugality and virtue had been a front to hide his selfish and indulgent lifestyle.

Naturally these accusations made the emperor feel betrayed by his once-cherished tutor. Raging and humiliated, Wanli had his officials confiscate Zhang's property and arrest his sons. They surrendered over 100,000 ounces of silver. After heavy beating, his eldest son confessed to hiding three times that amount somewhere. The next morning he hanged himself. The rest of his family was banished to the remote provinces of the empire. This silver was never recovered and, most likely, never existed. All of the talk of treason and bribery might have been nothing more than hearsay, a vicious attack on one faction by another to seek power at court. Eliminating Zhang's supporters from government offices would have made more positions for people from a rival faction.

The denouncement of his tutor as a traitor took a heavy emotional toll on Wanli. With the palace officials constantly accusing each other of bad faith and immorality, the emperor did not know whom to trust. Trapped as a virtual prisoner of the Forbidden City from which he could never leave, he felt powerless. His role was purely ceremonial, since an elite bureaucracy of scholars made the real decisions that directed the empire. These palace officials scrutinized every decision or movement that he made, and Wanli grew increasingly tired of their judgment.

A new concubine in the palace

One chronicle of the reign passed down an interesting story about how Lady Zheng entered the palace. It states that when her parents, commoners from Beijing, heard that eunuchs were recruiting concubines for the palace, they tried to marry her off quickly. Many parents feared the recruiters, knowing that if they selected their child, she would move to the inner palace of the Forbidden City, and they would never see her again. The Zheng family's marriage plan fell through, however, when the groom's family refused to provide the gifts her family expected. As the families quarreled, the daughter ran crying into the street just as the palace recruiters happened to be walking nearby. Impressed by her beauty, they selected her as one of nine new concubines for the palace in 1582.

Most likely, Lady Zheng's arrival in the Forbidden City had little to do with chance. Another account states that she was among three hundred girls between the ages of 9 and 14 who had been nominated by the elders of the precinct to win the honor of serving as an imperial concubine. The girls endured several rounds of screening and selection, and out of three hundred, Lady Zheng was among the nine who were chosen. Taking no chances with the future of the dynasty, the palace officials wanted only concubines of exceptional quality to serve as potential mothers for future emperors.

Lady Zheng entered the private chambers of the Forbidden City at the age of 14. Shortly afterward, she distinguished herself among her peers and was promoted to the rank of imperial consort. It was a great leap in status within the hierarchy of the court, which included five levels of palace women. According to the eunuchs who tended the secluded concubines, Zheng was not described as particularly beautiful, but she appeared to be intelligent, educated, and strong-willed. Most important, she came into the young emperor's life at the right time, when he needed emotional support after the death of Zhang Juzheng.

Wanli had, and would continue to have, numerous relationships at court. At age of 14, he had been formally married to Wang Xijie, a woman selected by his mother, the Dowager Li. The young empress gave birth to a daughter, but never produced a male heir. Some chronicles described the empress as proper and kind, but Liu Ruoyu, a eunuch who kept a diary during these years, claimed that she could be cruel to her subordinates, causing over one hundred palace women and eunuchs to be beaten to death. The Wanli Emperor paid little attention to the empress throughout his life.

The emperor's first male child was born to Lady Wang, the chambermaid of Dowager Li. One contemporary writer claimed that Wanli had met the woman while visiting his mother at her palace. He asked the maid for a basin of water for washing his hands, and when she brought to him, he rewarded her with a hair ornament. Later that day, the couple had intercourse, which was duly noted in the record book kept by the palace officials. When the maid gave birth to a son, Zhu Changlu, in 1582, the emperor denied the relationship. However, when Wanli's mother showed her son the record book with the date of the baby's conception, he reluctantly admitted that the child was his own. Despite Lady Wang's low status at court, the first son of the emperor gained the title of "eldest imperial son." Promoted to the level of imperial consort, Lady Wang nevertheless spent the rest of her life confined to her living quarters in the palace, utterly neglected by the emperor.

Wanli preferred the company of Lady Zheng, who filled emotional needs like no one else at the palace. The fact that he could have demanded the execution of

FIGURE 2.4   Court Portrait of Wanli Emperor. China: Emperor Wanli, 14th ruler of the Ming dynasty (r. 1572–1620).

Source: History/Bridgeman Images

anyone at any moment led many concubines to tremble in fear of him, but Lady Zheng teased and joked with him. Socially and emotionally, she treated him as an equal, even criticizing him at times. When he hesitated to make a decision, she was known to toss off angry insults such as, "You really are an old lady." These challenging statements seemed to increase his emotional attachment to her.

A lasting romance

Soon Lady Zheng and Wanli were inseparable. The couple enjoyed visiting the temples and villas in the Imperial City, the walled area within Beijing that surrounding the Forbidden City. Zheng enjoyed calligraphy and her beautiful and neat style was widely admired at court. In one case, she had written a passage about the bodhisattva Guanyin, a figure of Mahayanna Buddhism known as the "Goddess of Mercy." Written in gold ink on porcelain-green paper, the beauty of the work inspired one writer to compose four poems to celebrate it.

Reading together was another favorite pastime of the couple. In the late sixteenth century, a vast amount of popular literature in the form of poetry, plays, novels, and detective stories came off of the presses in Beijing. Some of this literature bordered on pornography, a genre which enjoyed great popularity in the late Ming dynasty. Many poems disguised erotic themes with natural images. One asked the question, "Does a flower love to have its ovary sucked by a honey bee?"

Stories about alluring concubines had enormous popularity in imperial China. The couple almost certainly read the "Song of Everlasting Regret," a famous poem about Yang Guifei (719–756), one of China's four great beauties. So lovely was Yang, it was said, that she made even flowers feel ashamed. Described as plump with ample breasts and hips, Yang Yuhuan (Jade Ring) was a real woman who lived during the Tang dynasty. Although she had come to the palace as the wife of his eighteenth son, Emperor Xuanzong fell in love with Yang and made her his favored imperial consort. Their love was shattered when a military governor stationed at the frontier, An Lushan, gained the trust of Yang, who adopted him as her own son. When he later mounted a rebellion against the emperor, she was implicated in the plot. The emperor was forced to order her execution by strangling. Before the order could be carried out, she uttered a tearful goodbye to the emperor and hanged herself with a silken cord. Devastated, the emperor spent the rest of his life mourning her death. At the end of the "Song of Everlasting Regret," Yang and Xuanzong are described as two birds, each with only one wing, that fly together into heaven. Although the poem captured the misery of romantic longing, the story also contained a warning about emperors who fall in love with beautiful concubines. Xuanzong eventually lost his throne and his dynasty fell into sharp decline because of his affair with Yang Guifei. Stories such as these warned Wanli to avoid falling deeply in love with a beautiful concubine.

No physical description of Lady Zheng remains. Having reached the elevated rank of noble consort, she must have been impressively adorned. Perhaps she wore light colored silk skirts, a waistcoat with jade buttons, and a rosy cloud cape that was the fashion of the time. One of the adornments she may have worn has survived as a museum piece: a spectacular golden hair pin embedded with rubies, sapphires, and pearls. Among her most alluring physical attributes were her tiny feet. For hundreds of years, foot binding was required for elite Chinese women. When their bones were still growing, little girls would have the toes and top half of their feet broken and folded under the other half. Afterward, the broken feet were bound so that they would grow into this constricting shape. The ultimate, and seemingly impossible, goal for fashionable ladies was a "golden lotus" foot that would fit into a three-inch shoe. Lady Zheng was reported to have tiny golden lotus feet. Disfigured in this way, Chinese women walked with great difficulty, but their careful shuffling along the floor in silk shoes added to their erotic attraction.

In the end, however, it was probably more than a physical attraction that Wanli felt for Lady Zheng. The father of eighteen children, he had numerous sexual encounters with beautiful women, and, if Liu Rouyu's diary can be believed, some attractive eunuchs. Only a strong emotional bond can explain his lifelong attachment to her. In 1590, he explained the real reason he loved Lady Zheng to his first grand secretary. "Lady Zheng is always with me whenever I retire to the palace quarters. She takes good care of me, day and night." That was enough for the emperor.

The strong relationship between the emperor and his favorite concubine posed a problem for the palace officials, who worried that the romance would take his mind off of his duties to the empire. When Lady Zheng gave birth to a son on New Year's Day, 1584, it caused the most important political crisis of the reign. Wanli favored this son, Zhu Changxun over his first son, Zhu Changlu. Refusing to honor Changlu with the appropriate ceremonies or provide the education appropriate to an heir to the throne, Wanli angered his court. Some palace officials were outraged when he raised the status of Zheng to *guifei* (imperial consort), a title only one rank below the status of the empress.

The issue of succession divided the palace officials. Some supported the emperor, but others thought that putting the third son before the first would undermine the entire social order. Inspired by the philosophy of Confucius, they believed that the universe demanded order in the family based on a strict hierarchy of age. Good behavior started at the top and trickled down to the lowest subject. Even the emperor had to obey these moral laws.

Confucius

Confucius (551–479 BCE) established the ethical foundations of the Chinese state. Having lived through hard times as a relatively unsuccessful bureaucrat in a time of political turmoil, he sought a way to bring order out of chaos. Hundreds of his sayings were collected into the *Analects* (selections), which served as a fountain of wisdom for individuals, families, and governments. Although completely secular, the book had been revered almost as religious scripture during the Ming dynasty.

Living through an age of endless, bloody warfare and political chaos, Confucius proposed that the broken world might be mended through kindness. He said, "If a man sets his heart on benevolence, he will be free from evil." Believing that every person needed courage and hard work to live a life of virtue and wisdom, he encouraged people to improve themselves. For example, one analect explains how one can learn from ordinary life. He said, "Even when walking in the company of two other men, I am bound to be able to learn from them. The good points of the one I copy; the bad points of the other I correct in myself." With such sayings, he repeatedly urged people to give up anger and resentment towards others. When asked to give the most important guide for living, Confucius said, "Do not impose on others what you yourself do not desire."

Confucius explained a means to establish harmony in families and the larger society. Linking individuals to their families, and families to the state were strong ties of obligation and obedience. On one hand, people needed to obey their superiors. On the other, those placed in authority had to rule in the best interest of the people below them. Obedience and kindness were two sides of the same coin. Harmony in a family and a state rested on obedience from the bottom up, and kindness from the top down. Children obeyed their parents, but parents looked after the well-being of their children. Wives obeyed husbands, but husbands acted in a way that benefitted their wives. The farmer obeyed his landlord, but the landlord protected the interests of his farmers. The landlord obeyed the government officials, but the officials ruled for the benefit of the landlords. Finally, government officials obeyed the emperor, but the emperor made decisions for the good of his officials. Indeed, at the top of the social pyramid, the emperor had to rule in the interests of all below him: officials, landlords, farmers, husbands, wives, and children. All peace and prosperity in the empire rested on the kindness of the emperor. If he acted selfishly, he would break the chain. Confucius understood that selfish leaders never commanded true obedience. Subjects who obeyed their leaders out of fear never gave their best effort. Selfishness caused turmoil and destruction in a family and a state. In this perspective, everyone had a moral obligation to fulfill their duties to others in order for the whole system to work.

The palace system

The government of imperial China under the Ming dynasty followed Confucian principles. Unlike the courts of France, Japan, and other states in the sixteenth century, where positions of power often went to the sons of royal and aristocratic families, the imperial court of China awarded important offices according to merit. The ministers who directed the government under Wanli had scored highest on a standardized test, the civil service examination. Originating in the Han dynasty (206 BCE–220 CE), the exam allowed members of every class and status an opportunity to rise in government service. The palace awarded positions to those with the highest scores. Although dynastic succession determined the emperor, the civil service examination decided who would actually rule the state.

The educational system of Ming dynasty China included over a thousand elementary schools, one for each region and district. About two million boys came out of the schools eligible to take the first round of exams, which were the first step to government office. Because these positions brought prestige, wealth, and fame, the Chinese referred to a job in government as the "golden rice bowl." Every three years in the autumn and winter, hundreds of thousands of 15-year-old boys sat for the qualifying exam in their province. If they passed, they could sit for the metropolitan exams in Beijing. Lodging in special examination cells in the capital, the boys brought their own brush, ink, water pitcher, chamber pot, bedding, curtain, and food. Passing these exams enabled them to sit for the palace examination given by the emperor himself. For this exam, the students wrote essays over the classic works of Chinese literature and history, including the *Analects* of Confucius. Clerks recopied the students' answers in order keep them anonymous. Nevertheless, fraud and cheating happened regularly, as one might expect in this high stakes competition.

Less than one percent of students passed the exams, but those who failed could retake them. It was not unusual to see grey haired men striving to pass the exam. The average age of those who passed the exam granting the degree of *jinshi*, or advanced scholar, was 35. Failing the exam caused such agony that some men sank into alcoholism, while others started riots. In the nineteenth century, one unsuccessful student who repeatedly failed the exam started an armed rebellion against the government. Known as the Tai Ping rebellion, the uprising caused the death of nearly twenty million people.

The office rank was determined by performance on the exams. These high offices brought honor to the student's entire family and ancestors. The scholars indicated their rank by wearing a "mandarin square" or piece of cloth with a particular bird embroidered on the front. Two cranes indicated the highest rank at the palace. Having excelled on the grueling series of civil service examinations, the government officials felt supremely confident to interpret the ideals of Confucius. They were certain that they knew what was best for the empire.

Controversy in the palace

Wanli's support for Lady Zheng's son put him at odds with Confucian ideals of order and hierarchy, which dictated that younger brothers must obey older brothers. In addition, for the emperor to favor the whims of a woman over the advice of his palace officials appeared to be a contradiction of the social order in which men ought to rule over women. Somewhat inconsistently, the palace officials did not consider their own disobedience to the will of the emperor, their superior, a breach of Confucian ideals.

As in other authoritarian states, palace officials who directly criticized the emperor risked death. For this reason, their reports often focused on attacking Lady Zheng, not Wanli. They called her nagging, stubborn, and selfish. Suspecting that certain tax ministers had encouraged her ambitions to further their own interests, her enemies denounced her faction at court as corrupt.

Further evidence of corruption appeared when Lady Zheng sided with palace women and eunuchs at court. Serving as her informants and carrying out her bidding, these women and eunuchs often sought her protection. In one story, the writer Shen Defu described an incident with Zheng's daughter, Princess Shouyang, and her husband. One night, the husband attempted to make an unexpected visit to his wife in her palace compound. Guarding her door was an intoxicated palace woman who refused to let him in and struck him in a drunken rage. When the husband threatened to complain to the emperor, he was beaten by two palace eunuchs. The emperor, eventually hearing of this case, took the side of his favorite consort. He assigned three months of moral training to his son-in-law, reassigned the palace woman to another location, and let the eunuchs off without any punishment. To Shen Defu, this case proved that Zheng encouraged Wanli to put favoritism above justice at the palace.

Palace officials also accused her of spending lavishly on her son. Granted the title, prince of Fu, when his older brother had been named heir in 1598, Zhu Changxun refused to leave the palace. According to custom, the younger brothers of the crowned prince moved to palaces in the provinces, where they were less likely to challenge the throne. Disregarding this custom, Zheng kept her son near her in the palace as long as possible. When she finally agreed to let him go, she spent ten times the allotted budget on his wedding and palace. The public also balked at the size of his domain, an incredible 600,000 acres, even if this grant only existed on paper. His allowances appeared to contradict the Confucian ideal of frugality.

In an effort to rehabilitate her reputation, Lady Zheng gave generously to charity and served as a patron of education. For example, she donated over 300 pounds of silver to relieve famine to Honan. She also spent money to publish a second edition of Lu K'un's *Lives of Exemplary Women*. In the preface she had written to this book, Lady Zheng discussed the importance of education for the common people. However, when she added twelve new biographies to her edition, she dared to include herself as an example of an illustrious woman and neglected to include the empress and Lady Wang. Not surprisingly, her efforts to promote herself backfired. Her critics accused her of using publicity stunts to make herself look qualified to be the mother of an emperor. Nothing she did could convince people of her sincerity.

As the palace officials continued to bombard Wanli with highly critical reports, the emperor grew increasingly distant from state business. He responded to the constant attacks with a strategy of passive aggression. He refused to appear at state ceremonies altogether, ceased to appoint new officials, and neglected to read the many reports written to advise him. Avoiding any public functions, he lived in the Forbidden City as a private man enjoying the company of Lady Zheng and other palace women while feasting on delicacies. Soon Wanli became so obese that he had to be supported by others simply to remain seated upright.

He also angered his ministers by not showing his mother, Empress Dowager Li, the respect he owed her. She, like the palace officials, favored his oldest son by Lady Wang. Wanli began to question his own mother's concern for him, feeling as though she treated him like an institution rather than a real human being. When he refused to attend her state funeral, officials were outraged. He claimed that he intended to mourn for her privately, but he did not want to play ceremonial roles in symbolic rituals simply to please the court.

Amazingly, the state ceremonies continued without him. Officials kowtowed by bowing and placing their forehead on the floor in front of an empty throne. For over forty years the imperial government conducted its business without any apparent leadership from the emperor.

The dynasty was able to withstand the lack of leadership at the top because the system of civil service education produced conscientious officials who cared about their moral duty to the state. Few emperors made decisions without the guidance of the bureaucratic scholars in the palace. Although the Ming dynasty began with two powerful emperors, many later emperors appeared weak, and some even seemed mentally unbalanced. Ming emperors did not always follow the advice of their ministers, and Wanli was not the first to carry on a strike against his court. In the 1540s, his grandfather, the Jiajing emperor, had been known for his alcoholism and cruelty. In 1542, several of his concubines tried to assassinate him by stabbing him with their hairpins and strangling him with a silk ribbon. Caught in the act by a eunuch, they did not succeed. Convicted of high treason, the Jaijing emperor sentenced the perpetrators to death by *lingchi* (slicing). In this terrible punishment, the prisoner endures the careful removal of hundreds, perhaps thousands of small slices of flesh causing a slow and painful death.

After the assassination attempt, the Jiajing emperor moved into seclusion away from the court. He practiced the fortune-telling and magical healing associated with Taoism, an ancient mystical philosophy. Obsessed with fertility and the search for immortality, he drank aphrodisiacs made of red lead and arsenic that eventually poisoned him. More disturbing, he believed that he could live forever by having sexual intercourse with virgins at the moment they entered puberty. Convinced that the onset of menstruation represented the perfect balance of life forces in the girl, he believed that he could absorb these precious energies through sexual intercourse and prolong his life forever. He selected 800 girls between the ages of 9 and 14 to serve this purpose. His terrible experiment illustrated how little value girls held at the imperial court, where they were seen as scarcely more than medical treatment for a deranged emperor.

Needless to say, the Jaijing emperor's efforts at immortality failed. His son, Wanli's father, took the throne after his death. Although not nearly as eccentric, Wanli's father also tended to neglect affairs of state. Compared to his predecessors, Wanli could not be considered the worst example of a Ming emperor. Indeed, despite a series of inattentive emperors, the economy of the Ming dynasty flourished. Modern historians look to Wanli's reign as one of China's golden ages. The first Spanish ships full of silver arrived in Manila, Philippines, in 1573. Europeans spent millions of silver coins on Chinese silks and porcelain. So popular were ceramic plates and bowls that they began to be called "China." Throughout the Middle East, blue and white porcelain inspired by China covered the walls of houses and domes of mosques. Even today, Ming dynasty vases are prized for their elegance and superior craftwork.

The massive influx of money from global trade changed Ming society. Fashion in clothes became more elaborate, and even poor country people appeared in town wearing silks embroidered with gold and silver. Class distinctions blurred as artisans and merchants could afford to live like landed gentry. They bought the finest brand name lacquer ware, bronzes, garments, and porcelains, as well as libraries of books providing education and refinement. For the first time, writers made the life of ordinary, middle class people the subjects of their novels.

Some moralists complained about money perverting relationships between men and women. Prostitution, it seemed, had gone upscale. By the Wanli era, the rich avoided ordinary prostitutes and sought the services of literate and refined courtesans who offered cultured conversation and romantic love. In an age when marriages were arranged as financial agreements, men wanted female companions who could understand them. Some of these ladies became famous poets and writers, as well as the subjects of best-selling fiction.

More rare and shocking, and reserved only for the most elite social circles in the late Ming dynasty, was the purchase of young boys for sex. Entrepreneurs often bought orphans or famine victims, trained them to sing and dance, and then hired them out or sold them as prostitutes. Traditional Confucian morality disapproved of pederasty, but many in the very highest social circles considered it an indication of good taste.

Some scholars blamed this increasingly commercial society, in which anything could be bought or sold, for corrupting the simple country morals that had built the dynasty hundreds of years earlier. In this time of unsettling change, many moralists blamed women for not adopting traditional roles in society. A Chinese book of omens published in 1599 listed the signs of a variety of disasters such as famine, drought, and invasion. Included among these misfortunes was the "chaos of women" foretold by a comet entering the constellation of the ox. The chaos referred to a situation in which women ruled over men. Was this a reference to Lady Zheng's influence on the emperor?

Three court cases

In the early seventeenth century, Lady Zheng, middle-aged but still a powerful presence in the court, played a role in three major scandals. In 1615 a young man entered the Forbidden City and attacked a palace eunuch with a thick club before being apprehended by guards. At first the details of the case seemed clear. The man with the club was insane and had a grudge against the eunuch because of an earlier incident that took place outside of the city. Not considering this explanation sufficient, some high-ranking ministers pressed for further interrogation of the intruder. A palace official who conducted a more thorough investigation found that the intruder had been perfectly sane and his attack had been coordinated by two eunuchs close to Lady Zheng. Without any real evidence, many suspected that Zheng had hired the intruder to murder Zhu Changlu so that her son could be named heir to the throne. Wanli ordered the immediate execution of the intruder, but took no action against the eunuchs or Lady Zheng.

The controversy caused the strengthening of one faction, the Donglin movement, whose members referred to themselves as "the good elements." Officials belonging to this faction attacked Zheng and the ministers who supported Wanli. Considering themselves a part of a moral crusade in the service of Confucian ideals, members of this secretive society hurled accusations and made insinuations about others without any real evidence. The rival faction soon sought to destroy the members of the Donglin movement. Every insignificant detail about palace life was used to point to the intrigue and corruption of the other faction.

The last years of the 48-year Wanli reign were filled with economic and military problems. The Manchurians from the northwest carried out invasions that threatened the empire, an influx of silver caused massive inflation, and rising taxes encouraged peasant rebellions. However, partisan bickering often prevented either of the factions from addressing these real problems. Instead, they spent time and energy dividing the bureaucracy into the "good elements" and the "bad elements" based on differing interpretations of Confucius.

Another famous court case happened shortly after the death of Wanli in 1620. His eldest son by Lady Wang, Zhu Changlu, acceded the throne as the Taichang emperor. He promised reform, and people felt optimistic about the new reign. However, about a week after he took the throne at the age of 38, he fell mysteriously ill. Suffering uncontrollable diarrhea for weeks, he took what was supposed to be a miracle drug, two doses of red pills prepared by a minor official. The following morning he was dead. Naturally, many at court suspected poison and accused a eunuch who had been associated with Lady Zheng. Her motive seemed clear; Changlu's death brought her son closer to the throne. However, Zhu Changlu had five sons of his own, and the prince of Fu was nowhere near the line of succession at that point. The court case did not present any solid evidence against Lady Zheng, but partisans continued to see her as a nefarious presence behind every misfortune at the palace.

The final court case involved Tianqi, the mentally deficient, poorly educated, and physically weak son of the late emperor who acceded to the throne in 1620. Illiterate, he allowed his favorite eunuch and his former nursemaid to rule the empire from his own palace in the Forbidden city. Government officials eventually forced the nursemaid to move away from the emperor's palace, but Lady Zheng was somehow accused of orchestrating the whole event to further the aims of her son. The evidence presented at the case had little to do with Zheng, but the controversy pitted a clique of eunuchs against the members of the Donglin movement. The power struggles between the factions led to the further weakening of the dynasty.

Lady Zheng outlived the Wanli Emperor by ten years. Unloved and accused of every crime, she spent lonely days in a desolate lodge in the palace complex. After Zhu Chanxun, the prince of Fu, moved to his domain in the provinces, the imperial consort never saw her son again. She died in 1630. Although Wanli had given instructions for her body to be interred next to his in his magnificent tomb, his palace officials refused. His body now rests in an enormous mausoleum between the tombs of his neglected empress and Lady Wang, mother of Zhu Changlu. Even in death, his ministers opposed him.

When the Tianqi emperor died at the age of 21, his younger brother, Zhu Youxiao assumed the throne at age 15. Under his reign, an army of Manchurians invaded China. When they entered Beijing, the last Ming emperor climbed a small hill in the Imperial City and hanged himself in the pavilion that housed the Imperial Hat and Girdle department. It was 1644, the end of the Ming dynasty, and the beginning of the Manchu, or Qing dynasty (1644–1912).

The fall of the Ming dynasty was not the fault of Lady Zheng, but she made a convenient target for contemporaries looking for a scapegoat to blame. No one can ever really know if her influence led Wanli to neglect his duties as emperor. Nor is there solid evidence connecting her to the assassination attempt and death of Zhu Changlu. These affairs and scandals appear insignificant compared to a number of problems and disasters attacking the Ming at the end of the dynasty. Some historians have debated whether Wanli's reign should be seen as a period of decline. They point out the emperor's successful defense against Hideyoshi's invasion of Korea as an example of Wanli's strength. However, if the empire had weaknesses, they stemmed in large part from an inflexible palace bureaucracy. Its rigid adherence to a strict interpretation of Confucian ideals made the palace officials unable to innovate and find practical solutions to concrete problems. These scholar bureaucrats refused to see their own part in the crisis of the late Ming dynasty. They, and subsequent historians, preferred to place the blame on one woman, an imperial consort, who led the emperor astray.

Chronology

c. 1568   Birth of Lady Zheng.
1582   Death of Grand Secretary Zhang Juzheng. Lady Zheng enters the Forbidden City. Birth of Zhu Changlu to Lady Wang.
1584   Birth of Zhu Changxun to Lady Zheng.
1615   Affair of the club.
1620   Death of the Wanli Emperor. Zhu Changlu becomes emperor of China.
1630   Death of Lady Zheng.
1644   Fall of the Ming dynasty.

Sources for further reading about Lady Zheng

Few primary sources about Lady Zheng have been translated into English. The most thorough discussion of the succession crisis during the Wanli reign is Ray Huang, *1587: A Year of No Significance: The Ming Dynasty in Decline* (New Haven, CT: Yale University Press, 1981). As yet, there is no biography dedicated to Lady Zheng. The most in-depth treatment of her remains Chaoying Fang, "Cheng Kui-Fei," in L. Carrington Goodrich and Chaoying Fang, *Dictionary of Ming Biography* (New York: Columbia University Press, 1976), pp. 208–211. Wang Caizhong and Shu Aixiang have written an entry, "Zheng Guifei," in Barbara Bennett Peterson, ed., *Notable Women of China: Shang Dynasty to the Early Twentieth Century* (New York: M. E. Sharp, 2000). A shorter entry with some different information on the consort is Lin Yanqing, "Zheng Consort of the Wanli Emperor Shenzon of Ming," in Lily Xiao Hong and Sue Wiles, eds., *Biographical Dictionary of Chinese Women, Volume II: From Tang to Ming 618–1644* (London: Routledge, 2015), although Keith McMahon, *Celestial Women: Imperial Wives and Concubines in China from Song to Qing* (Lanham, MD: Rowman & Littlefield, 2016) provides some interesting detail about her life based on writers, chroniclers, and diarists at the court. This work also includes a nice introduction that compares the lives of concubines in China to those of the harem in the Ottoman court. The controversies concerning the Donglin Movement are covered in John Dardess, *Blood and History in China: The Donglin Faction and its Repression, 1620–1627* (Honolulu, HI: University of Hawaii Press, 2002). For a general overview of the Ming dynasty see Timothy Brook, *The Confusions of Pleasure: Commerce and Culture in Ming China* (Berkeley, CA: University of California Press, 1999) and Frederick W. Mote and Denis Twitchett, eds., *Cambridge History of China, Volumes VII and VIII: The Ming Dynasty 1368–1644, Parts I and II* (Cambridge: Cambridge University Press, 1988, 1998), and John Dardess, *Ming China 1368–1644: A Concise History of a Resilient Empire* (Lanham, MD: Rowman & Littlefield, 2012).

Comparison between Hürrem Sultan and Lady Zheng

Hürrem and Lady Zheng illustrate how powerful women could impact policy in dynastic regimes. In courts dominated by family relationships, women played important roles as wives and mothers. Their greatest strength, however, seems to have been the hold they maintained over the male imagination. Historians have been telling their remarkably similar stories for five hundred years.

The Ming and Ottoman courts provided fertile ground for stories about women's sexual power, and it must be emphasized that these are stories and not true history. In autocratic states, all political decisions take place behind closed doors. This secrecy means that historians have no reliable record of foreign or domestic policy. The reports of diplomats and government officials can provide only speculation, rumor, and hearsay. In both of these empires, there were no representative institutions or rival sources of power to temper the absolute authority of the ruler, who had the power of life or death over every person in the state. This had a chilling effect on the flow of information.

Every dynasty suffers from the unavoidable problem of succession. Since a dynasty is a family that maintains control over a state for generations, it necessarily requires an obsession with sexual reproduction. Sexuality, therefore, existed as a political problem at the heart of the state. For the people who left records, especially the officials at court, succession was a matter of life or death. A legitimate heir was the greatest guarantee against a bloody civil war that might devastate the empire and topple the dynasty. When an heir's legitimacy was questioned, the court broke up into factions. A government official had to select carefully which heir to support, and which faction to join, and then to pour heart and soul into the fight. If one's chosen heir did not take up the throne, the rival heir might very well demand the execution of rival factions. To live at courts such as these was to live in constant fear for one's life.

Without the legal constraint of primogeniture (as operated in the royal families of France and England) the Ming and Ottoman dynasties required a large supply of potential male heirs. This necessitated the custom of keeping several hundred sexual partners on hand for the emperor. These women, voluntarily or not, lived as captives secluded in a harem guarded by eunuchs. Many never left the palace their whole lives. One can only hope that bonds of friendship, either with each other or with the palace eunuchs, provided emotional support for these concubines and consorts.

Although few sources remain of life in the harems of the rulers, plenty of documents recount the images they left in the imagination of the male officials. Here one sees images of ruthless and power hungry women willing to resort to any intrigue and even murder to put their sons on the throne. No firm evidence connects Hürrem or Lady Zheng to murder, and yet both stood accused. Indeed, the character portraits are so similar, it leads one to consider whether the officials reacted to reality or merely projected an archetype onto a certain political situation.

One thing is certain in both cases: Suleiman and Wanli developed strong emotional bonds with these women that lasted as long as they lived. The women adopted the role of friend, lover, advisor, and confidant to the ruler. Undoubtedly physically attractive, the women's main appeal for their lovers was based on education, refinement, and intelligence. Beyond these qualities, what seemed to matter most was their affectionate and steadfast devotion. The emperors responded in kind, by placing their confidence in them alone. Surely it must have been lonely for the ruler, who only existed as a public person without a personal or private life to call his own. Very possibly, loving a woman made him feel like a man, that is, as a real human being rather than an institution. Indeed, the ruler was just as much a captive to the dynasty as his concubine. A committed relationship was a way to transcend these limited roles and infuse one's life with meaning. Perhaps jealousy explains much of the animosity directed at them by the government officials. The bureaucracy could not stomach such a powerful force outside of its control. Fear may have also played a role, as a few words whispered into the ear of the sovereign by a consort could very well mean instant death for a previously trusted advisor.

In political terms, Hürrem experienced much more success than Lady Zheng. Not only did she make the journey from slave girl to sultana, she also managed to place her son on the throne. Lady Zheng was never promoted to empress, nor did she secure a place in the succession for her son. Indeed, other Chinese emperors had promoted imperial consorts to the rank of empress. That was Wanli's prerogative, but for some reason he did not do it. Perhaps the divergence of their fortunes might be attributed to differences in character between Suleiman and Wanli. Suleiman's active rule contrasted sharply with the passive complacency of the Wanli Emperor.

The religious and philosophical foundations of the court culture also had an impact on the lives of these women as servants of the dynasty. At the Ottoman court, the sultan ruled absolutely, but a sense of egalitarianism pervaded the government officials. Devoted to the principles of Islam, it was modeled on an army of religious warriors rather than an imperial bureaucracy. Nevertheless, the Ottomans, as they gained territories, began to develop a more impersonal, bureaucratic form of government. When power moved from the battlefield to the court, palace women played a larger role in directing policy. Women were increasingly expected to engage in charity and serve as patrons for the arts. Nevertheless, this transition was unsettling to many men, who perhaps took out their frustrations about a changing political structure on women who claimed power in the court.

In contrast, the Ming court, based on Confucian philosophy, sought to exemplify hierarchy over social equality. The rigid order was supposed to provide harmony to the state, but the court was also unsettled by social transformation. The prosperity and peace of the dynasty had ushered in magnificent wealth, new ideas, and luxury which many believed corrupted the court. A common way to complain about these trends was to place the blame on the harmful influence of women.

In both cases, officials facing social transformations beyond their control targeted the meddling of women in politics as the main issue facing the court. This had a long tradition in Chinese history, which viewed beautiful women as a distraction from the emperor's duties. In both Ottoman and Chinese courts, however, young women of childbearing age were considered the greatest threat to disorder. Once women entered into old age, however, their status rose considerably. They became sources of trusted and wise counsel, especially as the mothers of rulers.

Throughout the years, some historians have gone as far as to blame Hürrem and Lady Zheng for the decline and fall of their dynasties. This seems unfair, given that the Ming lasted until 1644 and the Ottoman dynasty lasted for another four hundred years, until the twentieth century. In reality, a combination of forces brought these dynasties into decline by the seventeenth century. The courts struggled to deal with the disruption caused by a new global economy, as well as the famine and disease caused by a mini-ice age. Increasingly, an inflexible and rigid imperial bureaucracy could not cope with practical problems such as floods, invasions, rapacious tax collectors, and peasant rebellions. Unable to diagnose these problems correctly, some government officials and chroniclers preferred to blame the "selfish" actions of individual women.

Such blatant misogyny is not confined to the Ottoman and Ming courts, nor to the sixteenth century as an era. Rather, it seems as though the same motives and impulses rise to the surface of history everywhere and always. Marie Antoinette did not cause the French Revolution and Yoko Ono did not break up the Beatles, and yet these women played a central role in the plot of such stories after so many years.

Questions to consider

1 Both the Ottoman and Chinese systems of bureaucracy claimed to be more meritocratic than governments based on feudal relationships as in Japan and France. Is this true? What are the benefits of each system? What are the disadvantages?

2 Compare the reputations of Hürrem and Lady Zheng to Catherine de Medici. Why do you think these women had a reputation for deceit? Refer to Henry IV's assessment of Catherine de Medici. Do you agree with him that motherhood is a justification for ruthlessness?

3 Do you think that absolute rulers such as Suleiman and Wanli were more or less susceptible to the influence of their lovers than ordinary people? Why or why not?

4 Discuss the role of factions in the four courts discussed in these chapters. What do you think leads to discord and partisanship? What can solve it? At the court of Wanli, one group accused the other of moral corruption. How can one prove or disprove this charge? Why do you think it is so common in politics?

5 In an age when women were formally denied access to political roles, what gave individual women the potential for power and influence over policy in dynastic states?

6 Chapter 1 presented two feudal states on the path toward nationhood, whereas Chapter 2 presented two large empires. How did they differ? Which political

system do you think is more stable? What are the advantages and disadvantages of these systems for the common people?

7   Hürrem and Lady Zheng were not warriors like Hideyoshi and Henry IV, but both exhibited a certain amount of courage. In what ways would you describe them as brave?

Note

1 Jayne L. Warner, ed., *Rapture and Revolution: Essays on Turkish Literature by Talat S. Halman* (Syracuse, NY: Syracuse University Press, 2007), p. 326.

3

AFONSO I OF KONGO AND ELIZABETH I OF ENGLAND

In their long reigns, Afonso I of Kongo and Elizabeth I of England brought prosperity, strength, and religious change to their kingdoms. Described by contemporaries as "instruments of divine will," Afonso and Elizabeth successfully merged new religious beliefs with the traditions of royal power. As the fifth king of Kongo, Afonso adopted and promoted the Catholic religion of the Portuguese. By the end of his reign, he had used Portuguese trade and military aid to consolidate and enlarge his domains in Africa. Queen Elizabeth I bolstered her royal authority as the protector of the Protestant faith in England. Both figures successfully used symbols to convey the majesty of their monarchical power to the people, while simultaneously keeping the elite content by distributing the profits from global trade as patronage. Despite enormous cultural differences, the people and rulers of Kongo and England engaged in a similar kind of magical thinking, which sought to bring down the power of the heavens to influence events on earth.

Afonso I of Kongo (c. 1456–c. 1543)

From 1506 to 1543 Afonso I ruled Kongo, one of the most powerful kingdoms of its time in Africa. Inspired and strengthened by Portuguese churchmen and soldiers, he made Christianity the state religion throughout his domains. Remembered by some as the "Apostle of the Kongo," Afonso blended Catholicism with elements of African religion to establish Kongo as a powerful Christian kingdom. His openness to aspects of a new and radically different culture combined with a sophisticated understanding of how to preserve the interests of his people allowed this African king to modernize his lands on his own terms. His political and religious legacy impacted millions of Africans dispersed throughout the Americas during the years of the Atlantic slave trade.

The origins of the kingdom of Kongo

The domains of the sixteenth-century kingdom of Kongo now lie divided between present day Angola, The Republic of Congo, and the Democratic Republic of Congo in Central West Africa. An enormous continent, Africa is large enough to hold the entire United States, China, and most of Europe within its land mass.

FIGURE 3.1   Olfert Dapper, *Alvaro I of Kongo receiving the Dutch ambassadors*, 1668. No contemporary image of Afonso I survives. This seventeenth-century woodcut portrays his grandson and heir, Alvaro I.

Source: Private collection/Bridgeman Images

Throughout its long history, Africa had seen the rise and fall of numerous kingdoms and empires. In the far north and northeast, the states of Egypt, Ethiopia, and the Sudan boasted cities that belonged to the cultures of classical antiquity. By 700 CE, the peoples of these regions had converted to Islam and were integrated into growing Islamic empires. South of the Sahara, camel caravans full of luxury goods began to make their way across the desert to the West African states of Mali and Benin around 1000 CE. Another empire, Zimbabwe, flourished in Central East Africa in the fourteenth century. Nearly two thousand miles from any other African kingdom or empire, the Kongo had little if any contact with other states and developed independently.

The people of Kongo spoke Kikongo, one of around 500 Bantu languages spoken south of the Equator in Africa. Over the course of millennia, the people of this language group had come from the northwest to form settlements in the savannah region below the Congo River. Skilled in agriculture and ironworking, the ancestors of the Kongolese people grew prosperous by controlling trade between the coastal, plateau, and forest areas in the region. By 1350, six independent states had united to form the kingdom of Kongo.

In the absence of written sources, oral traditions passed down by word of mouth for generations have served to establish the political foundations of the kingdom. Two surviving traditions present differing accounts of the first king of Kongo, who reigned about 150 years before Afonso I. One tradition holds that a warrior named Lukeni decided to collect tolls at a stream crossing. When his pregnant aunt refused to pay, he stabbed her in the stomach, killing both her and her unborn baby. Having transgressed the boundaries of social norms, the ruthless king conquered six entire provinces and built his capital, M'banza Kongo. The city sat perched on a high plateau protected by 200- to 300-feet-high cliffs overlooking the Luezi river.

Another account described the first king of Kongo as a blacksmith named Ntinu Wene. The people of the region believed that forging metals was a sacred activity. For them, ironworking had transformative powers, as the blacksmith had the skills necessary to transform liquid metals into powerful tools and weapons. In political terms, the iron symbolized the fortitude and strength of the ruler, while the activity of forging itself contained spiritual powers to heal and dispel evil influences. Only members of the high nobility were allowed to engage in ironworking. The blacksmith king established symbols of the Kongo monarchy that would remain for centuries: the iron bracelet, the hammer and anvil, and particularly the royal drum, whose beating recreated the sounds of the forge. Although historians now believe that ironworking had been in the region centuries before Ntinu Wene, the oral tradition of a founding king who brought special knowledge to his people gave political legitimacy to the rulers of Kongo.

By the late fifteenth century, the kings of Kongo collected tribute from all six provinces and taxed the goods exchanged from one side of the kingdom to the other. The capital of M'banza Kongo and its region grew to perhaps one hundred thousand residents, and the revenue collected by the crown created a ruling elite in the capital with a strong taste for luxury goods.

Religion and magic in Kongo

In every human society, a cosmology or worldview ties together religion, society, and political power. The foundation of Kongo society was the *kanda,* as association of family groups that also served as a district in a political sense. Each kanda had hundreds of members who called each other brothers and sisters. All of the younger members of the groups called the elder members mother and father and respected their authority. The elders of the kanda groups decided who worked what land and how the fruits of labor would be distributed. Not only did the kanda organize daily life on earth, they also extended their authority into the afterlife. The head of each kanda served as the major communicator with the spirits of their common ancestors.

The traditional religious beliefs of the Kongo people centered on spirits. These included ancestors, as well as territorial spirits connected to the land. Above all the spirits was one supreme being who lived in the sky, Nzambi Mpungu. Kongolese religion divided the world into two realms, one earthly, which could be seen and experienced by ordinary living people, and one spiritual, where the otherworldly spirits, both ancestral and territorial, lived. The separate realms of the living and the dead were imagined as two mountains separated by a body of water. On one mountain, living people went about their daily lives, while on the other dwelled the sprits. Every person had a soul, or *moyo,* and when a person died, the moyo passed through the water emerging on the side of the spirits as a ghostly white being. In the cosmology of Kongo, the color black represented life, white represented death and the supernatural world, and red represented the transition between two states of being.

As powerful forces, spirits controlled nearly everything that happened in the earthly world. These spirits influenced the living in both positive and negative ways. Magical thinking, nearly universal in the sixteenth-century world, played a large role in sixteenth-century African society. Called "conjuring," it involved the reading of natural phenomenon such as the flight of birds or intestines of animals for signs from the spirit world. The use of spells or the placement of special objects in special sachet bags was believed to allow the conjurer to harness the power of heaven for use on earth. In the traditional religion of Kongo, these magical powers could be used for good or evil ends. If used for bad purposes, the Africans called it witchcraft. Sometimes spirits lived in certain objects. When an object contained a spirit, it became an idol. In the traditional religion of Kongo, people worshipped these objects and believed that they had magical powers. Sometimes spirits came back to the earthly world and inhabited the bodies of living people. Because it was believed that spirits preferred to live in the bodies of dwarfs and albinos, many considered these kinds of people capable of performing magic.

The traditional religion of Kongo viewed the relationship between ancestors and their descendants as a chain. At the top of the chain were elders who had died. Below them were the living members of the kanda, from oldest at the top to the youngest baby at the bottom. Every member of this chain could curse or bless the member directly below, so the younger offered respect and gifts to those above them, whether in the world of the living or dead. Most people could not see or communicate with the spirit world, but it was believed that certain people had a talent or perception to read its messages or interpret its signs. Since spirituality lay at the heart of everyday life, from formal rituals on special occasions to a regular day in the fields, these specialists held enormous authority in Kongo. Just as younger people respected their elders, all people respected the wise men or women who could read the signs of the spirits.

Beyond the spirits ruled an all-powerful being who had created the world, Nzambi a Mpungu. Living humans could not communicate with him directly, but required spirits to serve as intermediaries. Messages or communications from the spirit world were understood as revelations, because they revealed the divine will. In this flexible religious system, believers were open to new religious specialists and ways of accessing the spirit world. Perhaps for this reason, they did not immediately reject the new ideas brought by the explorers from Europe who came with their own religious beliefs.

The Portuguese in Africa

Portugal, a small kingdom on the west coast of the Iberian Peninsula, shared a similar history with its neighbor, Spain. Both countries had been conquered and ruled by Muslims who came over from North Africa in 711 CE. The war that the Christian kings of Portugal and Spain waged to win back their peninsula, the *Reconquista*, took almost 800 years. It was not until 1492 that Ferdinand and Isabella of Spain retook the last bastion of Islam in Spain at Granada. To celebrate the victory, Isabella donated ships to an enterprising mariner named Christopher Columbus. Long before his journey to America, however, Portuguese sailors were exploring another new world, the west coast of Africa. Before that time, no European had ever ventured south of the Sahara desert.

Medieval Europeans held strange beliefs about geography. They knew the world was round, but some writers claimed that the lands south of the equator were so hot that humans would burst into flames if they tried to cross it. Others maintained that south of the equator, on the "bottom of the world," there were people called *antipodes*, who had feet coming out of their heads. They imagined the Atlantic as a body of water called the *Ocean*, which surrounded all of the land on earth. Nobody knew what lay beyond it. Sailors called the Atlantic the "Green Sea of Darkness." Not understanding its currents and trade winds, many explorers made their way down the coast of Africa and never returned.

However, several factors pushed the Portuguese toward the exploration of Africa. Many nobles considered the fight for African territory as a continuation of the *Reconquista*, a holy crusade of Christians against Muslims. In the course of this long fight, Iberians developed a wider view of war that included seizing the money and trade that supported their enemy's war effort. Heroic battles over land caught the attention of the epic poets, but the *Reconquista* also involved sea battles for control of maritime commerce. Both sides recognized that soldiers needed courage to fight, but rulers also needed money to pay the soldiers. For this reason, the Spanish and the Portuguese kings wanted to take over profitable trade routes that linked Asia and Africa with Europe. For 700 years, Islamic merchants of Southwest Asia had controlled global trade networks. By the 1300s, the Iberians started to explore ways to establish their own commercial empires and a new world.

Simply speaking, the Portuguese explorers sought three things in Africa: gold, God, and glory. They had heard legends of a mythical Christian king on the continent, known as Prester John, and sought his alliance against their Muslim rivals. Prester John never existed, but there were indeed a few Christian kingdoms in East Africa. Ethiopia and Nubia (modern-day Sudan) contained kingdoms that had converted to Christianity around 200 CE. The Portuguese had also heard stories of African kingdoms rich with gold. Reports from merchants in Southwest Asia and North Africa told of a rich king, Mansa Musa, from Mali. In 1324 he had traveled to Mecca to make his pilgrimage to the Kaaba, the holiest site in the Islamic world. Word soon spread of the African king and his dozens of caravans full of gold. It was said that he gave away his gold so generously in Cairo, that he depressed its value in the region for over a decade. His caravans of Arabian camels reached his kingdom by trade routes over the Sahara. The Portuguese tried to reach him by sea.

Prince Henry the Navigator, the third son of King John I of Portugal, became a great patron of overseas exploration in the early fifteenth century. He brought together a wide variety of people: sailors, merchants, astronomers, and noblemen to work on the enterprise of expanding into Africa. In 1415 he urged his father, King John I, to take the African city of Ceuta. For the next seven decades, the Portuguese gradually made their way further and further down the coast until 1488, when Bartholomew Diaz rounded the bottom of Africa, the Cape of Good Hope. He then entered the Indian Ocean and opened Portugal to a new world.

The Portuguese arrive in Kongo

Although the Portuguese went into Africa looking for gold and Christian kings, they also found something that would prove much more profitable to them, the slave trade. In the middle of the fifteenth century, the Portuguese trolled the African coast kidnapping and enslaving at least one African person from each area to take them back to Lisbon where they were taught the Portuguese language. The enslaved African would serve as a translator on future excursions, and perhaps even eventually win his freedom. When the Portuguese explorer Diogo Cão landed his ships in the estuary of the Congo River for the first time in 1483, the Kongolese had never seen Europeans. During their 23-day journey inland, the Portuguese explorers explained to the local people that they were looking to trade, not to conquer. Nevertheless, they arranged with a local governor in a coastal province to take four men as hostages back to Portugal to train as translators.

In his account of the expedition, the explorer Rui de Pina related that the four men from Kongo seemed exceptional. In the course of their journey to Portugal, the hostages indicated that they belonged to the Kongo nobility. It was clear to the Portuguese that they came from a society with a sophisticated political and military organization. Diogo Cão decided to treat the men differently, and promised not to enslave them. According to Pina, "after they had learned the language, customs and intentions of the king of Portugal and his kingdom, they would return to their country and through them the affairs of each side would be easily made known to the other." The men returned two years later, as eye witnesses who told the Kongolese about the European world. The Portuguese had brought writing, firearms, as well as well-crafted luxury goods of silk and glass as gifts for the king of Kongo.

Several years later, in 1491, the Portuguese captain, Rui de Sousa, followed the Congo River inland to the capital of the kingdom, Mbanza Kongo. The king, whom the Kongolese called the Manikongo, had been expecting them. About one hundred thousand people came out to greet the Portuguese, including noblemen, archers, and spearmen. The Portuguese explorers also described "a countless number of women, all of whom took part in war." The Africans received the Portuguese with ivory trumpets, drums, and other instruments. King Nzinga was seated on a high platform on an ivory throne. Bare-chested, he wore a long skirt of black cloth which had been brought to Africa by Diogo Cão. He wore a brass bracelet on his left arm, and held a fly whisk. On his head he wore a finely embroidered cap of palm raffia. Upon meeting the Portuguese ambassador, Nzinga gathered some dirt from the ground in his hand and touched the chest of the ambassador and then his own with it. This gesture possibly signified that the king regarded the light skin of the Portuguese man as a sign that he had a connection to the territorial spirits of the other world. The friendly meeting was followed by celebrations that included singing, dancing, and feasting with wine made from palm fruit. Shortly afterward, a Portuguese priest performed the ritual of baptism, which initiated the king into the Christian religion. Nzinga took the name João I, after the king of Portugal. Many other members of the nobility also underwent baptism, including Nzinga's son, Mvemba a Nzingo, the future Afonso I. The Portuguese renamed Mbanza Kongo the city of the Holy Savior, São Salvador.

King João may have converted so quickly to the new religion, because similarities in the African and Portuguese worldview made Christianity appealing to him. Both religions believed that the world had been divided into two realms: the earthly and spiritual. Although the Christians imagined the spirit world in the sky (heaven), and the Africans underground, the central division of the world was compatible. More important, both maintained a belief in an all-powerful figure who had created both realms. Christians called this divine entity, God, the father. As already noted, the people of the Kongo had a similar figure called Nzambi a Mpungu. They also shared similar ideas about the afterlife. In the Catholic faith, the spirits of special people, called saints, communicated with God as advocates for the living. A variety of spirits, angels, and demons caused miracles and disasters in the earthly world. The Kongolese readily understood this view of the spirit world, in which believers could supplicate the souls of ancestors to gain access to the supreme power of Nzambi Mpungu.

The traditional religion of Kongo did not recognize a divinity who acted as a personal savior, and the figure of Jesus Christ did not have an African counterpart. The Bible presented the account of Jesus as something new, literally, "good news." Perhaps because the message of Jesus appears as a revelation from heaven, Africans, who believed that the spirit world communicated with earth through revelations, seemed to respond positively to the new religion. The overall message did not appear to threaten their traditional beliefs. Moreover, several reports of signs seemed to indicate the will of heaven. In one, two men had a dream about a beautiful lady who told them to follow the new faith. The Portuguese interpreted this figure as the Virgin Mary. In another, a black stone was found in the ground in the shape of a cross. This striking object would stand at the altar of the first church in Kongo.

Even before the arrival of Christians, the symbol of the cross played a central role in the in Kongo religion. It symbolized the division between the living and the dead, the earthly and spiritual realms. In the African tradition, the crosses formed by the intersections of streets, or crossroads, served as places where individuals might go to communicate with the spirit world. People went to the crossroads to make vows or to plead for help from the spirits in the other world. When the Portuguese brought crosses that held the figure of Jesus at the intersection, the Kongolese recognized the symbolic representation of a savior who transcended the living and the dead. Such similarities encouraged many in Kongo to incorporate the new religion into their own worldview.

The Portuguese brought with them new tools that Africans could use to express their religious faith. Especially impressive to the Kongolese were the musical instruments. The people of Kongo used music as a way to communicate with spirits in the other world. It held tremendous importance in this culture and served as a language of its own. They had flutes, horns, and drums, but before the arrival of the Portuguese, they had never seen the lute, a stringed instrument similar to the guitar. New instruments provided more varied opportunities to express artistry as well as spirituality. One Portuguese observer described how a musician played the lute in the sixteenth-century court of the Manikongo:

> By means of this instrument, they [the musicians] express their thoughts and make themselves understood so clearly that almost anything that can be said with words they can render with their fingers by touching this instrument. To these sounds they dance, clapping their hands to mark the rhythm of the music.[1]

The common people of Kongo took a great interest in the new religion, but João, the former King Nzinga, originally wanted to keep it restricted to the royal family and the elite members of the nobility. He saw the religion as a source of power and realized that an alliance with the Portuguese could bolster his own authority. Adopting Christianity brought him a powerful ally. He also wanted the expeditions to continue, as they brought luxury items which he could distribute to his subjects in order to gain their allegiance. The king kept his noble vassals loyal through patronage, and the gifts provided a new way to show his power as a patron. Moreover, Portuguese trade provided a new source of revenue. As the king had made money from taxing the trade of the six provinces of his domain, he could now tax the trade between his realm and the Portuguese.

Not everyone favored the new religion. Christianity threatened the authority of the powerful African priests who presided over the rituals of the spirits. They feared that bishops and priests brought in by the Portuguese would usurp their important political and social roles. Also, some members of the royal family began to distrust the new religion. King João's son, Mpanzu, a half-brother of Afonso, started to stir up opposition to Christianity by calling it a form of witchcraft. Mpanzu did not deny the magical powers of the new religion. Instead, he claimed that the magic was real, but evil. Labelling the Portuguese priests witches, he called for their execution. He rallied relatives and others to his cause and started a movement to return the kingdom to the traditional religion of Kongo.

Soon even King João himself began to question the new faith. The priests who brought Christianity insisted that the king have only one, legitimate wife. Traditionally, kings had one principal wife, but they also married the sisters of the noble kanda chiefs. The successor to the throne was chosen from among the sons of these women. This system provided a strong bond between the royalty and the nobility that monogamy threatened. The nobility, made up of members of the twelve most powerful kanda, grew increasingly distrustful of the new religion thinking that it would distance them from the seat of Royal power.

King João's relationship with the Portuguese began to sour. He had little to export beyond some ivory, raffia cloth, and low quality copper found in the center of his kingdom. Without goods to exchange, the rich merchandise from the Portuguese ships began to slow to a trickle. By 1504, João had fully renounced Christianity and returned to the traditional religion. When João died in 1506, Mpanzu succeeded him as king. As the son of one of the sisters from a powerful kanda chief, he was eligible for the throne according to the traditions of Kongo monarchy.

Mpanzu's rival for the throne was his half-brother Afonso. Bitter enemies, the brothers fought a war to determine the direction of Kongo history. Because his mother came from the northern province of Nsundi and did not belong to one of the twelve central kanda of the kingdom, Afonso was excluded from royal succession. For this reason, he needed the Portuguese to help win the crown. As the eldest son of João's first and principal wife, the Europeans considered him the legitimate successor to his father's throne.

The Portuguese also supported Afonso as a Christian. The conversion of the Kongo to Christianity would expand Christendom and bring great honor to the king of Portugal. Religion would serve as a tie binding the two countries together, and good relations would bring the Portuguese substantial economic benefits. While the Portuguese clearly wanted a ruler they could influence to serve their interests, Afonso, for his part, regarded an alliance with the foreign power as beneficial to his own objectives.

A new king

In his many letters to Manuel I of Portugal, Afonso recounted remarkable details about his path to royal power. One learns from his correspondence that Afonso's adoption of Christianity eventually complicated his relationship with his father. "During the life of my father," he recalled, "I suffered a thousand million threats and injuries." Once he and his cousin, Pedro, had converted to Christianity, João I considered the boys a threat. One day the king summoned Pedro to his council. Afonso suspected that his father had brought him there to execute him, and he was not wrong. When Afonso tried to stop the execution of cousin, his father cynically told his son, "Let us see if God will save him." Somehow Pedro managed to escape death that day, but the king sent the two cousins into exile, deprived of income and left to wander the provinces of the kingdom homeless. The king declared them outlaws, and put out an edict allowing anyone to kill them without punishment as enemies of the kingdom. Seeking shelter with his mother, maternal uncle, cousin, and a few Portuguese priests, Afonso moved to his mother's home province of Nsundi. The region, although far from the capital, had many copper mines that produced a higher quality product than the central province. With this wealth, his African supporters and Portuguese allies, Afonso set out toward the city of M'banza Kongo, sometime around 1506.

In one letter to Manuel I, Afonso recounted the epic battle he waged against his brother for the throne of Kongo. With a small force of 37 Christians, both Africans and Portuguese, he marched into battle against Mpanzu's much larger army. Hopelessly outnumbered, Afonso's men gave out a loud shout calling for St. James (Santiago) to help them. Suddenly a white cross appeared in the sky above a vision of St. James wielding an iron sword and leading a cavalry charge between the two armies. Mpanzu's warriors quickly took fright and ran away. When Afonso recounted the miraculous vision to Manuel, he proudly proclaimed, "With this miracle battle, let Kongo serve as an example to the world of the progress of our faith and our glory."

Throughout his reign, Afonso made the miraculous battle of Mbanza Kongo the foundation of his new Christian kingdom. An avid reader of both history and scripture, Afonso understood that this vision placed Kongo within a powerful tradition. In the fourth century, the Roman emperor Constantine had seen an image of a white cross that set the empire on a path toward Christianity. In the 1100s Portugal's first king, Afonso Henrique, defeated the Moors thanks to the appearance of a vision of St. James at the battle of Ourique. In his description of the battle of Mbanza Kongo, Afonso portrayed himself as a crusader for the Christian faith. He included details that had symbolic meaning to the Africans: the color white, the sign of the cross, and the warrior with an iron sword, to bolster the legitimacy of the new religion as well as his own claim to the throne. On 25 July, the feast day of St James, subjects came to the capital to enjoy festivals, pay taxes, and perform military exercises. For centuries, soldiers reenacted the miraculous battle of Mbanza Kongo as a war dance or *sangamento*.

Once in power, Afonso I worked to put Christianity on a stronger footing in his kingdom. Although one report claims that Afonso executed his half-brother after his defeat, another claims that he spared his brother's life and allowed Mpanzu to serve in a lowly church office. Either way, the new king had destroyed his opposition. Shortly after the battle he addressed to his lords a speech in the central square of the city explaining the new religion. "My brothers," he said, "you know that the faith we have up to now believed in is nothing but an illusion and wind, because the true faith is that of our Lord God, creator of heaven and earth." He then explained the theology of the religion beginning with the creation of Adam and Eve in the Garden of Eden to the crucifixion of Jesus in Jerusalem. He explained the principle of salvation and the forgiving of sin. He concluded his inaugural address by foreshadowing his intention to destroy his subjects' faith in their old idols: "As for the stones and pieces of wood that you worship, [know that] our Lord has given us stones to build houses, and wood to burn." The last line was a thinly-veiled reference to the fire he would set to destroy the house of idols. Shortly after, his bewildered subjects watched as the sacred objects they had worshiped for centuries burst into flames.

In the capital of São Salvador he replaced the sacred spaces of the old religion with Christian buildings. He built a church on the holiest site in the kingdom, the graveyard of kings. People had believed that the whirlwinds circulating in the middle of these woods were the souls of kings and princes. Some had said that simply looking upon the site would bring immediate death. By building his church here, he was connecting the new religion to the sacred power of the traditional religion. Linking Christianity to the ancestor spirits of past kings served to enhance his royal authority.

The Portuguese emissaries at Afonso's court expressed admiration for the young king's devotion to his religious study. In 1516, the Portuguese vicar-general, Rui d'Aguiar, wrote to the king of Portugal:

> May Your Highness be informed that his Christian life is such that he appears to me not as a man but as an angel sent by the Lord to this kingdom to convert it, especially when he speaks and when he preaches. For I assure Your Highness that it is he who instructs us. Better than we, he knows the prophets and the Gospel of Our Lord Jesus Christ and all the lives of the saints and all things regarding our Mother the Holy Church . . . I must say, Lord, that he does nothing but study and that many times he falls asleep over his books; he forgets when it is time to dine, when he is speaking of the things of God.[2]

Afonso asked the king of Portugal to send teachers and priests to establish schools in the capital. He also sent his son, grandson, nephews and several other young Kongolese noblemen to Portugal to study both Portuguese and Latin. He believed that they might serve as more effective teachers than foreigners. When reports came back to the king that these youths spent too little time on their studies, Afonso was furious. In response, he sent a letter to Manuel I, asking that the students be separated from each other and dispersed throughout Portugal. However, before long the students began to take their studies more seriously. The monastery that hosted the scholars became a center for African studies in

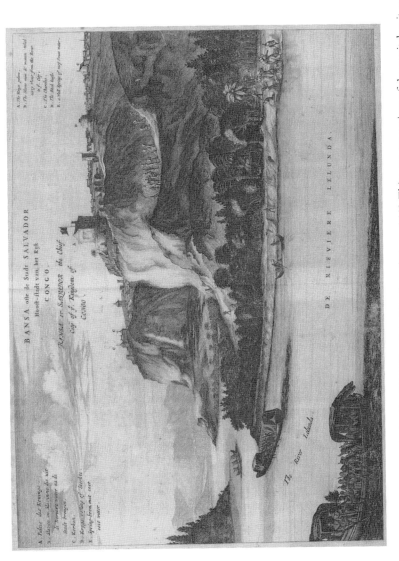

FIGURE 3.2 Olfert Dapper, *Bansa or Salvador, the Chief City of the Kingdom of Kongo*, 1668. This presents a view of the capital as it appeared in the seventeenth century.

Bansa ofte de Stadt Salvador Hoost- Stadt van het Rijk Congo from *Umbstandliche und eigentliche Beschreibung von Africa* 1670. Manuscripts, Archives and Rare Books Division, Schomburg Center for Research in Black Culture, The New York Public Library, Astor, Lenox and Tilden Foundations.

Source: New York Public Library

Portugal. In 1513–1514, his son, Henrique, led a delegation to Rome, the seat of the Catholic Church. One of the gifts presented to Pope Leo X was a live elephant, which caused a sensation in Rome and became a beloved pet. The pope welcomed the envoys graciously, and in 1518 he ordained Henrique a bishop, the first from Sub-Saharan Africa. At the same time, Afonso I pledged an oath of allegiance as a Christian prince to the pope establishing a direct line between his kingdom and the head of the Catholic Church. In political terms, this arrangement would later prove very beneficial to Kongo.

In addition to Christianity, Afonso appreciated and tried to implement other aspects of Portuguese culture, such as the legal system. For this reason, he requested a copy of the Portuguese code of law, the *Ordenações Manuelinas*. After reading all five volumes of the code, he decided that the laws of Portugal were too complicated for the needs of his own kingdom. Astonished by the number of petty crimes listed in the code, he jokingly asked a Portuguese envoy, "What is the punishment in Portugal for someone who puts his feet on the ground?" Afonso clearly understood what aspects of Portuguese culture to take and what to leave.

Kongo and the slave trade

Unlike his father, who had little to trade with the Portuguese, Afonso made the best use of Kongo's natural resources. He sent his loyal cousin Pedro to be governor of the province of Nsundi to secure and better develop the copper trade. The control of this high-quality copper provided a valuable export and enabled the king to trade for shipments of Portuguese goods. Increasingly, however, the Portuguese began to lose interest in copper and sought a far more valuable commodity: slaves. Eventually the slave trade threatened Afonso's hard-won royal authority.

Before the arrival of the Europeans, Kongo was economically self-sufficient. It had enough food, clothing, and shelter to sustain the life of its people. The Portuguese trade mainly provided luxuries, that is, expensive goods intended to show social distinction. In a hierarchical society like Kongo in the sixteenth century, these were essential for elites to maintain their position at the top of society.

The kings of Kongo were similar to many other rulers throughout the world who based their authority on a system of patronage. In this system, the king gave gifts to his governors, who passed on some of these goods to those who supported them in the provinces. The prestigious items enabled the elite to distinguish themselves from the common people. However, as the nobility grew accustomed to foreign luxuries like silk and glass, they began to demand more. Some began to trade directly with the Portuguese instead of relying on Afonso's patronage. The hierarchy only worked when there was one source of prestige. When Portuguese merchants began to exchange luxury items directly for commodities from Kongo, it greatly undermined the king's power over his subjects. To make matters worse for the king, the commodities most sought after by the Portuguese traders were increasingly human beings in bondage.

Almost all of the social systems around the world in the sixteenth century included some form of slavery. Because Africa was abundant in land, but limited in population, Africans valued labor more highly than property. The complicated social system of Kongo recognized eight distinct forms of compelled labor. These included war captives and criminals well as concubines paid as tribute to more powerful leaders. Owning slaves brought prestige and status to a family. When bought, owners considered their slaves as junior members of the household, often giving them the names of children. Africans used slaves to work the land on small family farms or serve as domestic servants. A few slaves with education and ability became government officials.

After the Arab conquest of North Africa in the 700s, the slave trade expanded to Sub-Saharan regions. Camel caravans crossed the Sahara desert to take West Africans to markets throughout the Middle East and around the Mediterranean Sea. By the 1300s there were enormous slave markets in the Ottoman Empire, which included captives from both Africa and Eastern Europe. As discussed in Chapter 2, so many slaves came from the Slavic lands of Poland, Russia, and the Ukraine, that the term *slav* became the origin of the word *slave*. Although the Arab slave trade never reached the equatorial region of the Kongo, it did provide inspiration for the early European efforts in the trade.

Europeans began to import slaves from far-off regions in the 1300s. Slavery had been widespread in the ancient Roman Empire, but had died out in the early Middle Ages, when labor was extremely cheap and land was the major source of wealth and status. By the Renaissance in the fifteenth century, cities in Spain and Italy that traded with the Middle East began to import slaves from other lands. Like the Ottomans, they bought both Europeans from Eastern Europe and Africans to serve as domestic servants in their opulent palaces. At that time, there were no more than a few thousand slaves in all of Europe. As in Africa, their main purpose was to show the wealth and status of the owner.

In the early sixteenth century, skin color did not signify slave status. Indeed, the concept of race hardly existed in the sixteenth century. Certainly people noticed a difference in skin color between Europeans and Sub-Saharan Africans, but this did not necessarily indicate a particular social status. Almost everywhere in the sixteenth century, societies divided people into two groups: nobility and the commons. The word *race*, which meant "stock" or "breed" in French, meant ties of blood or family. For example, there was a "race" of kings, as well as members of the noble "race." Both João II and Manuel I of Portugal recognized the noble status of certain Africans. The Portuguese language provided a way for Afonso to describe his own elite in terms recognizable to any European at the time. For example, when he recounted the miraculous battle for São Salvador, he described his men as "thirty-six captains who were of the purest and most noble blood." Elites from both societies imagined such distinctions as part of the natural order. Intermarriage among nobles of various skin tones was socially accepted. For example, in the middle of the sixteenth century, a nobleman from Kongo married into the royal house of Portugal.

As the Portuguese expanded their trade in Africa, the nature of the slave trade changed dramatically. In the 1480s they established a factory, or fort, on a nearby island, São Tome Principe. This became a center for the slave trade in central west Africa. At first, most slaves from Kongo stayed on the island to work on local sugar plantations. Eventually, however, slaves were held for a time in the factories of São

Tome and then packed tightly on to ships bound for Portugal and southern Spain. By the 1520s the trade expanded even further when the Portuguese established large sugar plantations in Brazil. The demand for African slaves to work Brazilian sugar plantations exploded, and the increased demand for slaves intensified the greed of the Portuguese. Some ruthless traders even reverted to illegal kidnapping rather than buying war captives legally from legitimate markets. Afonso expressed outrage at this behavior.

In 1526, Afonso sent an angry letter to the king of Portugal. "Thieves and men without conscience," he complained, seized "sons of our nobility and vassals" to sell as slaves to the Portuguese merchants. He explained that elites in Kongo had become too accustomed to the new luxuries from abroad and resorted to selling slaves on the black market to buy them. This illegal trading undermined his power of patronage. He complained, "Formerly I would have given them [the elites] these things in order to satisfy them and keep them under my suzerainty and jurisdiction" but now, since he could no longer distribute European goods, he faced rebellion. Exasperated, he informed the Portuguese that he would accept teachers and priests but no more traders and merchants, "for it is our will that in our kingdom there should no longer be a trade or export of slaves."

However, Afonso's disgust at the greed of the Portuguese traders did not extend to the institution of slavery in general. He disapproved of his subjects, especially nobles, being sold as slaves, but did not consider it wrong to sell war captives or Africans from regions outside of Kongo. He was also unwilling to support a slave trade that did not boost his own authority within his kingdom.

Facing the challenges of the Portuguese slave traders head on, Afonso found a way to stay in control of the slave economy in Kongo. He instructed his cousin Pedro, stationed in the northern provinces, to negotiate with a border region known as Tio. In the early part of the 1520s, Kongo fought numerous battles against the Tio and sold the war captives to the Portuguese as slaves. However, by the 1530s the Tio themselves started to purchase slaves captured from further into the interior of Africa. These slaves were cheaper than those of Kongo, so the Portuguese had an incentive to buy them, leaving the subjects of Afonso free from the fear of capture. Moreover, Pedro and Afonso arranged a way to direct the trade route from Tio through Kongo, so that the king could collect taxes on it. The kingdom of Kongo also made money by selling the Portuguese the cowrie shells that came from one of Kongo's coastal provinces. The Tio demanded these shells as currency for buying slaves.

By 1540, Afonso had adopted a new position on slavery. In a letter to the king of Portugal, he boasted:

> Put all the Guinea countries on one side and only Kongo on the other and you will find that Kongo renders more than all the others put together . . . no king in all these parts esteems Portuguese goods so much or treats the Portuguese so well as we do. We favour their trade, sustain it, open markets and roads . . . where the pieces [slaves] are traded[3].

The revenue from the trade allowed to Afonso to increase his territory, both by war and by patronage. The money funded his soldiers, which enabled him to engage in the conquest of nearby lands. Slavery, not copper and ivory, allowed Afonso to continue to give gifts to his officials and secure their loyalty.

There was one element of the Portuguese trade that lay beyond Afonso's control: guns. Kongo did not produce its own firearms, and so it had to rely on the foreigners for these powerful weapons. In an early letter to the king of Portugal, Afonso specifically asked for cannons and guns to "help us burn the great house of the idols." He continued, "Without the support of the Christians the pagans could return and kill us." Guns created a complicated situation for both sides. The Portuguese traders threatened to arm Afonso's rivals if he did not agree to their terms, and this would have been the end of his kingdom. Afonso, from his side, understood that in the long run, the Portuguese had more to gain from maintaining friendship with a powerful state. For one thing, trade works best when there is social stability in the region. Local rulers were in the best position to provide this stable situation. Moreover, Afonso recognized that the Portuguese ruler wanted to support Christianity in Africa. If Afonso's kingdom fell to non-Christian rivals, it would have been a stain on the king's honor as a defender of the faith. Both rulers considered the partnership mutually advantageous.

The European merchants and traders operating in Africa, however, seemed to think only of their short-term gain. They pressed for more exploitation of local peoples. When the traders demanded more and more merchandise from him, Afonso complained to the king, "As for us, your highness, we would have rather sent everything we have in this kingdom than lose faith in our Lord." In the same year, 1540, he recounted in a letter to the king that some Portuguese traders had tried to assassinate him in church during Mass. He said that they wanted to replace him with a king more agreeable to their financial interests. The attempt failed. Despite his disgust with the greed of individual Portuguese traders, Afonso never lost his faith in the religion brought from Portugal, nor did he doubt his relationship with Manuel I. The rulers spoke frankly with each other as equals, "king to king," and historians have described their close relationship as a "royal brotherhood."

In the sixteenth century, the Atlantic slave trade had barely begun. Of the estimated eleven million people who made the passage from Africa to the New World as slaves, only three percent came across the Atlantic before 1600. Nevertheless, the slave trade continued in Kongo for 400 years. Most of the enslaved who survived the brutal middle passage settled on sugar plantations in Brazil, but others reached the Caribbean islands, the American South, and even New England. It is unclear whether Afonso comprehended the enormous toll of the slave trade. Possibly he assumed that the enslaved would be treated as junior members of families, as they had in Kongo. Certainly he could not have foreseen the brutal dehumanization that characterized the practice from the seventeenth to the nineteenth century.

Afonso's accomplishments as a statesman impressed his contemporaries. Faced with a foreign incursion into his land, he responded with openness. His remarkable appetite for learning enabled him to solve complex political problems. He understood the power of symbols in rallying the people to his side. Economically and politically, he used the relatively scarce resources of his kingdom to his advantage. Even in terms of foreign affairs, Afonso showed his capacity to engage in sophisticated diplomacy. His adherence to the papacy gave his kingdom political leverage against Portugal. Moreover, he undoubtedly understood that the Catholic Church as an institution had as much to gain from Kongo as the reverse. By the second decade of the sixteenth century, the papacy was under attack. The invasion of Spain and the Protestant Reformation caused a great deal of damage to the prestige and influence of Catholicism in Europe. Expansion into new areas such as Africa and the Americas strengthened the institution at that difficult time, and the future of the Catholic Church lay in the wider world.

Afonso's legacy

According to a legend which circulated in the eighteenth century, Afonso had buried his mother alive for keeping a small idol around her neck. Although no supporting historical evidence supports this story, oral traditions such as this were rooted in symbolic meanings understood by the people of the kingdom. From one side, it presented Afonso as an individual who was willing and able to go beyond, and indeed break, accepted social norms. These were skills required of Kongo's kings. At the same time, the story highlights his dedication to the Christian faith, so much so that he would judge and condemn his own mother for violating its rules. Both elements of the tradition reinforce the long-standing belief that Afonso's ultimate source of power, worldly and otherworldly, derived from his embrace of Christianity and his ability to spread it among his people.

Afonso made every effort to convert his subjects to the new faith, and within six years after his death, there were churches in every province in the land. Several hundred children were learning how to read and write in order to follow Christian teachings. Afonso had also invested in the education of women. His sister became a teacher at one of the schools he opened for girls. He himself remained devout, but had created a form of Christianity that was highly syncretic, accommodating Christianity to his own culture. Despite the disapproval of the priests from Portugal, he refused to remain monogamous and kept several wives. The king's polygamy was essential to the traditional political system in Kongo, which demanded that he marry women from the twelve central kanda. A new king would be chosen from among their sons. The Portuguese did not press the marriage issue with Afonso. They were willing to overlook this sin in order to keep a strong ally in the region. The historical record contains no reference to his wives, but sources indicate that he had over three hundred grandchildren and great grandchildren. Such a large amount of children would of course require numerous wives.

Afonso died an old man after nearly forty years of rule. His grandson, from his daughter Nzimba, succeeded him. The kingdom remained strong and unified for almost one hundred years beyond his death in 1542 or 1543. However, by the end of the seventeenth century, civil wars carried out between the provinces of the kingdom ripped apart the country. These wars were made worse by the increasing demand for slaves in the sugar plantations of Brazil. Rival factions started wars simply to create instability in order to gain more slaves rather than for the purposes of gaining true political power. Nevertheless, Kongo retained its independence until the nineteenth century.

Despite the civil wars, the people of Kongo still remembered the time of the good king Afonso. In the early eighteenth century there was a woman named Doña Beatriz who emerged as mysterious and powerful figure in Kongo. She claimed that she had died and her body was possessed by the spirit of St. Anthony. Claiming to speak with his voice, she pleaded with the rival factions to end the destructive wars, and hearkened back to the time of Afonso as a golden age of the Christian kingdom. Although she was eventually burned at the stake as a witch by Jesuit priests, her story shows that Afonso remained a symbol for his country of unity, Christianity, and pride for centuries.

The memory of the powerful kingdom of Kongo survived even in the New World. In the Stono Rebellion of 1739, Kongolese slaves in South Carolina rose up on a feast day of the Virgin Mary, stirred into action by the sound of their drums. It was the largest slave revolt in colonial America. Fifty years later, during the Haitian Revolution in 1793, a leader of a slave rebellion named Macaya refused to support the French, who had recently overthrown their monarchy in the revolution. He wrote: "I am the subject of three kings: the King of Kongo, master of all the blacks; the King of France who represents my father; the King of Spain who represents my mother. These three Kings are the descendants of those who, led by a star, came to adore God made Man." Centuries later, and ten thousand miles away, Afonso's dual legacy of powerful royalty and Christian spirituality lived on in the African imagination.

Chronology

c. 1456 Birth of Mvemba a Nzingo, the future Afonso I.

1483 Diogo Cão lands in the Kongo region.

1491 Rui de Sousa lands in Mbanza Kongo. King Nzinga converts to Catholicism and changes his name to João I. Mvemba a Nzingo baptized as Afonso. City of Mbanza Kongo renamed São Salvador.

c. 1506 Battle of Mbanza Kongo. Afonso I becomes king of Kongo.

1518 Pope Leo X appoints Henrique, son of Afonso I, as bishop. He becomes the first bishop from Sub-Saharan Africa.

1526 Afonso I writes a letter to João II of Portugal complaining about the abuses of Portuguese slave traders.

c.1543 Death of Afonso I.

Sources for further reading about Afonso I

Sources about Afonso in English are unfortunately rare. There is no English biography of Afonso I, but the most in-depth discussion of his reign is in Anne Hilton, *The Kingdom of Kongo* (Oxford: Oxford University Press, 1985). An earlier book focusing on the social history of Kongo is George Balandier, *Daily Life in the Kingdom of Kongo from the Sixteenth Century to the Eighteenth Century*, trans. Helen Weaver (New York: Pantheon Books, 1968). John Thornton provides a wealth of information on early Kongo and its political history in a variety of books. His *Africa and Africans in the Making of the Atlantic World, 1400–1800* (Cambridge: Cambridge University Press, 1998) provides a good overview of the political, economic, and religious aspects of West African kingdom before the age of imperialism. His *The Kingdom of Kongo: Civil War and Transition, 1641–1718* (Madison, WI: University of Wisconsin Press, 1983) covers the seventeenth century. His *The Kongolese Saint Anthony: Dona Beatriz Kimpa Vita and the Antonian Movement, 1684–1706* (Cambridge: Cambridge University Press, 1998, 2009) provides a great introduction to religion and culture in the kingdom. A more recent article by the same author, "Afro-Christian Syncretism in the Kingdom of Kongo," *Journal of African History* 54 (2013), pp. 53–77, is more specifically focused on the role of Afonso in converting his state to Christianity. General information about African religious traditions can be found in Molefi Kete Asante and Ama Mazama, eds. *The Encyclopedia of African Religion* (Los Angeles, CA: Sage, 2009). Two interesting books focus on the culture of Christian monarchy in Kongo from the standpoint of art history: Alisa LaGamma, *Kongo: Power and Majesty* (New York: Metropolitan Museum of Art, 2015) and Cecile Fromont, *The Art of Conversation: Christian Visual Culture in the Kingdom of Kongo* (Chapel Hill, NC: University of North Carolina Press, 2014). On the Bantu migration into west-central Africa, see Kairn A. Klieman, *"The Pygmies Were Our Compass": Bantu and Batwa in the History of West Central Africa, Early Times to c. 1900* (Portsmouth, NH: Heinemann, 2003). The relationship between Africa and Europe from an African standpoint is covered in David Northrup, *Africa's Discovery of Europe 1450–1850* (New York: Oxford University Press, 2009). An overall text on Africa is Christopher Ehret, *The Civilizations of Africa: A History to 1800* (Charlottesville, VA: University of Virginia Press, 2002). Good sources for information on the Portuguese slave trade are P. E. Russell, *Portugal, Spain and the African Atlantic, 1343–1490: Chivalry and Crusade from John of Gaunt to Henry the Navigator* (Brookfied, VT: Variorum, 1995) and A. R. Disney, *A History of Portugal and the Portuguese Empire* (Cambridge: Cambridge University Press, 2007). See also John Thornton, "Early Kongo–Portuguese Relations: A New Interpretation," *History in Africa* 8 (1981), pp. 183–204. For the slave trade specifically, see Hugh Thomas, *The Slave Trade: The Story of the Atlantic Slave Trade, 1440–1870* (New York: Simon & Schuster, 1997).

Elizabeth I of England (1533–1603)

With her flaming red hair, pearl-studded dresses, and white lace ruff collars, queen Elizabeth I of England is one of the most recognizable figures in the English-speaking world. During her 44-year reign, England became a Protestant kingdom, strong and united within its borders, and on its way to establishing itself as a world empire.

A turbulent childhood

The strange circumstances of Elizabeth I's childhood provide an interesting contrast to her future glory. Her birth was a disappointment to her father, Henry VIII of England, who had wanted a son. Indeed, he had divorced his first wife, Catherine of Aragon, because she had not produced a son and heir—only a daughter, Mary. When Pope Clement VII (profiled in Chapter 4 of this book) refused to grant an annulment of his marriage, King Henry broke away from the Catholic Church, taking the entire kingdom with him. Having fallen in love, he married Anne Boleyn, a lady of the court, hoping she would give birth to a son. She did not. Her only living child was Elizabeth, born in 1533.

FIGURE 3.3   Unknown, *The Armada Portrait* (c. 1590). One of the most famous images in British history, this portrait of Elizabeth is rich with symbolism. The pearls and bows on her dress represent virginity, while her hand rests on a globe indicating imperial claims in the New World.

Source: Woburn Abbey, Bedfordshire/Bridgeman Images

Three years later, Henry VIII looked for a way to end his marriage to Elizabeth's mother, accusing her of committing adultery with five other men, one of whom was her brother. A court found her guilty of treason (a queen's adultery is treason against the king), for which she lost her head. The day after the execution, Henry married Jane Seymour. Although she gave Henry a son (Edward), soon after she died due to complications of childbirth. Henry's fourth wife was Anne of Cleves, but their marriage was annulled after only six months. Catherine Howard became number five. She, like Anne Boleyn, was tried for adultery and beheaded. Finally, Henry's sixth and last wife, Catherine Parr, survived her husband and served as an affectionate stepmother to the three children, Mary, Elizabeth, and Edward. A popular rhyme provides an easy way to remember the fate of Henry VIII's six wives: "Divorced, beheaded, died, divorced, beheaded, survived."

Elizabeth I inherited her father's bright auburn hair, fair skin, and bold self-confidence. She, like Henry, could be stubborn and headstrong. Throughout her life, Henry served as a role model for her in terms of strength and vitality. She had no living memory of her mother, Anne Boleyn, but she had inherited her striking brown-black eyes. By all accounts, Elizabeth was a sprightly and precocious child. She took as her personal motto the Latin phrase, *semper eadem* (always the same).

The young princess had the good fortune to be born at a time when powerful people considered women capable of learning and ruling. Educating girls was fashionable during the Renaissance era, when Europeans rediscovered the culture of ancient Greece and Rome. Anne Boleyn had greatly admired the Greek philosopher Plato (c. 428 BCE–c. 348 BCE), who believed that women had the same talents as men and should be trained for leadership. For this reason, Anne insisted that her little girl study French, Italian, and Spanish, Latin, Greek, and Hebrew. Elizabeth loved learning new languages and frequently gave her translated works as gifts to her family members. At the age of 11, she translated Marguerite de Navarre's *Mirror for a Sinful Soul*, a French book of evangelical Christian meditations written by the grandmother of Henry IV (profiled in Chapter 1). The same year she translated her stepmother's prayer book into Latin, French, and Italian and presented it as a gift to her father. The 12-year-old boldly wrote in her dedication to Henry VIII, "May I, by this means, be indebted to you not as an imitator of your virtues, but indeed as an inheritor of them." As a young teenager, she prided herself on her intelligence rather than appearance. When she sent a portrait of herself to her brother, King Edward VI, she told him, "For the face, I grant, I might well blush to offer, but the mind I shall never be ashamed to present."

King Edward had always been sickly. He died at the age of 14, leaving the eldest sister Mary as the new queen of England. Mary Tudor (1516–1558) also suffered a difficult childhood. After the divorce of her mother, Catherine of Aragon, Mary (unlike Henry, Elizabeth, and Edward) maintained a strong Catholic faith. The English Parliament, a powerful assembly of representatives who enacted laws in the kingdom, did not consider a Catholic eligible to inherit the throne. Henry agreed, and even discussed executing his own daughter. After Henry's death, however, Parliament passed a law that allowed Mary to reign as queen.

Mary faced a great deal of opposition as the first queen to rule England. It often happened that a queen consort (the wife of a king), or a queen regent (the mother of a king who was too young to rule), had ruled in the name of a male relative, but no woman had headed the government in her own name. Protestants, who made up a majority of the population, resented Mary as a Catholic. Nevertheless, Mary came to the throne in 1553. Although only in her late 30s, she looked prematurely aged; years of worrying showed in the wrinkles and the constant frown she wore on her face. As queen, she wanted most of all to return England to the Catholic faith. She married Philip II of Spain, the son of Charles V, who aimed to spread Catholicism around the globe. In her effort to rid England of what she considered heresy, she sentenced hundreds of Protestants to burn at the stake. This hard line against religious dissent earned her the nickname "Bloody Mary."

During her reign, some Protestants worked secretly to overthrow her government and put her Protestant sister, Elizabeth, on the throne. Fearing this conspiracy, Mary locked Elizabeth in the Tower of London and then held her under house arrest at a number of country estates for several years. When Mary died in 1558, a tradition claims that royal officials found Elizabeth standing outside beside an old oak tree when they gave her the royal ring and saluted her as queen of England. She knelt down and recited Psalm 118, "*A domino factum est mirabile in oculis nostris*" (The Lord has done this and it is marvelous in our eyes). The image of the young woman held symbolic meaning for the oak tree served as a metaphor for the strength and resilience of the British people. The phrase, "heart of oak" refers to a person of exceptional courage and valor.

What was England?

Elizabeth took the throne with the title "Elizabeth by the grace of God Queen of England, France and Ireland." How exactly could she claim these lands as her kingdom? A complicated history led to these titles.

England is the largest kingdom on the island of Great Britain, which lies to the northwest of continental Europe. The island also includes Wales and Scotland. The large island of Ireland lies directly to the west. Thousands of islands surround the two larger islands, whose craggy coastline has provided safe harbors for its seafaring inhabitants for thousands of years. Today, England is part of a nation whose official name is the United Kingdom of Great Britain and Northern Ireland.

The islands have suffered waves of invasions by various peoples for thousands of years. In the early Stone Age, Celts built a mysterious circular rock formation known as Stonehenge. The Romans invaded the island of Great Britain in 43 CE, conquering the local tribes in all but the northern region of Scotland. Under Emperor Hadrian, the Romans built a wall to keep the "barbaric" tribes of the north out of their province, the ruins of which remain today.

When the Roman Empire fell in the fifth century CE, the islands suffered another wave of invasions from German lands, including tribes of Angles and Saxons. King Arthur was believed to be a mythical king of the Saxons, but he was undoubtedly more like a tribal chieftain than a real king. These tribes adopted the religion of Christianity around 600 CE. Two hundred years later, a new wave of invaders came, including the Vikings, Danes, and Jutes. Around 890, one leader, Alfred the Great, had taken over many of the other tribes and established himself as a king. His son, Edward, was the first to claim the title of King of England.

A hundred and fifty years later, the island suffered yet another invasion, when a wave of Normans came over the English Channel from Northern France. Their leader, William (the Conqueror) defeated King Harold at the battle of Hastings in 1066. The English king died as a result of an arrow shot through his eyeball. William took the crown of England, divided up the royal domains, and distributed them among his French-speaking warriors. The descendants of these feudal warlords became members of the English nobility, who spoke French for centuries. Because of the Norman invasion, French words make up about half of today's English vocabulary.

Following the Norman Conquest, England remained a feudal society where noble warlords rewarded their loyal vassals with land to rule as their own. William of Normandy kept two-thirds of the land for himself and his royal descendants. By doing this, he insured that English kings would always control more land than the other warlords. England developed a powerful and centralized monarchy after the Norman invasion.

Living on an island helped to give the English a sense of common identity, separate from the European continent. Nevertheless, English kings often claimed to inherit lands in France. The English army fought the Hundred Years' War (1337–1453) to keep half of France under the English crown. Despite some heroic battles, the French armies managed to push the English out, thanks largely to the inspiring leadership of a 15-year-old girl, Joan of Arc. Dressed as a soldier, the young woman claimed divine inspiration to free France from English domination. Unfortunately, she was burned at the stake as a witch in 1412. By the end of the war, all that remained of the English dominion in France was the town of Calais, which fell to the French in 1558. Nevertheless, English kings and queens continued to call themselves rulers of France until 1803.

English monarchs waged endless wars for centuries in order to dominate Scotland and Ireland, but in Elizabeth's time, English kings ruled only England and Wales. Scotland only became part of the United Kingdom in 1707, and the southern half of Ireland remains an independent nation today.

Elizabeth Regina

Even under Mary's rule, the common people of England adored the young, energetic princess Elizabeth. Kept in captivity, she could only been seen when moving from one residence to another. Whenever she appeared in public, crowds would come out to see "young Bess." In her early twenties, she would smile and wave, while churches rang their bells and townspeople offered her flowers and cakes they had baked themselves. She understood from these remarkable displays of public affection that her real strength would ultimately come from the common people rather than from the nobility, the Church, the Parliament, or marriage to a foreign prince.

Her coronation on 15 January 1559, was a magnificent pageant. The procession from the Tower of London to Westminster Abbey included a thousand horsemen. The streets were lined with fences draped with tapestries, velvets, and silks. Elizabeth wore a royal robe of golden cloth, and her litter was escorted by gentlemen in bright red velvet. Their vests were studded with silver gilt and embroidered with the red and white rose that symbolized Tudor family and the two letters "E" and "R" for Elizabeth Regina: Queen Elizabeth. Despite the snow, thousands of Londoners had waited several hours to catch a glimpse of the princess, to speak to her or offer her little bouquets of flowers or rosemary. Overcome with emotion, one old man cried when he saw her; his tears, he said, flowed from gladness. After the ceremony in Westminster Abbey, she was presented to the people with a fanfare of organs, trumpets, bells, and drums. She had captured the hearts of the people with her charm and majesty. Some wondered, however, whether or not she would be able to rule effectively.

Not everyone accepted the idea of a queen as the head of the government. During the reign of Mary, a Protestant minister, John Knox, wrote an influential book about the evils of female rule, *The First Blast of the Trumpet against the Monstrous Regiment of Women*. In it he claimed that women were weak, unstable, greedy, and foolish. "That a woman should reign and bear empire above man," he wrote, was a "monster in nature" and an inversion of God's order. He had written this when Mary, the Catholic, ruled as queen over England. Now that the woman ruler in question was Protestant, he changed his mind. He, like many Protestants, now argued that God had sometimes raised women into positions of power. For example, Deborah was a prophet and judge in the Old Testament who delivered her people from their enemies. Elizabeth and her supporters promoted her rule as an exception that did not threaten true religion and the "natural" order; instead, she protected them. Believing her to be an instrument of God's will, one contemporary wrote, "God sent us our Elizabeth."

Religion was a thorny problem for any ruler in the age of the Reformation. The Protestant queen had Catholic enemies who resented her as a heretic. Powerful forces stood against her, potentially the armies of Catholic France and Spain. At the other extreme were the Puritans, Protestants who wanted the Church of England "purified" of all rituals and images of Jesus. The most ardent of those on both sides saw the world as a battlefield between the forces of God and Satan. Such a view had soaked the soil of France with blood for years.

Elizabeth plotted a moderate path and made compromises on the question of religion. A firm Protestant, she believed that one's faith in Jesus led to salvation and eternal life in heaven. In her view, devout Christians strengthened their faith through careful reading of the Bible rather than performing the rituals of the Catholic Church such as confession and the Mass. She considered the pope in Rome a foreign prince with no say in the religion of England. As a Protestant, she did not offer prayers to the Virgin Mary. When Elizabeth found a small statue of the Virgin at a country house in 1578, she ordered it to be burned as an idol.

On the other hand, Elizabeth wanted to keep many ceremonial aspects of the Catholic ritual. The priests of the Church of England wore the clothes of Catholic priests, burned incense, and offered communion. These rituals, she believed, maintained the majesty of God. As she said, "Almighty God is at all times to be honored with all manner of reverence that may be devised." She believed that respect for religion encouraged a culture of obedience that supported the monarchy. Maintaining familiar rituals also served to comfort the people as they transitioned from one religion to another. Under Elizabeth's rule, England managed to avoid the scourge of religious warfare. Forty years after her death, however, Puritans who wanted to eliminate Catholic structure and rituals in the church would incite a civil war, overthrowing the monarchy and causing King Charles I to lose his head.

The marriage question

Nearly everyone expected Elizabeth to marry, but the young queen had little interest in finding a husband. Even in her youth, she claimed that she wanted her tombstone to read, "A virgin pure until death." When her sister Mary and her husband, Philip II of Spain, urged her to marry the Catholic Duke of Savoy, she threatened to commit suicide. When she acceded to the throne, she promised to consider marriage, but only for the benefit of her subjects. As an unmarried queen in Europe, foreign princes from Spain, France, Germany, and Sweden tried to woo her into marriage. She kept them in suspense with hopes and expectations, but never committed. She knew her subjects did not want to be ruled by a foreign king. They had bitter memories of Mary and Philip II. While marriage to an Englishman solved that problem, there were too many noble suitors competing for so great an honor. She could not choose one without causing spite and resentment among the others.

Elizabeth remained unmarried throughout her life, but was the "virgin queen" really a virgin? Historians have been asking this question for 500 years. Although most scholars agree she lived up to her reputation, she did indulge in scandalous behavior at times. She showed strong romantic feelings for men, particularly those who were attractive, energetic, and daring.

As a 15-year-old, Elizabeth seemed to have been infatuated with a man named Thomas Seymour, the brother of Jane Seymour, third wife of Henry VIII and uncle of the King Edward VI. The extremely ambitious and charming 38-year-old flirted with the teenage princess. In the end, however, he married Catherine Parr, Elizabeth's stepmother. When Elizabeth and Thomas lived in the same house, he used to enter her bedchamber, which was highly unusual at the time. There they "played games" which included tickles and slaps on her bottom. At one time, Elizabeth, Thomas, and Catherine played a strange game in the garden of the manor.

Catherine held the young princess while Thomas cut Elizabeth's gown into a hundred pieces with a pair of scissors. Eventually, Catherine began to suspect that such foolishness posed a threat to her marriage, and she sent Elizabeth away from the household. When Catherine died after giving birth to a daughter, the newly widowed Thomas Seymour asked Elizabeth to marry him. She refused. Even at a young age, she was clever enough to sense real danger. Her instincts proved accurate: a few years later Thomas was arrested for treason. He had been involved with a plot to overthrow the government. Elizabeth served as a witness during his trial, where she confessed embarrassing details of their relationship. Found guilty of high treason, Thomas Seymour was beheaded, drawn, and quartered.

Even as queen, the young woman in her twenties had a difficult time hiding her affection. It was widely known at court that Elizabeth had fallen in love with Robert Dudley, a well-dressed, tall, and handsome courtier with a reputation for excellence in jousting. Dudley's marriage to another woman, however, made his romance with the queen scandalous. His wife, Amy Robsart, lived in the countryside, far away from the royal court. Considering an affair with a married man extremely dishonorable, people close to Elizabeth begged her to break off their close relationship. The outrage intensified when Amy Robsart was found dead at the foot of large staircase. Was the fall an accident or did she commit suicide? Did Dudley push her? Rumors circulated that Dudley had killed his wife in order to be free to marry the queen. A thorough investigation determined that her death had been an accident, but the damage had been done to Dudley's reputation. There was no honorable way for Elizabeth to marry him. In the end, the queen's head overruled her heart. For the good of her subjects, she renounced this scandalous love affair.

The last potential suitor for the queen was the Duke of Anjou, brother of French king Henry III. He and Elizabeth flirted with each other during his brief visit to England in 1579, and the courtship ended in a marriage proposal and exchange of rings before his departure back to France. According to royal doctors, Elizabeth, then 45 years old, could still produce children, and the queen rightly considered the French duke her last chance at marriage. Her advisors counseled against it, however, arguing that the marriage would put England under a foreign and Catholic king. They also feared that an heir might serve as the focal point for a rival faction at court. More important, the people of England opposed the marriage. Although Elizabeth forbade discussions of her marriage outside of court, one printer, John Stubbs, wrote and published a pamphlet on the subject, *Discovery of a Gaping Gulf whereunto England is like to be swallowed by another French Marriage if the Lord forbid not the banns.* For this crime, Stubbs paid the heavy penalty of the loss of his right hand. After the royal official severed the hand with a cleaver and a mallet, the unfortunate printer raised his hat in his left hand and shouted, "God save the queen" before he passed out. After several months and not a few bouts of tears, Elizabeth fulfilled the wishes of the court and her people by renouncing the marriage proposal. She would remain the virgin queen until her death.

Enemies

Mary Stuart, Queen of Scots (1542–1587), Elizabeth's cousin, friend, and rival, had a very good claim to the English throne as the niece of Henry VIII. Although she inherited the kingdom of Scotland, she spent her youth in France, where she adopted the Catholic religion. A teenager at the court of Catherine de Medici during the religious wars, she grew up in the midst of plots, conspiracies, and mysterious deaths. She married the second son of the French king, who became King Francis II in 1559. For two years, she reigned as queen of France, until the untimely death of her husband two years later. She then returned to Scotland to rule as queen.

In Scotland she married her cousin, Henry Stuart, Lord of Darnley. In 1566, she gave birth to a son, James Stuart. However, Mary grew tired of her husband's lying, drinking, and constant insults against her. When he was found strangled to death in a garden a day after she had left his side, many thought Mary had plotted against him. She made the scandal worse by marrying the man believed to have committed the murder, the Earl of Bothwell. This so outraged Mary's Scottish subjects that they stripped her of her crown and exiled her from the kingdom 1567. With few other options, she found safety in England with her cousin, Elizabeth I.

Although deprived of her kingdom, Mary still posed a real threat to Elizabeth. Many at court accused her of conspiring with Catholics in England or abroad to overthrow her rule. For this reason, Elizabeth kept her cousin in captivity for nineteen years. When Catholics in France and the Netherlands allied with Spain to crush the Protestant religion in their lands, Elizabeth's closest advisors warned her that Mary plotted with her Catholic allies against her. When a Catholic assassinated William of Orange, the Protestant ruler of the Netherlands, in 1584, many feared such a fate threatened Elizabeth. Reluctantly, Elizabeth allowed the Parliament to put Mary on trial for treason. The judges ruled her guilty and sentenced her to death. At first the queen refused to sign the order of execution for her cousin, but eventually she succumbed to pressure and gave her signature. In February of 1587 the former queen of France and Scotland went to the scaffold as a martyr to the Catholic faith. She walked to the scaffold wearing a black gown and rosary, holding a crucifix in her hands. As she calmly placed her head on the block, her little dog hid under her skirt. With two drops of the broad, heavy axe, the executioner severed her head, then raised it to the air and shouted, "God save the Queen." The poor dog refused to leave the headless body of its mistress.

By eliminating a potential rival, Elizabeth's execution of Mary helped to consolidate power within her kingdom. The leaders of the opposition movement had been silenced. However, Catholic forces outside of England, considering Mary a martyr for their faith, vowed to destroy the Protestant queen. Phillip II, her former brother-in-law, considered Elizabeth a heretic with no legitimate right to the English throne. Beyond the religious difference between them, Philip also considered England a menace to the Spanish Empire. English ships had preyed upon Spanish colonies around the world. The English called the frequent raiding and plundering of Spanish ships and seaports, "privateering," but the Spanish considered it piracy.

FIGURE 3.4   Anglo-Netherlandish school, *Robert Dudley, Earl of Leicester, 1532–88,* c. 1564.

Source: Art Collection 2/Alamy Stock Photo

England, an island country with a seafaring tradition, increasingly challenged Spanish shipping on the high seas.

Despite these ongoing attacks, the most important factor leading England to war with Spain was the English support of Protestant armies on the European continent. English soldiers fought alongside their Protestant enemies in France and the Netherlands, a Dutch-speaking collection of provinces which had been part of the Holy Roman Empire. After the death of Emperor Charles V, Philip II inherited the Dutch provinces as the king of Spain. Protestants in the Netherlands, many of whom had become rich from shipping and global trade fought a war for independence from Spanish rule in 1566. They declared themselves the United Provinces in 1579. When Philip II tried to crush the revolt, Elizabeth sent troops and resources to aid the revolutionaries. In response, Philip II decided that Spain had a strategic interest in overthrowing Protestant rule in England.

The Armada

Philip II called his grand plan to invade Great Britain the "Enterprise of England." In the sixteenth century, Spain had established dominion over Italy, Mexico, and Peru. Treasure fleets coming into the Spanish port of Seville from the New World had brought Spain incredible wealth and seemingly unlimited resources for war. Moreover, the king of Spain believed that he fought for the glory of God and the true Catholic faith.

At the time, Spain had the most fearsome army in Europe. England, on the other hand, had no professional army at all. Instead of relying on paid soldiers to protect it from invaders, England put its defense in the hands of a citizen militia, a volunteer army, in which all male subjects between the ages of 16 and 60, whether rich or poor, served. Each village and town had an arsenal stocked with guns and artillery to use in case of invasion. Most kingdoms in the sixteenth century restricted gun use to the nobility, as rulers feared that arming the common people would lead to rebellions and uprisings. By custom and tradition, however, Englishmen considered participation in the militia a fundamental right guaranteeing their freedom. At the same time, they felt a strong sense of duty to defend their island. English rulers had faith in the loyalty of their subjects to the crown.

In the end, the Spanish invasion never happened. Philip had sent a fleet of 130 ships, called his *gran armada*, through the English Channel in July of 1588. By August his fleet docked off of the coast of the Netherlands intending to carry Spanish soldiers to England, but due to poor planning and communication, the army never reached the fleet. Instead, smaller, more maneuverable English gunboats attacked, blasting the large and cumbersome galleys of the Spanish flotilla. Confusion set in until a massive wind from the southwest drove the Spanish fleet into the North Sea. Forced to circumnavigate Great Britain, one-third of the Spanish ships slammed into the rocky islands off the coast of Scotland and Ireland. The rest of the fleet retreated in defeat. Miraculously, it seemed, England had been saved.

On August 8, before the fear of invasion had passed, Elizabeth visited the troops at Tilbury. Riding a white horse, and wearing a white velvet dress with a breastplate of shining silver, Elizabeth gave the most important speech of her life:

> My loving people, we have been persuaded by some that are careful of our safety to take heed how we commit ourselves to armed multitudes, for fear of treachery. But I assure you, I do not desire to live in distrust of my faithful and loving people. Let tyrants fear! I have always so behaved myself that, under God, I have placed my chiefest strength and safeguard in the loyal hearts and goodwill of my subjects; and therefore am come amongst you ... in the midst and heat of battle, to live or die amongst you all, and to lay down for God, for my kingdom, and for my people, my honor and my blood, even in the dust. I know I have the body of a weak and feeble woman, but I have the heart and stomach of a king.[4]

The speech, which expressed Elizabeth's courageous faith in the love of her people, brought tears to the eyes of the audience.

The defeat of the Spanish Armada in 1588 was a turning point in English history. England had withstood the most powerful state on the European continent. The island would not face another invasion for 352 years, in 1940, when the Royal Air Force successfully defeated the German Blitzkrieg in the Battle of Britain.

A golden age

The domestic peace and unity enjoyed by Elizabethans encouraged economic expansion, exploration and overseas commerce. As a Protestant, Elizabeth did not respect the Treaty of Tordesillas (1494) in which the pope decreed that all the lands of the New World be divided between the kingdoms of Portugal and Spain. Instead, she encouraged her subjects to explore and colonize any land in the New World not directly inhabited by other European countries.

The greatest explorer of the Elizabethan age was Sir Francis Drake. Born into a poor farming family, he made his fortune through privateering, the state-sponsored form of piracy. Using massive gunboats he raided coastal villages as well as Spanish ships filled with gold and silver on the high seas throughout the world. The people of coastal communities in the New World grew to fear Drake and nicknamed him *El Draque* (the dragon). Since he gave a portion of his plunder to the crown, Elizabeth endorsed and even invested in these raiding expeditions. In 1577 Drake set sail from England and circumnavigated the world with his fleet. He returned three years later with Spanish treasure and precious spices.

Another merchant explorer, John Hawkins, had started slaving raids off the coast of West Africa. These predatory incursions into the slave trade (at that time controlled by the Portuguese) were limited in the sixteenth century. In his four voyages, Hawkins had acquired hundreds of slaves by kidnapping, negotiation, or stealing from Portuguese ships. Although Elizabeth approved of his expeditions, she seems not to have understood the brutality of the enterprise. She commented that she hoped the Africans would not be enslaved without their consent, "which would be detestable and call down the vengeance of Heaven upon the undertakers." Despite this small beginning, the British would eventually dominate the Atlantic slave trade in the eighteenth century.

England's economy benefitted from new commercial enterprises carried out by joint-stock companies, which were associations of investors who funded risky overseas expeditions. When war between the Dutch and the Spanish closed the port of Antwerp, where English merchants had traded for centuries, English merchant adventurers looked for new areas of trade around the world, expanding even into Turkey and North Africa. Commercial ties with Muslim governments led to friendly diplomatic relations. Setting aside religious differences, both England and France regarded the enemy (Ottoman Empire) of their enemy (Spain) a useful ally.

While English merchants ventured out into the world, the island itself absorbed a great influx of people from overseas. Persecuted in their home countries, Protestants escaping religious oppression from the Netherlands, France, Spain, Italy, and Portugal sought freedom in London, where one in twenty workers were foreign born in 1571. Although the local population complained that they brought 'strange' beliefs and values, these immigrants carried with them new technologies and expertise that led to innovations in a number of enterprises.

Elizabeth, herself a scholar, encouraged education and the arts throughout her kingdom. It was the age of the Renaissance. The rivival revival of the works of ancient Greece and Rome that started in Florence in the fifteenth century moved to England in the sixteenth, and English publishers printed hundreds of English translations of ancient books. Ancient historians such as Thucydides and Tacitus provided a new way of looking at the world that seemed to energize the mind. The philosopher Plato, who wrote about beauty, justice, and love, inspired Elizabeth's supporters to portray her as the epitome of these ideals. Royal propagandists represented her as allegorical figures named Gloriana, and Astrea, the personifications of glory and justice. As for Elizabeth, she remained open to learning new things throughout her life. She faithfully continued to study Greek into old age. Her open-minded approach toward knowledge set the tone for a cultural flourishing that created timeless works of literature as well as scientific progress.

It is to Elizabeth's credit that William Shakespeare, whom many believe to be the greatest poet and playwright in the English language, emerged during her reign. The 1590s were a golden age of theater. From 1590–1603, there were almost 400 plays and entertainments first performed or published in England. The son of a small-town glovemaker, Shakespeare wrote around 37 plays and 154 sonnets. His works have had tremendous force and universal appeal for several reasons. First, he used an unusual variety of sources (stories and histories from around the world), and themes (love, sex, murder, money, class, gender). More important, he intended his plays to include dialogues, not only between characters, but within people's minds. His characters experience moral dilemmas, that were not easy to solve. For example, his most famous quote, from Hamlet—"To be or not to be, that is the question"—is from a character considering suicide. Such difficult themes continue to touch the human heart across the centuries.

Magic and witchcraft in Elizabethan England

Despite remarkable advancements in education, commerce, and technology, magical thinking permeated almost all aspects of society in sixteenth-century England. For centuries, the common people had sought protection from the harmful effects of supernatural powers. They trusted "cunning" men and women who sold charms, prescribed medications and ointments, and performed rituals to ward off evil spirits and counteract the harmful effects of witchcraft. In the past, the Catholic Church had provided "good magic" as protection, but English Protestants increasingly shunned Catholic rituals such as exorcism used to cleanse a person of demonic possession. Although they dismissed the "good" magic of Catholicism as superstition, they continued to fear the harmful effects of "bad" or "black" magic.

Using magic to cause harm to others was the crime of witchcraft, and Elizabeth and her contemporaries believed that it was an ever-increasing threat to Christian society. The late sixteenth century was the height of the witch trials in Europe. Between 1550 and 1650, perhaps 90,000 people were tried and 45,000 executed as witches. England's witch-craze was comparatively mild compared to the continent (only about five hundred people were put to death for witchcraft in England), but an Elizabethan statute of 1563 made it a capital offense to cause death by magic. It also spelled out lesser punishments for other magical acts.

The witch craze was a response to a belief in a worldwide conspiracy of witches allied with Satan to overthrow the religious, political, and social order. Medieval Europeans had believed in the crime of witchcraft, but they did not believe that their evil deeds, or *maleficium*, had anything to do with a larger conspiracy led by a secret association of witches (who were always allied with political or religious enemy groups). The sixteenth century, with its religious and political upheaval, caused a great deal of fear among the people. This fear became the moral panic that led to the witch trials. Some Protestant ministers tried to assure their congregations that the devil could not do anything without God's permission. Accordingly, they advised people to accept misfortune as God's will instead of blaming witches for their problems. Despite this advice, many people continued to believe that Satan had taken over the world and that evil reigned on Earth. They were looking for a scapegoat, and elderly women, the most vulnerable people in society, often made the most convenient targets.

According to testimony given at English witchcraft trials, witches made a pact with the devil and frequented assemblies of witches called "sabbaths." Sometimes witches kept a "familiar" to do evil deeds. This could be any small creature such as a cat, bug, or "imp." Because these "imps" were believed to suckle from a hidden witch's teat, those accused of witchcraft were searched for protrusions or moles supposedly used for this purpose. The courts sentenced those found guilty to execution by hanging. This happened only rarely in England, however, because of its unusual legal system. English Common Law required every case to go through a lengthy judicial process involving a justice of the peace, grand jury, full jury trial, and an appeals process, all of which served to protect the defendant. Those accused of witchcraft in continental courts that used torture were not as fortunate.

Many of the most educated Elizabethans developed a fascination with the occult aspects of ancient knowledge. John Dee (1527–1608), a talented mathematician, spent most of his time dabbling in the magical arts. In the sixteenth century, scholars made little distinction between science (natural philosophy) and magic, as both sought out the hidden forces of the universe. Dee, influenced by the mystical Hebrew *Cabala,* believed that numbers expressed the sacred language of God. In his view, understanding this spiritual "code" could bring a scholar closer to unlocking the mysteries of God's creation as well as mystical revelations. Dee and others believed that celestial beings such as angels and demons filled the heavens. In an effort to harness the power of these beings, Dee used a crystal ball to communicate with angels. The goal of any *magus* (wise man) like Dee was to use supernatural forces to influence events on earth. Elizabeth, believing in Dee's magical abilities, kept him at court as her astrologer and close advisor. He drew up her horoscope and calculated the most auspicious days on which to conduct important business. At the time, Elizabethans distinguished between good and bad magic and many did not consider the occult sciences as contradictory to the Christian faith. They permitted communicating with angels, but strongly forbade the practice of calling on demons by name.

The end of her reign

By the end of the sixteenth century, Elizabeth's face had begun to reflect her age. Her hair, however, remained an unnatural shade of red thanks to dye, and her official portraits portrayed her as eternally young. She continued to have the energy of a much younger person, riding her horses ten miles a day. Moreover, she still had the hearts of her people. Some have suggested that her popularity had developed into a cult of personality and that the queen, who had detested the worship of idols, had actually become one herself. Indeed, many of Elizabeth's symbols, such as the rose and the pearl, had previously been associated with the Virgin Mary. The Queen's birthday, 7 September, replaced the feast of the Virgin as a national holiday, which was celebrated with festivals and fireworks. The bond between the queen and the common folk was real, but how much of her success was due to propaganda and how much was due to effective policy?

More than a figure head, she had always taken an active approach to state policy. With her fluency in French, Spanish, and Italian, she negotiated with foreign diplomats directly. She also favored innovation and exploration. Nevertheless, she ruled at a time when the greatest kings had also been successful warriors. As a woman, she had never fought a battle. She solved this problem by inspiring soldiers with her words rather than her example.

Elizabeth increased her authority by attracting the best and brightest to a glittering and extremely opulent court. She made sure that her courtiers were well dressed and well paid. To the nobility of the kingdom, she offered generous patronage in the form of government offices, gifts, or salaries. The patronage system, although not exactly fair or just, satisfied and pacified the aristocracy of the kingdom. Peace enabled a prosperity, that extended to the lower ranks of society.

Elizabeth's reign was not without failures and mistakes. Her armies had suffered defeats in Scotland and France, and her navy had failed in Portugal. She never managed to conquer Ireland or establish a permanent settlement in the New World. The Roanoke colony established during her reign mysteriously disappeared. Nevertheless, the land it claimed still bears the name of the virgin queen who inspired the colonists: Virginia.

By the end of her long reign, some members of Parliament grumbled that she had not done enough to reform the royal monopolies that many considered corrupt.

Her last speech responded to this complaint in 1601. As she faced an angry and oppositional assembly, she gave a memorable speech:

> To be a king and to wear a crown is a thing more glorious to them that see it, than it is pleasant to them that bear it. For myself, I was never so much enticed with the glorious name of a king, or royal authority of a queen, as delighted that God hath made me His instrument to maintain His truth and glory, and to defend this kingdom from peril, dishonor, tyranny, and oppression . . . And though you have had, and may have, many mightier and wiser princes sitting in this seat, yet you never had, nor shall have, any that will love you better.[5]

With this moving oration, called by posterity the "Golden Speech," Elizabeth turned an angry assembly of 140 men into a joyful and grateful group of loyal supporters. She had a talent for leadership that never left her.

From time to time during her life, Elizabeth had suffered from low moods that were then called melancholy, but today might be diagnosed as depression. In May of 1602, the year in which she turned 70, she complained that she was tired of living, and that nothing gave her pleasure anymore. By spring of 1603 she had refused to dress for the cold, eat, or take any medicine. Her last act was to name the son of Mary Queen of Scots, James, as her successor. On March 24, 1603, she died.

Elizabeth was the last ruler of the Tudor dynasty. James I established the Stuart dynasty, which was much less prosperous and peaceful. James I and his son, Charles I, believed in the "divine right of kings" to rule. In this view, kings had been established by God and therefore did not have to consider the wishes of Parliament or their subjects. In 1640, an angry Parliament deposed and decapitated Charles I. The result was civil war and several years without a king or queen. In 1660, Charles II took the throne, but his son, James II, faced a new revolution and left the kingdom. The Parliament brought in a new dynasty in 1689. Under William and Mary and their successors, England kept its constitutional monarchy, but gradually moved increasingly toward democracy. England's growing power and prestige would enable the rise of the British Empire, which stretched across the globe under the rule of another memorable queen, Victoria, in the nineteenth century.

Chronology

1533	Birth of Elizabeth I.
1534	England officially breaks from the Roman Catholic Church.
1536	Death of Anne Boleyn, mother of Elizabeth.
1547	Death of Henry VIII. Edward VI becomes King of England.
1553	Death of Edward VI. Mary I becomes Queen of England.
1558	Death of Mary I. Elizabeth I becomes Queen of England.
1587	Execution of Mary Queen of Scots.
1588	Defeat of the Spanish Armada.
1603	Death of Elizabeth I.

Sources for further reading about Elizabeth I

Biographies of Elizabeth I in English are legion. A classic work which provides a lively introduction to the queen is J. E. Neale, *Queen Elizabeth I* (Chicago, IL: Academy Chicago Publishers, 1992), first published in 1933. A useful compilation of articles is Christopher Haigh, *The Reign of Elizabeth I* (London: Macmillan Press, 1984). A more recent compilation is Susan Doran and Norman Jones, eds., *The Elizabethan World* (London: Routledge, 2011). It has great chapters on witchcraft and foreign policy. Several useful multi-volume sets are John A. Wagner, *Historical Dictionary of the Elizabethan World. Britain, Ireland, Europe, and America* (Chicago, IL: Fitzroy Dearborn Publishers, 1999), and John A. Wagner and Susan Walters Schmid, eds., *Encyclopedia of Tudor England* (3 volumes; Santa Barbara, CA: ABC-CLIO, 2012). There is also a lengthy article by Patrick Collinson, "Elizabeth I," in H. C. G. Matthew and Brian Harrison, eds., *Dictionary of National Biography, Volume 18* (Oxford: Oxford University Press, 2004), pp. 95–130. A classic social and economic study of the sixteenth century in England is Lawrence Stone, *The Causes of the English Revolution 1529–1642* (New York: Harper & Row, 1972). For foreign policy, see R. B. Wernham, *Before the Armada: The Emergence of the English Nation, 1485–1588* (New York: W. W. Norton, 1966), and more recently Susan Brigden, *New Worlds, Lost Worlds* (New York: Penguin, 2000). For lively discussions of some important battles see Garrett Mattingly, *The Armada* (Boston, MA: Houghton Mifflin, 1959). A popular history of England from its origins to the end of Elizabeth's reign is Simon Schama, *A History of Britain: At the Edge of the World? 3000 BC–AD 1603* (New York: Hyperion, 2000). A fun book about daily life in the Elizabethan age is Ian Mortimer, *A Time Traveler's Guide to Elizabethan England* (New York: Penguin, 2014).

Comparison between Afonso I and Elizabeth I

The passing of five centuries has clouded the modern understanding of Africa and England as they were in the early modern era. In between the sixteenth century and the present lie centuries of atrocities related to the slave trade, invariably described as a narrative in which the English were the predators and the Africans the victims. This set of biographies does not attempt to illuminate the nature of the slave trade, but to provide an analysis of the motives of two historical figures engaged in similar situations. Both Afonso I and Elizabeth I were successful rulers who used the tools available to them to consolidate power within their kingdoms.

The most obvious common link between them was religion, the ultimate source of their power. Unlike Henry IV and Hideyoshi, they did not build their powerbase on conquest. Rather, they claimed to be instruments of divine will, exceptions to the normal order of things. If they had followed ancient customs, neither would have ruled. Afonso's mother did not belong to the kanda, that supplied royal heirs. Elizabeth was the product of what the Catholic Church considered an illicit affair. Therefore, both rulers needed a new belief system to establish their claims to legitimacy.

The adoption of a new religion may have established their rule, but it did not necessarily secure their success. If there is one quality that distinguishes them in their approach to leadership, it is openness. New worlds appeared beyond their shores, and Afonso and Elizabeth embraced them. Rather than recoiling from outside forces, these two sought out opportunities and used them them to their advantage. Intense in their scholarship and open to new ideas, Afonso and Elizabeth made the best use of their own resources, while always seeking improvement in themselves and their subjects. Despite setbacks and troubles, they never ceased to look toward the future with optimism.

The cultures of England and Kongo had some notable similarities. Both acted as a crossroads and an entrepôt for the transportation of goods. Government revenue depended heavily on taxing trade rather than agricultural products or tribute. When the Portuguese came to Africa, Afonso understood the advantages of contact from the perspective of trade. So too did Elizabeth recognize the necessity of trade networks, even though they differed greatly in scale. For both England and Africa, land was less valuable than it was in many other countries. Labor and commerce were the bases of wealth. After several hundreds of years of European contact with Africa, the British economist, Adam Smith, maintained that labor, not land, was the primary foundation of wealth. He revealed this "revolutionary" element of the capitalist system in his eighteenth-century work, *The Wealth of Nations*. Two hundred years earlier, both Afonso and Elizabeth also considered their wealth in people.

In both kingdoms, the dispensing of gifts played a large role in linking the monarch to the nobility. Afonso saw the Portuguese as a supplier of luxury goods with which he insured his "sovereignty and jurisdiction." Elizabeth, too, realized how insatiable the nobility was for cash as well as honor or favor. Both held a remarkably practical attitude toward political power.

Although they took a realistic approach to royal authority, they did not discount the magical thinking common to both societies. Elizabeth and Afonso burned idols, considering certain figurines to hold supernatural forces of evil inside them. Their powers were real. Otherwise, why burn them? Burning is an act of purification. One does not need to burn something inert and powerless, one can simply ignore it. Their treatment of idols indicates that both viewed the traditional religion as real, a dangerous and potentially evil force in the world.

The nature of the spiritual world they inhabited was remarkably similar. Africans and Europeans divided the world into heaven and earth, the realm of the spirits and the world that could be seen and experienced by ordinary people. Both believed that the occupants of heaven influenced the world of living people, but it did so in unusual and mysterious ways. Only a few, talented people could read the signs of the spirit world and translate their "revelations" to the living. In England and Kongo, the process of naming the spirits was seen as a way to harness their magical power to use on earth. Cunning men and women in England and as well as witch doctors in Africa used spells, rituals, divination, and conjuring to tell the future or influence the outcome of events in much the same way. It was believed that the celestial world, including the stars, somehow controlled events on earth. The transmutation of metals figured in John Dee's studies of alchemy, as well as in African traditions of blacksmithing. And in both cases, the symbolic value in each society was to underline the potential for positive change. The alchemists searched for immortality, while the African blacksmith sought a monarchal power that united the discordant wills of his subjects into an orderly human society.

Historians are not exactly sure about the origins of magical thinking. Perhaps similar ideas about the nature of the supernatural world in Africa and England had common origins, or they may have been expressions of ancient, universal beliefs. Interestingly, Europeans of the sixteenth century considered Africa as a great source of magical wisdom. Indeed, when a duke from Milan met an ambassador of Ethiopia for the first time, he asked him whether or not he had a copy of a mysterious magic book, *The Key of Solomon*. The Europeans of the Renaissance imagined an African among the three Magi from the East. They associated Africa, as well as the Middle East, with ancient wisdom from which they might learn.

For too long, historians have portrayed Elizabethan England as being in the forefront of modern science, while Africa remained behind as a superstitious and and backward-thinking society. In reality, the people of these societies did not experience the world so differently, nor was there an unfathomable gulf between how the rulers of each kingdom approached problems of religion and politics.

Questions to consider

1 Why did Afonso I not consider the Portuguese a threat? Why did he choose to adopt the language and religious beliefs of outsiders?

2 Discuss Afonso's participation in the slave trade. What lines did he draw concerning its abuse? What were its advantages and disadvantages from the standpoint of his rule?

3   Both Afonso and Elizabeth claimed to rule by divine right in some sense. Was this enough to secure the loyalty of their subjects? Why or why not? What were some other strategies they used to gain support?

4   Compare Elizabeth I with Catherine de Medici (Chapter 1) in terms of leadership. Why was one able to prevent civil war, and the other unable to prevent it?

5   What elements of Elizabeth's character and situation contributed to her exceptional charisma?

6   Compare the figure of Elizabeth to Hürrem and Lady Zheng. Would marriage and family have damaged her popularity?

7   The biographies of Henry IV and Elizabeth contain salacious stories. What role did sexuality play in each case? How was sex central to the identities of both rulers?

8   Magical thinking permeated the societies of both Kongo and England throughout the sixteenth century. In what way might Afonso and Elizabeth be considered magicians in terms of their strategies of leadership?

9   Chapters 1–3 have presented a simplified picture of three political systems: feudal, imperial, and commercial. Does each system of government encourage or require a particular leadership strategy?

Notes

1 George Balandier, *Daily Life in the Kingdom of Kongo from the Sixteenth Century to the Eighteenth Century*, trans. Helen Weaver (New York: Pantheon Books, 1968), p. 231.

2 Ibid., p. 52.

3 Hugh Thomas, *The Slave Trade: The Story of the Atlantic Slave Trade 1440–1870* (New York: Simon & Schuster Paperbacks, 1997, p. 110.

4 John A. Wagner, *Historical Dictionary of the Elizabethan World: Britain, Ireland, Europe, and America* (Chicago, IL: Fitzroy Dearborn Publishers, 1999), p. 303.

5 Ibid., p. 124.

4
POPE CLEMENT VII AND MOCTEZUMA II OF MEXICO

Despite their positions of power, neither Clement VII nor Moctezuma II of Mexico successfully managed to prevent the Spanish Empire from establishing a new regime in their regions. Born Giulio de' Medici at the height of the Italian Renaissance, Clement VII ascended to the highest office in the Catholic Church. As a spiritual leader for the majority of Europeans and a political ruler of lands in central Italy, Clement tried to unite a variety of states against the threat of imperial domination. Fear, indecision, and untrustworthy allies undermined his ability to lead a successful resistance. Moctezuma II, an Aztec prince, had proven himself to be an effective ruler over the Mexican Empire. However, he ultimately remained helpless against a Spanish-led coalition of his enemies. Despite some positive qualities and good intentions, both Clement and Moctezuma had the misfortune to witness the massacres and atrocities that accompanied the occupations of Rome and Tenochtitlan, respectively. In the end, however, both managed to provide a means for their family members to enter the elite of newly established regimes.

Giulio de' Medici, or Pope Clement VII (1478–1534)

Stunning artistic beauty and extreme violence marked the life of Giulio de' Medici. Born in the city of Florence at the height of the Renaissance, he rose through the ranks of the Catholic Church and assumed the throne as Pope Clement VII in 1523. Having found himself at the pinnacle of power in Europe, his fate would take a sharp, downward turn. His papacy suffered the calamities of the brutal sack of Rome and the end of Catholic unity in Europe. His contemporaries described him as intelligent, refined, and fundamentally honest, but also fearful and indecisive. Posterity has viewed him as a weak and troubled leader, partially responsible for the disasters that befell his homeland.

FIGURE 4.1 Sebastiano del Piombo, *Portrait of Clement VII*, 1526.

Source: Art Collection 2/Alamy Stock Photo

A tragic beginning

From its very beginning, Giulio de' Medici's life had been marked by tragedy. On 26 April, 1478, Florentine citizens gathered to celebrate mass at the Cathedral of Santa Maria del Fiore in the heart of the city. The magnificent cathedral boasted the largest dome in the world and stood as a symbol of the greatness of the Florentine Republic. Two Medici brothers, Lorenzo and Giuliano, were attentively following the service as it reached its most sacred moment. When the priest raised the bread to the sky as the very body of Jesus, two men in hooded cloaks unsheathed their daggers and plunged them into Giuliano's side and chest. Giuliano bled out on the ornate marble floor of the sacred church, the victim of multiple stab wounds and blows to the head. On the other side of the altar, two priests made an attempt on the life of Lorenzo. Protected by a few supporters and wielding a dagger of his own, Lorenzo survived the attack with only superficial wounds. The murdered Giuliano had left an unmarried lover who gave birth to Giulio de Medici, the future Clement VII, within months of the assassination. Lorenzo de Medici, his uncle, raised the boy as his own child.

By the fifteenth century, the Medici family had amassed a fortune as bankers in Florence. Giulio's great grandfather, Cosimo de' Medici (1389–1464) built the family's banking empire. What began as a simple wooden table for money lending in the central market of medieval Florence became a multi-national financial enterprise with branches throughout Europe, and members of the family bank served as financiers to kings and popes. The family's increasing status and wealth, however, had created personal and political enemies in the republic.

Without a duke, king, or emperor as an overlord, Florentine citizens governed their republic according to a constitution, and elections determined who held offices in the city council. Although bitter and sometimes bloody disputes arose among political factions, the special freedom the Florentines enjoyed encouraged the growth of commerce and industry. The fiercely independent citizens who took pride in the liberty and public spirit of their city feared that if one family rose above the others in wealth and power, it might seek to rule the city as a monarchy and establish itself as a dynasty. Understanding that these fears were directed toward him, Cosimo de' Medici carefully continued to respect the traditions and institutions of the republic. Wearing simple clothes and riding a mule around the city, the head of the Medici family greeted people from all walks of life with the same friendly smile. By downplaying his wealth and status, he reassured the citizens of Florence that he had no intentions of ruling as a prince.

Cosimo himself seemed to embody the self-confident exuberance of the Florentine Republic. Under his generous patronage, artists, engineers, and scholars felt free to explore all areas of human knowledge. He built libraries and encouraged the study of ancient Greece and Rome. The flourishing culture he helped to inspire became the movement known as the Renaissance, a rebirth of ancient civilization. At the same time, he showed exceptional ability as a statesman who worked to bring peace and prosperity to his city. For all of these reasons, the Florentines granted Cosimo de' Medici the title *pater patriae* (father of his country).

Behind the scenes, however, the Medici family worked to establish themselves as undisputed leaders in the city. They used their vast financial resources to influence elections and secure loyal supporters. As heir to the family fortune, Cosimo's grandson, Lorenzo de' Medici (1449–1492), continued and expanded the financial, political, and artistic influence of the Medici family. Known as Lorenzo the Magnificent, he presided over the city at the height of the Florentine Renaissance.

The palace of Lorenzo the Magnificent, where Giulio de' Medici spent his childhood, served as a banking headquarters, political court, and cultural epicenter. Lorenzo and his wife, Clarice, a noblewoman from an old and powerful and powerful Roman family, raised Giulio and their own children among scholars and artists. Lorenzo, who kept an extensive collection of ancient statues in the courtyard of his palace, used to invite the apprentices of local workshops into his home to practice their skills. One of these was the 15-year-old Michelangelo Buonarroti. Recognizing his amazing potential, Lorenzo invited the young artist to live at the Medici palace among his children. With the support of the Medici family, the city of Florence, and several popes, Michelangelo would go on to create some of the most iconic works of Western art, including the statues, *Pietà* and *David*, as well as the magnificent frescoes adorning the ceiling of the Vatican's Sistine Chapel.

A writer of poetry himself, Lorenzo the Magnificent supported writers and philosophers. He especially favored the study of the Greek philosopher, Plato (c. 428 BCE–c. 348 BCE), whose heady vision of beauty, truth, and goodness intoxicated the Florentines at the end of the fifteenth century. Plato had taught that such ideals were reflections of a divine essence he called the "Good." Artistically, these platonic ideas encouraged artists such as Leonardo da Vinci and Michelangelo to aspire to create images so beautiful that they might be considered divine in themselves. Their spellbinding masterpieces entrance the world to this day.

Lorenzo's extensive patronage of the arts and culture helped to make Florence a shining jewel among cities. His investment in art also increased the power and prestige of his family. Although he held no official title as prince, Lorenzo the Magnificent's influence and authority allowed him to decide who would win elections and what laws would pass. Bending the constitutional laws that governed the city, Lorenzo's opinions gained so much weight that before long, no one dared to make any political decisions without his approval. Though unofficial, his rule had become tyrannical. Few complained. As the Florentine historian, Francesco Guicciardini, commented, "If Florence was to have a tyrant, she could never have found a better or more delightful one." From 1454 to 1494, most of Italy enjoyed an extended era of peace that allowed money to flow into the economy. Rich people spent lavishly on luxuries, and built elegant palaces and gardens throughout Italian cities, while libraries and universities, industries and mills, churches and banks flourished as never before. Although nobody used the term "Renaissance" at the time, many described the age as one of *renovatio* (renovation).

Beneath the surface of what seemed to be a golden age of cultural revival, however, flowed a dark undercurrent of political intrigue. The resentment and fear of powerful rivals had led to the murder of Lorenzo's brother in 1478. Allied against the Medici was a group of conspirators that included Pope Sixtus IV, the Duke of Urbino, and the Pazzi, a rival Florentine banking family. Although they all had personal, financial and strategic reasons to bring the Medici down, the conspirators believed that the citizens of Florence would support them as liberators of the city from the increasingly tyrannical Medici. After the brutal murder in the cathedral of Giulio's father described earlier, the assassins attempted to incite a revolution. They rode horses through the crowds yelling, "Liberty! Liberty!" But the common people strongly supported the Medici. The crowd angrily shouted back at them, "Balls! Balls!" It was a reference to the Medici coat of arms bearing five balls on a shield. As in English, however, the Italian word for balls, *palle*, also holds another, more vulgar meaning.

The prosperous fifteenth century came to an abrupt end when Lorenzo de' Medici died of natural causes in 1492, and two years later, in 1494, the first of many foreign invasions shattered the peace established among the city-states of Italy. North of the Alpine mountains, the powerful kings of Spain and France had begun to notice that the rich commercial cities of Italy, Milan, Venice, Genoa, and Florence had little in the way of military defenses. Below the Alps, some Italians themselves realized that they might use these foreign armies from the north to settle their own scores against long-standing enemies. When the Duke of Milan invited the French king to cross the Alps to attack his enemy in Naples in 1494, the army of Charles VIII of France encountered hardly any resistance as it marched down the peninsula. In response, the King of Naples called the Spanish army into Italy to fight the French. For the next thirty-five years, the armies of French and Spanish kings would reduce Italy to a confused, bloody, and often desolate battleground.

Surrendering without a fight to the French in 1494, Piero de' Medici, head of the family after Lorenzo's death, provoked a revolt against Medici power in the city. The Florentines exiled the Medici, forcing 16-year-old Giulio, the future Clement VII, to spend several years traveling from city to city. No longer in control of Florence, the Medici used their financial networks to expand their base of operations across the peninsula and Europe. They soon found a new source of power and authority in the city of Rome, the seat of the Catholic Church.

The Church

According to Catholic tradition, Jesus created the institution of the Church when he approached a fisherman named Simon and told him, "You are a rock, and on this rock I build my church" (Matthew 16:18). Because the Greek word for rock is *petros*, Simon changed his name to *petros* (Peter). After the crucifixion of Jesus in Jerusalem, Peter moved to the city of Rome where he served as the first bishop, or overseer, of the Roman congregation. By the third century CE, many cities in the Roman Empire had Christian congregations headed by a bishop. Among these, the bishop of Rome held an honored place.

Peter, whom the Romans crucified upside down upon a cross, became an important saint after his death. According to Catholic tradition, St. Peter held the keys to heaven and determined which souls might enter the gates of paradise. The bishop of Rome eventually claimed superiority over the other bishops and claimed the title of pope, meaning father. They claimed to serve, like St. Peter, as Christ's deputy on Earth; just as Peter decided who would enter heaven, the pope served as gate keeper for the Church. By the tenth century, the papacy claimed to have the authority to make the final decisions concerning doctrine in the Roman Catholic faith, which dominated in the Latin-speaking regions of Western Europe. In the Greek-speaking lands of the Byzantine Empire, the Eastern Orthodox Church arose as a separate branch of the Christian faith. With its capital in Constantinople, it did not recognize the authority of the pope in Rome.

The pope, also known as *pontifex maximus* and Holy Father, served as the head of the largest religious institution in Europe. As the only Latin governing body remaining after the fall of Rome in 476 CE, the Church filled an administrative power vacuum. Every city and village had a church with a priest, while larger towns and cities had cathedrals with bishops. Above the bishops and archbishops in the church hierarchy were the cardinals. Appointed by the pope, the cardinals formed a college that served as an advisory council. When a pope died, the cardinals chose his successor from among its members. In the Middle Ages, cardinals and bishops lived like lords on large domains with money and status. The pope's ability to appoint people to fill these offices made him extremely powerful. In order to pay the salaries of these officials, the church collected money from rents and taxes, called tithes, throughout Europe.

In the Middle Ages, the pope's authority and prestige rivaled that of European monarchs. With little separation between Church and state, popes, kings, and emperors held both secular and religious authority. This caused endless conflicts that lasted hundreds of years. Sometimes rulers threatened to depose popes by calling church councils to unseat them. In response, popes often used the punishment of excommunication, which separated them from the Catholic Church so that neither they nor their subjects could participate in any ceremonies. Deprived of the services of a priest in the rituals of baptism, marriage, and burial, common people often revolted against their king. Wishing to appease their subjects, and boost their popularity, rulers strove to appear loyal to the Church. This, in turn added to the pope's considerable power.

People often complained about the corruption of individual priests and popes, but generally regarded the institution itself as a necessary part of the Christian religion, especially in the chaotic world left after the fall or the Roman Empire. However, by the sixteenth century, calls to reform the Church grew louder from both common people and kings. The printing press invented in 1453 proved to be the most powerful weapon opposing the power of the papacy, as it gave more people access to the Holy Scripture. This intensified the desire of many Europeans to pursue a more personal and spiritual approach to Christianity, outside of the influence of a church hierarchy.

Pope Leo X

To further strengthen the position of the Medici family, Lorenzo the Magnificent had directed his son, Giovanni, toward a career in the church from an early age. He used money and connections to acquire church offices for Giovanni beginning at the astoundingly young age of eight. By 13, the boy had been appointed cardinal. In 1489, Giovanni began his studies in theology and canon (church) law at the University of Pisa. After three years of study, Giovanni moved to Rome to accept his office as cardinal, and Giulio, who had also entered the Church at an early age, followed his older cousin to Rome at the age of 13.

Exiled from Florence, the Medici cousins made a ten-year journey through the lands of Italy, Germany, and France acting as agents of the family beginning in 1499. Giovanni and Giulio worked continuously to reestablish the family's political leadership in Florence. The Medici had friends inside the city working secretly to overthrow the popular government and reclaim their family's position. Giulio took part in initiating this conspiracy, by sneaking his letters into the city. To do this, he employed a farmer as a messenger. This man rolled up tiny letters into a small brass tube which he hid in, as one contemporary described it, "the most secret part of his person." The messenger then deposited the container into a hole located in a church cemetery, where his friends found the messages and brought them to fellow conspirators.

At that time, one of the chancellors of the Florentine Republic was Niccolò Machiavelli. Better known to posterity as a statesman, political theorist, historian, and playwright, the author of both *The Prince* and *The Art of War* was fervently devoted to the republic. Inspired by the histories of ancient Rome, he wanted Florence to remain independent and self-governing, and he believed the key to freedom was a strong and dedicated citizen militia. He advocated for and even trained a citizen army to defend the Republic against a potential Medici assault.

In an aggressive bid to take control of the city in 1512, Cardinal Giovanni arranged the support of a Spanish army to attack the Florentines. In the battle of Prato, a small town about ten miles outside of Florence, the professional Spanish soldiers, then considered the most effective fighting force in Europe, slaughtered about two thousand Florentine soldiers who had surrendered without much of a fight. The Spanish army then sacked the city and the streets of Prato ran red with the blood of thousands of massacred citizens. Panicked, defeated and politically divided, the city council of Florence agreed to let the Medici return. When Giovanni, Giulio, and the other leaders of the family reentered the city, they brought soldiers with them. Mercenary troops paid by the Medici family occupied the town squares, public buildings, and even the halls of government. Their presence gave Florence the atmosphere of a police state.

When an assassination plot against the Medici was discovered in the following year, 1513, the Medici controlled government executed the ringleaders and rounded up a number of suspects. One list of conspirators included the name of Niccolò Machiavelli. Arrested and jailed, he endured the *strappado*, a torture in which his wrists were tied behind his back and lifted into the air by a rope. His whole body hanging by the arms twisted behind him, the torturers let him drop several feet before pulling up the rope again and dislocating his shoulders. Machiavelli, who confessed nothing, was released but excluded from employment in the government. Having returned to his house in the country, he passed endless days engaging in card games and arguments with the local villagers. Every night, however, he relieved his boredom and frustration by reading the classic works of antiquity, dressed in the robes he used to wear as a government official. As a mental escape from his difficult circumstances, he imagined his reading as a pleasant conversation with ancient writers who seemed to come to life and speak with him. He believed time spent with historical figures, if only in his mind, was essential to his life, stating: "There I taste the food that alone is mine, and for which I was born." He recorded the insights gained from these imaginary conversations in *The Prince*. Containing his reflections on fate, human nature, and the dark side of political strategy, the short treatise is considered one of the most celebrated and controversial books of all time.

As Machiavelli's fortunes sank to their lowest point, those of the Medici cousins continued to climb. Later in 1513, Cardinal Giovanni was elected as Pope Leo X. For the first time, a Florentine would sit on the throne of St. Peter. Proud to have a fellow citizen in a position of great authority to further their interests, Florentine artists and writers were especially optimistic that his patronage would provide jobs for them in Rome. in Rome. Leo X expressed the general sense of jubilation by affirming, "Since God has given us the papacy, let us enjoy it." His papacy strongly reflected the Medici style of rule. He invited hundreds of artists, scholars, musicians, poets, court jesters, courtesans, and a variety of entertainers to the Vatican palace, the residence of the popes. His banquets were legendary—one of them even featured a feast of peacocks. An extravagant host, Leo X's shows of magnificence amazed his guests. His antics sometimes involved his favorite pet, Hanno, a white elephant given to him by Manuel I, king of Portugal. Despite his fun-loving persona, Leo X took his religious office seriously and faithfully observed the fasts, rituals, and ceremonies required by the Church.

However, a revolt against the powerful and opulent papacy that began to simmer under Leo X would have grave and chaotic consequences for his successors and all of Europe. This movement came to be known as the Protestant Reformation led by the German monk, Martin Luther. Arguing that certain key Catholic traditions and rituals had no basis in the scriptures, he maintained that faith was the only true path to salvation. In Luther's view, faith mattered more to God than good deeds done in the name of religion. Viewing salvation as granted by the grace of God alone, he considered much of the institution of the Catholic Church as irrelevant to the faith. On October 31, 1517 he made a public statement of his radical ideas, supposedly by nailing his "95 Theses" to the door of the Wittenberg cathedral. Eventually, Luther and his followers openly declared the papacy itself as evil, corrupt, and in league with the devil. The bold proclamation of the German monk changed the course of history.

Believing that persecuting Martin Luther's followers would "fan the flames" of a revolt, Leo X hoped the movement would die out on its own. The Catholic Church had faced heresies for over a thousand years while maintaining religious unity. The pope had no reason to think the Protestant revolt differed in any signifi-cant way. He was wrong. At this time in European history, Martin Luther's religious ideas spread quickly and soon took on political importance that could be used for a variety of purposes. Peasants used Luther's words to justify a revolt against their landowners in 1525. Some townspeople wanted to establish their cities as inde-pendent Protestant communities. At the top of society, a few German princes no longer wanted to pay heavy taxes to a Church they considered foreign, and aimed to keep church revenues in their own states. Clement VII and all of Europe would soon face the dire results of this religious and political revolt.

Meanwhile, the election to the papacy of Leo X had beneficial consequences for Giulio de' Medici. Realizing that illegitimacy prevented his cousin from filling the highest offices in the church, Leo formed a commission to look into the conditions of his birth. Through testimony of certain family members, the commission found, not surprisingly, that Giulio's parents had been secretly married before the couple conceived their son. Rendered legitimate, Giulio was promoted to cardinal and provided with the revenues of over a dozen other offices throughout Italy, France, England, and Spain. The massive collection of church positions was an extreme example of *pluralism*, an abuse of power very common in the Renaissance Church. Essentially, Giulio took the titles and the revenues from the offices, but never com-pleted the required duties. Instead, he hired deputies to lead the faithful, thereby committing another abuse, *absenteeism*.

From 1517 on, Giulio also served his cousin Leo as vice chancellor of the pope, an office that put him second in command to his cousin. Throughout his entire life, Giulio had served his cousin as a faithful servant. Serious and responsible, he pro-vided a much needed complement to the fun-loving Leo X. His intelligence and talent for management made Giulio an excellent administrator. He had a mind for details and an ability to see both sides to every question. Although some cardinals disliked him personally, as one who lacked the friendly and easy-going manner of his cousin, Giulio managed to gain the respect of a majority of cardinals who appreciated his abilities.

When he gained the office of archbishop of Florence, in 1519, he moved to the city of his birth with a contingent of troops. Clothed in his scarlet robes, Cardinal Giulio was modest and accommodating as the unofficial ruler of the city. As an indication of his ability to forgive and forget past injuries, Giulio gave Niccolò Machiavelli the opportunity to submit a plan for a new constitution for the city of Florence and a position as official historian. Giulio also hired Francesco Guic-ciardini; another prominent statesman and scholar, as his lieutenant and governor for several cities under papal rule including Parma, Reggio, Modena, Piacenza, and Forlì. He would serve as an advisor to Giulio throughout the course of his career. Posterity remembers Guicciardini for his monumental history of the era, *History of Italy*, widely considered one of the most profound explorations of human motiva-tion ever written by a historian. Machiavelli and Guicciardini, having served as lawyers, diplomats, politicians, and historians, excelled at describing politics in a refreshingly realistic style. Their works convey the despair over the dramatic events that would ultimately destroy the liberty of their state and place the Italian peninsula under subjection to a foreign power.

The second Medici pope

In 1521, Leo X died of a sudden illness, or, as some suspected, poison. Giulio was in a good position to follow his cousin, but in 1522 the cardinals elected an outsider, Adrian VI, who had been the Dutch tutor of Charles V, Holy Roman Emperor but also king of Spain. A serious and pious man, the new pope had little interest in Italian politics or the arts. When Adrian died in September of 1523, few Italians mourned his death. Giulio again appeared to many as the obvious choice as successor. He had proven himself as a competent administrator and he also had the support of the Emperor. Moreover Giulio had presented himself as a leader. When Adrian was still alive and had called Giulio to leave Florence and come to Rome, the cardinal made a triumphal entry into the city in April of 1523. With over one thousand knights on horseback surrounding him, his arrival looked more like the triumph of a Roman general than the arrival of a religious figure.

Giulio was confirmed as pope in 1523 and took the papal name Clement, from clemency, the virtue of forgiving one's enemies. The Florentines were happy to see another of their fellow citizens claim the seat of St. Peter, expecting a shower of patronage for them individually and as a city. They were disappointed. Clement had to put the papal finances in order after the lavish spending spree of his cousin, Leo X. Taking his duties seriously, he worked to alleviate hunger by redistributing land from the noble families near Rome to small farmers and by creating a fund to provide money for economic investment. In terms of service to the poor, he proved himself a devout and committed pope.

Nevertheless, Clement's papacy seemed destined to result in tragedy, as dangers surrounded him on all sides. Within Europe, the new Lutheran movement continued to gain strength in the German lands. As Christian unity threatened to crumble from the inside, it also faced a major threat from the East. Suleiman the Magnificent, Sultan of the Ottoman Empire, expanded the borders of Islam into Eastern Europe. To face this threat, the pope tried to enlist all of the Christian princes to launch a crusade against the Turks, but Emperor Charles V, Francis I of France, and Henry VIII of England could not agree on who would lead the crusade. They continued to fight each other for hegemony in Europe.

Because Francis I of France and Charles V of Spain had the most powerful armies and largest sums of money, they dominated the political situation in Europe. Accordingly, the weaker powers, which included England, Venice, and the papacy, tried to angle for power by playing each state against the other one. In the end, though, victory would go to the army able to field the largest, most successful army. The weaker powers watched the battles and hedged their bets almost daily. Although Clement claimed neutrality among the princes, he found himself switching his allegiance back and forth, making treaties with one, then breaking it, then striking a new one with another. In the end, this made him seem increasingly indecisive, weak, and untrustworthy.

The fight for Italy

By the end of the 1520s, Charles V (1500–1558) made the conquest of the Italian peninsula the keystone of his global empire. A bizarre series of marriages and events positioned the young Charles V as the most powerful monarch in sixteenth-century Europe. As the grandson of Ferdinand and Isabella of Spain, he inherited the Spanish throne in 1516. Three years later, as the grandson of Holy Roman Emperor Maximilian I, he won the imperial election and was designated the new Holy Roman Emperor. The domains of his empire, which traced its origins to Charlemagne, included Spain, Austria, Burgundy, the Low Countries, and the German lands.

Raised as a feudal knight, Charles V's primary aims were limited to defending his honor and reputation as a Christian prince through military valor. However, his main advisor, the grand chancellor Mercurino di Gattinara, convinced him to aim for world domination. An Italian himself, Gattinara assured the emperor that God had prepared his way toward "universal monarchy." According to biblical prophecies, he claimed, Charles would united all of Christendom under his authority and then conquer the Holy Land from the Muslims. He would establish world peace by bringing all of the lands and peoples of the globe under his rule. In a propaganda campaign directed by Gattinara, Spanish pamphlets promised peace and prosperity to those submitting to the Spanish empire. Few in Europe took the grand chancellor's vision of world domination seriously, but then Spain suddenly found itself with more land and resources than anyone could have imagined. After Hernán Cortés had conquered the empire of Mexico in 1521 (as discussed later in this chapter), hundreds of ships laden with gold and silver began arriving back at the Spanish port of Seville. Aztec gold and silver provided the collateral for bank loans needed to pay for Charles's massive imperial armies.

The armies of France and Spain collided on February 24, 1525, at the battle of Pavia near Milan in northern Italy. Although King Francis I of France had bravely led his own troops into the battle, his army suffered a terrible defeat. The Spanish took the French king into captivity, and this spectacular victory gave Charles V a clear path toward the domination of the Italian peninsula.

Fearful of unchecked Spanish dominance in the peninsula, the remaining European powers soon united to form a defensive league. The League of Cognac included England, France, Venice, and Florence. Clement VII wavered on whether to join the league and betray his patron. In the end, however, Guicciardini convinced him to join the league and establish an alliance with France. At the time, France claimed to be the defender of the free states of Italy against an oppressive imperial power.

Clement VII also considered the interests of his family when he decided to ally with France. The Medici had been successful in contracting marriages with relatives of the French royal family. Leo X had married his nephew, Lorenzo (the Younger), to a high-ranking French noblewoman. Although he and his wife died of the plague in 1519, they left an orphaned daughter, Caterina. Raised with the Medici family in Florence, the Florentines called her the *duchessina* (little duchess), and Clement called her "a pearl beyond value." This was not only out of his fondness for her, but also because of her potential as a marriage pawn. Hopes for an advantageous marriage for Caterina possibly helped to push him toward making an alliance with the French king.

Meanwhile, the Spanish court, outraged by Clement VII's apparent betrayal, prepared for a full invasion of Italy. As Holy Roman Emperor with authority over the German lands, Charles V was able to recruit tens of thousands of *Landsknechts* (German infantrymen) to fight in Italy. With rather bizarre and colorful uniforms, these mercenaries were among the most fearsome in Europe. Many of these soldiers had converted to the Protestant faith, which made them heretics in the eyes of the Catholic court in Spain. Nevertheless, the advisors of Charles V were willing to overlook their religious dissent for the sake of the larger mission, the conquest of Italy.

High-ranking officials at the Spanish court had used religion as a tool to recruit these Protestant soldiers. They portrayed the fight for Italy as a holy war against a corrupt church and a renegade pope. According to widely published pamphlets, the emperor wanted this war only to establish a greater peace in Christendom. He promised to call a council of the church, where all Christians could discuss their differences and establish the "evangelical truth" of the faith. Naturally, Clement VII felt threatened by the ugly rhetoric aimed against him, and especially dreaded the convening of a church council. He feared it might reopen the issue of his illegitimate birth, which had had originally disqualified him from the holy office.

Clement VII trusted the armies of the League of Cognac to protect him from the Spanish threat. His calculation proved fatal, however, as Spanish armies, fortified now with Germans and even some Italian allies, moved down the peninsula with little opposition. The commander of this imperial army, Charles, Duke of Bourbon, had recently switched his allegiance from France to Spain. A close relative of the French royal family, Bourbon had betrayed his natural lord, Francis I, when Charles V had presented him with a generous bribe: his sister Eleanor in marriage, 200,000 ducats, and general command of the imperial armed forces.

As Bourbon led his army in the winter of 1527, he begged the Spanish king for money to pay his soldiers. No money came. Without pay, the soldiers had to make do by "living off the land," or forcing the inhabitants of villages and towns to give them food, shelter, and clothing as they marched south. In an age when people lived in the countryside on the edge of starvation, the already impoverished population often had no choice but to abandon their farms and towns to become wandering beggars. Bourbon next directed his starving army toward Rome, one of the oldest, richest, and most respected cities in the world, in search of food and plunder.

Many Italians viewed Rome as a sacred city, a New Jerusalem, and refused to think Christian soldiers would invade or pillage it as they had other Italian cities. As the army drew closer and the threat became more real, Clement grew fearful. When a fleet of imperial ships was spotted along the coast of Italy, he knew that he had been out-maneuvered. One advisor reported that the pope "sees nothing ahead but ruin, not just his own, which he cares for little, but that of the Apostolic See (papacy), of Rome, of his own country, and of the whole of Italy." An ambassador from Milan commented that the pope "seemed struck dead." Clement responded by turning to diplomacy. He wrote urgent letters to Francis I calling for help, but the French king simply ignored them. He then sent letters to another League member, Venice, for money to bribe the commanders. They too refused. Clement could not rely on the support of the leaders of smaller cities such as Urbino and Ferrara, as they had cast their lots with Spain. Indeed, many smaller states viewed an alliance with Spain as protection against the territorial ambitions of more powerful enemies. Resentment against the overbearing papacy, Florence, and the Medici were strong in many cities of Italy.

Desperate and afraid, Clement abruptly switched sides again. In January 1527 the pope hastily revoked his alliance with France and signed a treaty of alliance with Spain. Not long after, Clement learned of a minor Spanish defeat in the area around Rome. Panicked, he tore up the treaty with Spain and sent another letter—a plea to renew the alliance with France. The French king wrote back:

> For the love of God he [Clement VII] must keep up his courage, and meddle no more with truces or negotiations. To tell the truth, his incessant practice of making terms, his projects of flight, have kept me undecided and made me always afraid that I should lose my time and money[1].

Clement VII's lieutenant, Guicciardini, considered the pope's constant indecision a major fault of character. He noted that once he made a decision, Clement hesitated to follow through with it. Instead he thought about the lost opportunities caused by his chosen path. This had the effect of making him change course often or resist taking any firm action, as though he were paralyzed by his own intelligence.

In a last-minute effort to halt Bourbon's imperial army as it headed toward Rome, Clement signed a truce with Spain. Among other stipulations, it required a payment of 150,000 ducats and the disbanding of the pope's mercenary troops. The Spanish emissary promised the pope that the agreement would stop Bourbon's army, but it was ultimately a scam. In reality, the emissary and Bourbon were acting in collusion to extort even more money from Clement. Bourbon had no intention of halting the march to Rome, because he had promised his soldiers all of the plunder they could take from a rich and opulent city.

That fateful decision to make a truce with Spain left the city of Rome without any professional soldiers to defend it. Instead, the pope appointed a local commander to train a citizen militia, enlisting about 10,000 men to defend the city. He asked the richest inhabitants of the city to contribute to the war effort. Despite their millions, few contributed more than a few hundreds of ducats. Believing that they would need money to bribe their way out of a military occupation, they buried their gold and silver in the ground. Stashes of money hid in this way were found even up until the eighteenth century.

The sack of Rome

On Holy Thursday, 18 April, 1527, just as Clement was giving his blessing to a crowd of thousands at St. Peter's Cathedral, the voice of Brandano, a wondering street preacher, broke the silence. Skin and bones, with long shaggy hair, and wearing nothing but a leather apron, he shouted, "Bastard, sodomite, because of your sins Rome will be destroyed. Confess and mend your ways. If you do not believe this, wait and see in two weeks' time." In the years leading up to the sack, astrologers had predicted the destruction of Rome, and several omens seem to foretell disaster. For example, in the days leading up to the sack, lightning struck the Vatican and a calf had been born with two heads.

As the imperial armies gathered and surrounded the city, the Romans put faith in their ancient fortifications. Built in 271 CE, the ramparts were over 10 meters high and four meters thick. On May 6, the Duke of Bourbon led the assault himself by scaling the Roman walls, but a bullet from an arquebus killed him before he could enter the city. Nevertheless, Bourbon's death did not stop his soldiers, who continued to scale the walls with tall ladders, and chip away at the city's defenses with pick axes. As the fortifications failed, imperial soldiers streamed into the city. The Roman defensive commander quickly abandoned his position and urged his fellow soldiers to retreat and save themselves.

With no one to stop them, the Spanish, German, and Italian soldiers of the imperial army put the city to the sack. Clement had spent the entire morning in his chapel saying mass, but with danger rapidly approaching, he took the passageway from the Vatican to the Castel Sant' Angelo, a round, imposing fortress that had originally served as the tomb of the emperor Hadrian. Disguised in the purple robes of a bishop, Clement safely reached the castle to find that almost three thousand refugees had already sought shelter there, including most of the cardinals and other high-ranking church officials.

Protected by soldiers armed with heavy artillery, the clergymen within the castle found safety. It was their unhappy fate, however, to gaze down and witness helplessly as those on the outside faced death and destruction on an unimaginable scale. As he manned the cannons defending the castle, the goldsmith and autobiographer, Benvenuto Cellini, gave a horrifying account of the scene:

> I went up to some guns that were in charge of a bombardier called Giuliano the Florentine. He was staring out over the battlements to where his poor house was being sacked and his wife and children outraged. He dared not fire in case he harmed his own family, and flinging the fuse on the ground he started tearing at his face and sobbing bitterly. Other bombardiers were doing the same.[2]

Shouting "Empire! Spain! Victory!" the imperial soldiers looted, burned, and slaughtered. For several months commanders had promised their marching soldiers all they could plunder from a city renowned for its wealth and luxury. After 6 May, without effective military commanders to stop them, the soldiers went through the city at will, extracting wealth from the citizens by any means available. Everywhere, the soldiers demanded ransoms from their victims, and killed any who could not pay whatever amount the soldiers ordered.

Knowing that many Romans had buried their money, soldiers often used torture to force their victims to reveal their hiding places. Witnesses recounted several tactics including beating, and ropes to suspend people, either by their feet or genitals. In some of the most terrifying accounts, the soldiers cut their victims with red hot irons, or forced them to eat their own ears, noses, or roasted testicles. Soldiers forced parents to pay ransoms for the corpses of their tortured children.

Roman women of all ages and conditions endured shocking and lamentable sexual assaults. Although rape had been an expected part of any successful siege, standard military protocol limited the amount of time an army could rape and pillage, usually to three days. With the death of the Duke of Bourbon and without clear direction, no one could enforce military discipline, and the rape of Roman women continued for months. Soldiers sold nuns in the streets as sex slaves and converted convents and palaces into brothels.

The Lutherans among the German soldiers added sacrilege to the robbery, rape, and murder. Without any respect for traditions of the Catholic Church not based on scriptural authority, Protestants destroyed statues and paintings of the Virgin Mary, melted down reliquaries, scattered the sacred bones of saints, and exhumed the bodies of the previous popes. Looking for rings and other valuable items, they left the exposed corpses to rot and spread disease. Although the treasured manuscripts of the Vatican Library survived, soldiers throughout the city burned books, libraries, and precious works of art for their own amusement.

Many of the invaders viewed Rome as a polluted swamp of corruption, or a "new Babylon," and that perspective appeared to justify treating its residents as sub-humans. By committing these atrocities, they believed they were acting as the agents of God's will by punishing a corrupt church and its supporters. One Spanish witness explained this attitude in his description of the city: "The streets are changed into dunghills, the stench of dead bodies is terrible, men and beasts have a common grave and in the churches I have seen corpses that dogs have gnawed." Nevertheless, he justified the situation: "In Rome all sins are openly committed—sodomy, simony, idolatry, hypocrisy, fraud. Well may we believe, then, that what has come to pass has not been by chance but by the judgment of God."

As Clement looked over the death and destruction from the fortress of Sant'Angelo, he raised his hands to the sky and cried to God in Latin, *Quare de vulva eduxisti me?* (Why did you lead me out of the womb?). The castle had guns and cannon for its defense, but food soon became scarce. The guards did not permit anyone to give aid to the prisoners. When an old woman tried to bring the pope the gift of a basket of lettuce, she was strangled to death by an imperial soldier. The pope, priests, diplomats, and officials kept prisoner in the castle waited for relief from the army of the League of Cognac. It never came. As lieutenant, Guicciardini urged the commander of the League to rescue Rome, but his pleas failed to move him. As Duke of Urbino, he held a longstanding grudge against the Medici family and refused to engage his army. Despite reports of atrocities coming out from Rome in the weeks after the invasion, there would be no hope from the League, Venice, or France. Clement was left at the mercy of the Spanish emperor who held him captive.

The Spanish demanded 400,000 ducats to end the occupation, but the treasury of the church had been largely depleted. Although Clement detested the practice of simony, the sale of church offices for money, he had begun to offer the office of cardinal for ready cash. When this failed to raise enough, he had the goldsmith Cellini construct a huge cauldron to melt down the treasures of the church including gold and silver chalices, staffs, and other liturgical items. He even melted down his own papal tiara, although he removed the jewels from it beforehand and hid them in case he might need them in the future.

As spring turned to summer, the piles of dead bodies brought a disgusting stench and terrible disease. Many soldiers retreated from the city, but they came back to sack the city again in September. The pope was forced to sign a punishing treaty with Spain in November, but he still remained a prisoner. Clement, once an attractive and vigorous young man, had become a skeleton with shaking hands, a long white beard, and a dull empty stare. At last, with the help of some sympathetic imperial commanders, the pope escaped the Castel Sant' Angelo in the dead of night, 7 December, 1527, disguised as the head servant of his household. Troops under the imperial commander, Luigi Gonzaga, escorted him from the fields outside of Rome to the city of Orvieto. In an old, decaying, bishop's palace with a roof that was caving in, Clement set up his court. By February, he had found enough money, 40,000 ducats, to bribe the imperial soldiers to leave Rome and attack the French army in Naples. After nine months, the occupation officially ended. Very slowly, the city started to rebuild.

Recovery

Newly released from captivity in Rome, Clement again sought a way to place his family firmly back in control of Florence. In 1527, upon hearing reports from the sack of Rome, the city had once again revolted against their Medici overlords and re-established their republic on more democratic foundations. The exiled Medici family would not be able to defeat the new government and rule the city as a dynasty without the help of a powerful army. True to his name, Clement quickly forgave the atrocities committed by the Spanish troops in Rome and made an agreement with Charles V. In 1529, Clement signed the Treaty of Barcelona that created an alliance between Spain and the Catholic Church and the treaty gave Charles V effective domination over much of the Italian peninsula. In exchange, Clement VII gained the emperor's support for the establishment of a Medici dynasty in Florence.

The citizens of Florence prepared to resist the Medici and their imperial allies and fight for their liberty. Ironically, Michelangelo designed the fortifications that defended the republic against the Medici, even though Clement had been one of his oldest and dearest friends. As leverage against attack, the Florentines held Clement's niece, the little duchess Caterina de Medici, as a hostage. Some extremists in the government even suggested subjecting the 11-year-old to a variety of horrors that included lodging the girl in a soldiers' brothel or hanging her naked on the outside of the city walls as target practice for the imperial army. Fortunately, Caterina remained sheltered safely in a convent. After a brutal siege, when starvation eventually caused the city to surrender the republic, city leaders put themselves at the mercy of the emperor and pope.

In 1532, the Medici dismantled the republican government of Florence once and for all and established a hereditary monarchy. The first duke would be Alessandro de' Medici, the half-brother of Caterina de' Medici and the nephew of Clement VII. Although he had been born the illegitimate son of an African servant or slave who had worked in the Medici household, Alessandro's mixed race did not hinder his promotion to head of the family. Rumors, but no strong evidence, suggested that his father was Clement VII himself. Alessandro married Margaret of Parma, the illegitimate daughter of Charles V, and by agreement with the emperor, their children, if they had any, would rule Florence as a hereditary dynasty.

FIGURE 4.2 Pontormo, *Portrait of Alessandro de Medici*, 1534–1535. Although contemporaries referred to Alessandro as the nephew of Clement VII, many suspected that he was his son. He became the first duke of Florence.

Source: Hulton Fine Art Collection/Getty Images

Caterina de' Medici, the little duchess, survived a traumatic childhood to emerge as a major figure in sixteenth-century history. In 1534, Clement secured a crowning victory for his family when he negotiated her marriage at fourteen to the second son of Francis I of France. When her husband, Henry II, acceded the throne in 1547, she became queen of France. Known in France as Catherine de Medici, she gave birth to three French kings and ruled the country as queen regent for several decades, playing a major role in the French Wars of Religion (described in Chapter 1). By arranging this marriage, Clement had completed the gradual elevation of the Medici family from middle-class bankers to French royalty.

Clement VII died of illness in 1534. In the office of pope, he proved ineffective in many respects. After the sack of Rome, his greatest defeat came when Henry VIII of England broke away from the Catholic Church. Bound to the interests of Charles V, Clement refused to grant Henry an annulment from his marriage to Catherine of Aragon, the aunt of the emperor. As a result, Henry VIII declared England independent, and placed himself at the head of a new church, the Church of England, or the Anglican Church, in 1534. During his term of office, large regions of Western Europe had turned to the Protestant faith, never to return to Catholicism. The religious split led to 150 years of civil war in Europe.

Giulio de' Medici had a variety of leadership abilities, but they did not prove to be the ones he needed in his difficult circumstances. Instead, he appeared to be the victim of larger, uncontrollable forces. As Pope Clement VII, he witnessed the devastation and foreign domination of his homeland, as well as the departure of England from the Catholic Church. However, Giulio's life did not ultimately end in failure. The ever-dutiful nephew, cousin, uncle, and family patriarch finally succeeded in establishing his relatives as rulers over Florence, and linking the Medici dynasty to royalty. In this respect, by putting family first, Giulio de' Medici succeeded on his own terms.

Chronology

1478   Assassination of Giulio de' Medici's father, Giuliano de' Medici. Birth of Giulio de' Medici.

1492   Death of Lorenzo de' Medici, "The Magnificent."

1494   French Invasion of Italy. Beginning of the Italian Wars 1494–1559.

1512   Medici take over the Republic of Florence with help of Spanish soldiers.

1513   Giovanni de' Medici becomes Pope Leo X.

1523   Giulio de' Medici becomes Pope Clement VII.

1527   Sack of Rome by imperial army.

1529   Treaty of Barcelona between Spain and papacy. Florence given to the Medici family.

1530   Siege of Florence.

1532   End of the Florentine Republic. Alessandro de' Medici, nephew of Clement VII, becomes the first duke of Florence.

1534   Catherine de' Medici marries the future Henry II of France. Death of Clement VII.

Sources for further reading about Clement VII

The classic account of the history of Italy during the term of Clement VII is written by Clement VII's advisor and lieutenant, Francesco Guicciardini, *The History of Italy: Sidney Alexander, ed. and trans.* (Princeton, NJ: Princeton University Press, 1969). The dense, dry account of battles, massacres, and complex diplomatic negotiations is actually a profound meditation on human agency and fate. The work provides a negative perspective on Clement VII, who is blamed for the disasters which befell Italy. A true biography of Clement VII in English does not yet exist, but a detailed account of his papacy is in the multi-volume set by Ludwig Pastor, *A History of the Popes from the Close of the Middle Ages*, trans. Ralph Kerr (London: Kegan Paul, Trench, Trübner & Co., 1910). A more recent work is a collection of scholarly essays that emphasize more positive aspects of his papacy. Sheryl Riess and Kenneth Gouwens, eds., *The Pontificate of Clement VII: History, Politics, Culture* (London: Routledge, 2005). Clement VII and his role in the Medici takeover of Florence is well documented in J. R. Hale, *Florence and the Medici: The Pattern of Control* (London: Thames & Hudson, 1977). The assassination of Giuliano and its impact on Florentine politics is covered in Lauro Martines, *April Blood: Florence and the Plot against the Medici* (Oxford: Oxford University Press, 2003). Marcello Simonetta provides a lively narrative of the complex intrigue that led to the Pazzi Conspiracy in *The Montefeltro Conspiracy* (New York: Doubleday, 2008). Lorenzo de Medici's consolidation of power is discussed in Melissa Bullard, *Lorenzo Il Magnifico: Image and Anxiety, Politics and Finance* (Florence: Leo S. Olschki, 1994). The sack of Rome in 1527 is covered in Judith Hook, *The Sack of Rome 1527* (New York: Palgrave Macmillan, 2004). From the standpoint of art history, there is André Chastel, *The Sack of Rome, 1527*, trans. Beth Archer (Princeton, NJ: Princeton University Press, 1983). More recently, Kenneth Gouwens has provided a study of literary perspectives on the sack in *Remembering the Renaissance: Humanist Narratives on the Sack of Rome* (Leiden: Brill, 1998). A good, readable popular history of the Medici and Florence is Christopher Hibbert, *The House of Medici: Its Rise and Fall* (New York: William Morrow & Company, 1975). A new study of Alessandro de Medici is Catherine Fletcher, *The Black Prince of Florence: The Spectacular Life and Treacherous World of Alessandro de' Medici* (Oxford: Oxford University Press, 2016).

Moctezuma II (1466–1520)

Moctezuma II ruled as the ninth emperor of Mexico when Europeans first arrived on the continent of North America. Under his rule, the boundaries of the Mexican, or Aztec, Empire expanded to their greatest extent. Trained from childhood as a warrior and priest, he wielded absolute authority over his people. Nevertheless, the Spanish invasion and the revolution it sparked toppled his regime. His untimely death spared him the misfortune of witnessing the destruction of his empire at the

FIGURE 4.3   Antonio Rodriguez, *Portrait of Moctezuma II*, c. 1680. Painted in New Spain over a century after Moctezuma's death, this unusual portrait reveals an interesting blend of European and indigenous influences. The depiction of the ruler's face and body reflect a classical European approach to beauty, while the adornment, which appears to be authentic and well-researched, provides a traditional image of Aztec rulership.

hands of the Spanish Conquistadors. After his death, however, a new society evolved as the Mexica people maintained their heritage under Spanish rule.

The Mexica

Sometime between 30,000 BCE and 10,000 BCE, a small group of people migrated from Asia into North America by way of a land bridge that connected the two continents. By 1500 CE, the descendants of these tribes, numbering in the hundreds of millions, had settled throughout all of North and South America. When Europeans first arrived in the Americas in the early sixteenth century, they encountered two complex and powerful empires. The Aztecs dominated Central America from the Pacific Ocean to the Yucatan peninsula, while the Incas ruled from the Andes Mountains to the Pacific along the western coast of South America.

The tribe of people who founded the Aztec civilization called themselves the Mexica. According to legend, they wandered as nomads from a mythical place in the north called Aztlan, meaning "the place of the white feathered heron." By the fourteenth century they had settled in Central America, where a high mountain ridge surrounded a large plateau. Although close to the equator, the high altitude of the plateau provided a temperate climate, with predictable rainfall and fertile soil. Massive irrigation projects led to the rise of many ancient civilizations in the same region over the course of millennia, and ruins of ancient cities with grand and mysterious temples scattered the plateau. The remains of one city, deserted for centuries before the arrival of the Mexica, contained enormous pyramids, wide streets, and stately apartments painted with beautiful frescoes. Local people called it Teotihuican, or "city of the gods," because they imagined that gods had built it. The ruins of a glorious past provided inspiration for the present, but they also served as a reminder that civilizations, no matter how grand, both rise and fall.

The history of the Mexica, long chronicled in pictographic books and oral traditions, was put into writing shortly after the Spanish conquest in the sixteenth century. Written in Nahua (the language of the Mexica) and Spanish, these accounts described the astonishing rise of outsiders to imperial domination over the course of two centuries. In the 1300s, the Toltec kingdom controlled the region surrounding the great lake Texcoco in the middle of the Central American plateau. Although they worshipped many gods, the Toltecs felt a special bond with a feathered serpent god named Quetzalcoatl, who had brought songs, books, and other aspects of civilization to the people. When the Mexica tried to settle in the region, the Toltecs looked down on the newly arrived nomadic tribespeople as aggressive and uncivilized barbarians. Whereas the Toltecs revered a peaceful god of culture and knowledge, the Mexica followed their violent war god, Huitzilopochtli, who often took the form of a blue hummingbird.

The Mexica had gathered strength in their settlements near Culhuacan, the capital city of the Toltecs. Grudgingly, the Toltecs granted the newcomers some of their territory: a rocky region infested with snakes. They hoped the snakes would eat them, but instead the Mexica ate the snakes and grew stronger.

Seeking prestige and greater status in the region, the Mexica started to inter-marry with the Toltecs. In 1323, the newcomers had gained enough strength to marry into the royal family. According to legend, Huitzilopochtli told the Mexica leaders to ask the king of the Toltecs for his virgin daughter. Obeying their patron god, the leaders told the king that they wanted to bring the princess into their set-tlement so that they could worship her as a living goddess. The king granted their wish, and a few days later the Mexica invited him to their temple in order to wor-ship her. Thick smoke filled the air of the temple as the old Toltec king sacrificed a quail to the image of his daughter. However, as the smoke disappeared, he could see clearly that the vision was not his daughter, but instead a priest wearing the skin of the dead princess. They had sacrificed and flayed the girl. The grieving king declared war against the Mexica and pushed them into the marshes of the great lake Texcoco.

On an island in the middle of the lake the wandering tribe saw a sign from the gods. An eagle perched atop a prickly pear cactus held a snake in its mouth. The Mexica understood this as proof that the gods intended this island to be their homeland. They dredged the lake and built a city connected to the mainland by three wide causeways. Tenochtitlan, their capital, grew to hold at least 200,000 people. At first the Mexica paid tribute to the surrounding states and served as mercenary soldiers. However, by 1468 they had used their superior skills as warri-ors to demand tribute from others. As their empire grew, a massive influx of goods entered Tenochtitlan including gold, jewels, crystal, feathers, cacao beans, embroi-dered cloth, furniture, caged animals, and fruits and vegetables of all kinds. The powerful Mexica began to refer to themselves as the people of the sun.

Religion, empire, and human sacrifice

In the traditional religion of the Mexica, human blood had life-giving properties. One ancient myth held that four previous ages of man existed before the current age. The present world (the fifth age) began when Quetzalcoatl took and ground up the bones of the old generations and gathered them into a bowl. To give them new life, he slashed his penis with a sharp blade and drizzled the life-giving blood over the bones. When the mixture came to life he provided it with a perfect form of food: maize, or corn. Traditional beliefs required that the sacrifices made by gods for humanity had to be reciprocated with similar offerings made by humans to the gods.

The Aztec calendar provided another justification for human sacrifice. Combin-ing the calculations of the orbit of the planet Venus with those of the sun and moon, it organized time as a series of fifty-two-year cycles. At the beginning of each cycle the Mexica celebrated a New Fire Ceremony, which reenacted the creation of the world. With each new cycle, or "bundle of years," a burst of energy enabled the sun to rise and the rain to fall. However, this source of energy declined with every year that passed. Human sacrifice was a way to fortify the universe with the energy found in human life. For this reason, priests sought out the most vigorous victims in the form of young, strong, warriors. Other gods required different kinds of victims such as young maidens. Most chillingly, sacrifices made for the rain god, Tlaloc, required the lives of young children. The tears that fell during the sacrifice insured sufficient rain for the crops.

Although the Mexica believed that the rituals of human sacrifice reenacted their religious myths and insured the rising of the sun each day, they also served a political purpose. Even after the surrounding lands had submitted to Mexica authority, they were not entirely at peace. Emperors declared "flower wars," or wars waged specifically for the purpose of capturing warriors for human sacrifice. Placed in cages for days or even weeks to "fatten up," the captives awaited the public ceremony. On the day they were to be sacrificed, priests took the victims up the steps of the temple of Huizlopochtl, the grand pyramid in the heart of Tenochtitlan. As four men stretched the victim over a large stone slab holding each arm and leg, the high priest sawed through the sternum of the victim with an obsidian blade. His hair knotted by clumps of clotted human blood, the priest then reached into the chest cavity to pull out the still palpitating heart as an offering to the gods. Afterward, the body was tossed down the bloodied steps of the pyramid to the crowd below. The limbs of the victim became the meat in stews, or *mole*, that the Aztecs flavored with peppers and chocolate. Perhaps an average of over 20,000 people died as human sacrifices each year in Mexico. The flower wars enabled the empire to keep its subjects in a state of fear.

Nevertheless, the Mexica did not build an empire over the other Mesoamerican states by blood alone. They provided incentives for the elites of the older, more established cities such as Tepanecs and Culhuacan. The Mexica married their elite with the aristocracy of these older cities. From these marriages emerged a noble caste, the *pipiltin*, which distinguished itself from the commoners, or *macehualtin*. The *pipiltin* carried out offices in the priesthood, administration, justice, education, and the army. They made up around twenty percent of the population of the Mexica Empire. As in Europe, books carefully recorded the lineages of the members of the nobility.

The common people, those who served the *pipiltin*, also enjoyed some benefits of empire. The artisans earned a living by supplying the elites with a variety of expensive luxury goods, such as feather arts. Woven into tapestries, textiles, and elaborate headdresses, feathers held the greatest value among the Mexica. Many commoners in the middle ranks of society also enjoyed a certain peace and prosperity that favored trade in the bustling markets. At the bottom of society, the poor field hands often had to sell themselves or their family members into slavery to avoid starvation. The Mexica sold slaves at their markets as any other commodity.

A strong emperor

Moctezuma Xocoyotzin, or Moctezuma the Younger, acceded to the throne after the death of his uncle, Ahuizotl. Born into the royal family, Moctezuma prepared from childhood for a life as a priest and warrior. He learned how to read books in the manner of the Aztecs, which required the memorization of both symbols and pictures. At his school, the sons of noble families were trained to endure great hardships, much like the ancient Spartans. Serving as a soldier in his youth, he gained recognition for his capture of enemy warriors destined for sacrifice. Simultaneously, he studied religion and joined the priesthood in his early twenties.

When it came time for him to marry, Moctezuma followed the tradition of his family and married a Toltec princess. Poets described the Lady Tezalco as the "gliding jewel" of the palace. The marriage was the occasion of a great festival with gifts of finely embroidered clothes, jewels, and feather work. Older guests enjoyed a frothy bowl of *pulque*, a milky white alcoholic beverage made by fermented agave sap. The servants of the palace worked for days preparing turkey with *mole* sauce, corn, tamales, and tortillas. On the day of the wedding, Moctezuma sat on special mats in the middle of a grand hall surrounded by nobles. His uncle, the emperor Ahuitzotl, watched the ceremony from his turquoise throne. A procession of young women with torches came in the room to the sound of flutes, rattles, and horns. Behind them a large woman carried on her back a bundle wrapped in white linen. As she approached the prince, she kneeled and untied the cloth so that the bride Tezalco fell to the floor. Her face painted yellow with two red flowers on her cheeks, she wore golden earrings and a jade nose ring. To symbolize their union, bride and groom sat with their capes tied together. After three days the couple consummated the marriage. The cloth upon which they had sexual intercourse was displayed at the feast that evening as a proof of the bride's virginity. Publically declared husband and wife, they plowed and sowed a few hills of corn to symbolize the fertility of their union.

After many successful war expeditions, around the age of 30, he was appointed commander and chief of the army. His fortunes rose even higher as he built a number of palaces and sat on the emperor's high council. At this time his wife gave birth to her first child, a daughter named Tecuichpo. Although Moctezuma had numerous wives, mistresses, and children, Tezalco remained his principal wife, and Tecuichpo, as first daughter, maintained a privileged position in the family. When his uncle Ahuitzotl died, the royal council elected Moctezuma to the position of emperor, or *tlahtoani*. The dignitaries charged with giving him the news found the prince in his private room in the temple of Huitzilopochtli, where he often went for meditation and quiet study. He acceded to the throne in the year Ten Rabbit (1502). At his coronation, he accepted the royal cloak and turquoise crown. He then used the sharpened bones of a jaguar and eagle to draw blood from his ears, arms, and legs. As emperor he promised to defend the gods and nourish the sun with human blood.

The modest, valiant, and wise 34-year-old proved to be an effective leader. Under his rule, the empire expanded to its greatest extent. He waged war aggressively, engaging his army in campaigns that stretched from the Atlantic to the Pacific Ocean, over 150,000 square miles. However, history remembers him differently, as the primary victim in the conquest that would put an end to his rule and transform his civilization.

The Spanish path to Tenochtitlan

In the year Twelve House (1509), a comet appeared in the sky with a tail like "a flame or tongue of fire." It rose in the east, climbed to the middle of the sky, and stayed the whole year. Witnesses recounted other unusual events: a thunderbolt hit the temple of Huitzilopochtli, though unaccompanied by rain, Lake Texcoco started to boil, and several people heard the mysterious sounds of a woman wailing and weeping, "O my children, we are about to go forever." Such omens seemed to foretell the coming of the Europeans.

Although Vikings had reached North America in the tenth century, lasting and meaningful contact between the western and eastern hemispheres began when ships commanded by Christopher Columbus landed in the Bahamas in 1492. The explorer sailed around the islands of the Caribbean, believing them to be islands off of the coast of Asia, but he never set foot on the mainland. Shortly afterward, explorers, soldiers, and adventurers seeking fortune in the New World began to settle the islands and establish control over their inhabitants. In those early years, the continents of North and South America remained unknown to the Europeans.

Hernán Cortés (1485–1547) was one of many who sought his fortune in the New World. Born into a poor but noble family in Medellìn, Spain, he studied law at the University of Salamanca. After two years the restless youth abandoned his books to take up arms and the life of a soldier. Although he considered joining the Spanish army in Italy, he decided to venture overseas to America. He settled in Cuba, where he married, managed a farm, and eventually held the office of mayor in the town of Santiago. His life took another radical turn when explorers came back from Yucatan peninsula with stories of cities of gold. Having secured an authorization from Diego Velásquez, governor of Cuba, to make an expedition to the mainland of North America, he gathered ships, provisions, and men. He put all the money he had into the expedition, and bought the rest on credit. The governor and other volunteers also made contributions. With eleven ships, around five hundred men, and sixteen horses, Cortés left Cuba in the early part of 1519. Although his official commission was limited to exploration and bartering for gold with the local inhabitants, Cortés most likely had larger plans in mind.

Upon landing on the island of Cozumel, he searched for translators to communicate with the local tribes. He found Jerònimo de Aguilar, a Spaniard who had been shipwrecked off the coast of Jamaica. Enslaved by Mayans, he wore cropped hair, a loincloth, and a cape. Aguilar broke into tears of joy when he saw Cortés and his men, and asked "Is it Wednesday?" For fifteen years he prayed for rescue, keeping a small book of prayers with him always in his cape in which he had kept track of the days. The rescued Spaniard told the story of his companion, the only other survivor of the shipwreck. His life had taken another path, having married a Mayan woman with whom he had three sons. Adopting the local culture, this Spaniard had tattooed his face and wore a lip stud. His whole village honored him as a fierce Mayan warrior, and he had no interest in returning to the Spanish way of life.

Cortés left Cozumel with Aguilar as his Mayan translator. In the Yucatan he found a second translator who spoke Nahuatl, the language of the Mexica. This was Malinche, an adolescent girl. The daughter of a local *cacique*, or ruler, she had been born a princess. When her father died, however, Malinche's mother remarried and had a son. Wanting her son to inherit the crown in place of her daughter, the mother plotted to get rid of her. She found the corpse of a young girl and buried it, claiming that it was Malinche. Meanwhile, her mother secretly sold the princess into slavery to a Mayan lord. Several years later, the same Mayan lord made a peace agreement with Cortés, giving him twenty female slaves as an offering. Malinche was among them. Cortés gave the girl to his closest friend as a reward for his loyalty.

Malinche soon converted to Christianity and took the name Doña Marina. Contemporaries described her as attractive, bright, and self-confident. She wore the garments of a Mexica noblewoman. Speaking Nahuatl, Maya, and Spanish, she had a profound understanding of the many cultures of Mesoamerica. When her master returned to Spain, Cortés kept her as his own. She became his most important advisor, diplomat, nurse, and lover throughout the conquest. By all accounts, her help was indispensable to the conquest.

Landing on the mainland of Mexico, about 250 miles east of Tenochtitlan, Cortés sent a party ashore to explore the terrain. They found some evacuated towns with large pyramids. As they wandered into the blood-splattered temples, they first encountered the corpses of sacrificial victims: open chested torsos without heads or limbs. They had known tribes that had performed sacrifices and even cannibalism in the Caribbean, but they had never seen it practiced on such a large scale.

Meanwhile, Aztec spies who had seen the fleet of ships reported back to Moctezuma. From their perspective, the ships resembled mountains or moving houses with giant white wings. Although some of the men had faces the color of limestone with yellow-reddish hair, others had dark skin and tightly curled black hair. When the men rode what looked like deer, with armored steel that glistened in the sun, they looked like a single animal. Stranger even still to the messengers were the huge and ferocious Spanish war dogs with "eyes like coals, yellow and fiery." They went about panting with their tongues hanging down, with spots like a jaguar. Compared to the only dog domesticated in Mexico, the Chihuahua, the Spanish bullmastiffs seemed like demons. Most frightening of all, the invaders had sticks that made the sound of thunder. The Mexica had never seen guns or cannon.

Moctezuma sent imperial ambassadors to meet the Spaniards docked on the coast of Mexico. The Aztec embassy met the Spanish captain on his anchored ship. Both sides treated each other with cordiality and respect. Cortés asked the Mexica if they were subjects of Moctezuma. Looking perplexed, one ambassador replied, "Who isn't?" They believed their emperor was lord of all the world.

Over the next few days, the ambassadors brought food for the Spanish: white tortillas, poultry, and fruit. They also brought precious gifts: a turquoise serpent mask, a quetzal feather headdress, and a chest containing finely worked gold items such as ear and lip plugs in the shape of animals. According to one legend, Cortés asked if their master had any more gold. He explained, "We Spanish have a disease of the heart that can only be cured with gold."

The explorer talked to the Aztecs about the emperor Charles V and the Christian religion. He showed them images of a young woman with a baby, and a man extended on a cross. Despite an outwardly friendly demeanor, he put Moctezuma's men in chains while his soldiers fired a cannon at a tree. It disappeared as if by magic. He sewed bells to the breastplates of his horses and had them gallop across the shore. After such dramatic and frightening displays, Cortés sent the ambassadors back with gifts: a richly carved chair with inlaid precious stones, a red velvet cap, a chalice, and some glass beads. The envoys asked to take one of the iron helmets worn by the soldiers. Cortés agreed, and asked them to send it back, if possible, full of gold.

When the ambassadors reported back to Moctezuma, the emperor had them sprinkled with the blood of two sacrificed warriors. This provided a ritual cleansing in case the unusual visitors were gods. According to native accounts, the news about the strangers pained him greatly, as though chili peppers had burned his heart. Apparently sinking into a depression, the emperor no longer ate, drank, or took delight in his usual activities. He devised another strategy to turn back the invaders. This time, instead of sending ambassadors, Moctezuma sent out conjurers, soothsayers, and witches, hoping to counteract the strange "magic" of the Spaniards.

This second group of messengers presented the Spanish with a great feast. The sight of the food greatly pleased the Europeans until the priests drizzled human blood over it. This turned their stomachs, as they grew nauseous from the bloody stench. Although the messengers cast spells and tried to repel the invaders with their magic, it had not worked. The group returned to Moctezuma with the news that his magic had no effect on the strangers. At this point, the emperor gave the orders to treat the Spanish as guests.

In some accounts, Moctezuma considered the Spaniards gods. He viewed Cortés, in particular, as the human incarnation of Quetzalcoatl, the god of the Toltecs who had come back to claim his throne from the Mexica. Nahua sources recounted the predictions of Quetzalcoatl arrival in the year named "One Reed." They said he would come from the east, out of the water, and have white skin. Perhaps also, Malinche, familiar with the Nahua religious beliefs, encouraged Cortés to dress in black velvet (as a god), and to hold back his landing to the first day of the year One Reed. Some historians doubt that Moctezuma believed that the Conquistador was a god, claiming that the prophecies of Quetzalcoatl might have been invented well after the conquest to provide legitimation for the Spanish takeover after the fact. Whether or not Moctezuma really thought of Cortés as Quetzalcoatl, he did appear to treat the Spanish as divine. As they made their way further inland, he offered little resistance.

On 28 June, 1519, Cortés officially founded a city, Vera Cruz, on the coastline of Mexico. Although the conquistador established the city under the jurisdiction of Emperor Charles V, he had no legal authority to do so. Nevertheless, he built an altar and a fortress, while a majority of his men elected him captain and chief justice of the expedition. Shortly thereafter, largely in response to threats of mutiny and desertion, Cortés beached and disabled most of his ships. He assured the stranded men that "they would conquer and win the land, or die in the attempt." Leaving around 150 men in Vera Cruz, the captain took the rest with him farther inland. Along the way, he met the subjects of Moctezuma's vast empire. He learned that many of them felt oppressed by the need to supply tribute, especially in the form of human sacrifices. He found subjects willing to ally with him in order to defeat their Aztec overlords. Before long, he had added hundreds of native soldiers to his small army. From these local allies, he learned that the main rival to the Mexica was Tlaxcala, and independent republic close to Tenochtitlan.

As in sixteenth-century Italy, the city-states of Mexico had long histories of local resentments. Moctezuma's envoys called the Tlaxcalans lying traitors and had advised Cortés against trusting them. Venturing into their capital city would be a mistake, they warned, as the Tlaxcalans intended to trap and kill them. Cortés dismissed the warning, stating that if he were attacked in the city, he would fight and win, whether night or day, in the fields or in the city, or in any way the opportunity for battle presented itself. The captain recognized the discord between Mexico and Tlaxcala as an opportunity. Writing to Emperor Charles V about the situation, he quoted the biblical passage, "Every kingdom divided against itself is brought to desolation." Dissention among the Mesoamericans cities aided his strategy to divide and conquer.

The Spanish and their allies made their way up the snowy mountains that surrounded the Mexican plateau. Whereas the weather in the tropical regions of the coast had been hot and humid, now they faced bitter cold. They marched through miles of corn and agave plantations searching for Tlaxcala.

Important allies

The first Spanish encounter with the Tlaxcalans was on the battlefield. The three hundred or so Spanish soldiers found themselves surrounded and greatly outnumbered in three brutal engagements. The conquistadors had iron swords and crossbows, whereas their enemy only had slingshots with stones, bows and arrows, and javelins. The native warriors also fought with *macuahuitl*, wooden clubs studded with obsidian blades that were sharp enough to sever a horse's head with one blow. After serious hand to hand combat with heavy casualties on both sides, Cortés managed to chase the Tlaxcalan army away with his cavalry. The Spanish then retreated to an abandoned village to tend to their numerous wounded men. They dressed their wounds with the fat of a dead Tlaxcalan they had cut open for this purpose. For food, they cooked the dogs they found in the houses. Although the villagers had taken their dogs with them as they evacuated, they had returned to their homes in the night.

Fearless and resolute, Malinche served as a nurse for the wounded soldiers and helped to build the morale of the Spanish army. According to Bernal Dìaz (a soldier of Cortés who later wrote a history of the conquest):

> She had heard every day how the Indians were going to kill us and eat our flesh with chili, and had seen us surrounded in the late battles, and knew that

all of us were wounded and sick, yet never allowed us to see any sign of fear in her, only a courage passing that of a woman[3].

The Spanish wondered how they would defeat the mighty Mexican warriors if they fared so poorly fighting Tlaxcalans. They decided to send a messenger to the Tlaxcalans to ask for a peace agreement.

Longstanding enemies of the Mexica, the Tlaxcalan leaders had already been looking for powerful allies when the Spanish arrived. They explained that they were free and independent, but surrounded by the empire of Mexico. In terms of government, Cortés compared the republic of Tlaxcala to city-states of Venice or Genoa. When he entered their capital city, he was at a loss to explain how great and wonderful it seemed to him. He marveled at a market with perhaps 20,000 people actively engaged in trade of all kinds. He described public baths and shops for everything one could ask for, whether shoes, fine china, or a haircut and a shave. An efficient police system kept good order in the city. In a letter to Charles V, Cortés claimed, "Your Majesty may well call himself Emperor of it with no less reason and title than he now does of Germany."

On its continued march to Tenochtitlan, the Spanish army planned to stop in the city of Cholula, an ally of Mexico. The Tlaxcalans distrusted the Cholulans, their traditional enemies, about whom they warned Cortés, referring to them as 'lying merchants who never kept their word.' In case of treachery, the Tlaxcalans sent thousands of their own warriors to accompany Cortés. When the conquistadors and their allies came to Cholula, the local rulers greeted them as friends. They offered them a feast of tortillas, turkey, quail, and prickly pear fruit. Cortés offered his friendship, and for a few days, peace reigned between the hosts and their guests. Uneasy feelings arose, however, when several seemingly unremarkable details hinted at a trap. Stones piled up on the rooftops and the absence of women and children in the town indicated an approaching attack. Speaking with the local women, Malinche had heard that Moctezuma's army had camped nearby. One woman offered to provide shelter for her, as escape from the town would soon be impossible. The Mexica had closed off the roads from Cholula to Tenochtitlan.

Cortés carefully hid any awareness of a potential attack. Instead, he expressed interest in the local traditions of the city and invited the local dignitaries, priests, and warriors to greet him in the central courtyard near the main temple. The Cholulan elite, clothed in their finest costumes and headdresses, paraded with a great fanfare of trumpets and horns. When all had assembled, Cortés ordered his soldiers to block the entrances on all four sides of the courtyard. With no means of escape, and no arms to defend themselves, the Cholulans fell prey to the Spanish, who brutally massacred them all. With all of their leaders slaughtered, the Tlaxcalans entered the city and sacked it, burning and looting the stores and houses, for two days. When the Cholulans surrendered to the Tlaxcalans, many believed the attack had been premeditated, and that the Tlaxcalans had used the Spanish to settle scores with their enemies.

When word reached Moctezuma about the Cholulan massacre, the emperor fell into great despair. The common people also feared the alliance of Spanish army with their traditional Tlaxcalan enemies. Anxiety led to anger and rebellion. The state seemed to be coming apart, as though the world started to quake and spin. Moctezuma's family members urged him to leave the capital, and the emperor thought about hiding in nearby caves. In the end, however, he decided to stay.

Moctezuma sent more emissaries to the Spaniards in an effort to appease them. The highest nobles of the land served as ambassadors to Cortés bringing gold banners, golden necklaces, and precious feathers. The Mexica considered the Spanish reaction to the gold unusual. One Nahua historian recounted, "Like monkeys they grabbed the gold. It was as though their hearts were put to rest, brightened, freshened. For gold was what they greatly thirsted for: they were gluttonous for it, starved for it, piggishly wanting it." In one story, Moctezuma tried to send a well-dressed emissary trying to pose as Moctezuma himself, in order to deter the invaders from the city. Malinche, recognizing the dialect of the Mexica lower class, revealed the emissary as an imposter. Cortés told the embassy that he intended to continue on to the capital city, where he would see Moctezuma himself, face to face.

Tenochtitlan

As the Spanish army descended from the snow-capped volcanoes that surrounded the plateau, they first glimpsed at Tenochtitlan from high above the city. One Spanish observer expressed his amazement:

> When we saw so many cities and villages built in the water and other great towns built on dry land and that straight and level causeway going towards [Tenochtitlan], we were amazed and said that it was like the enchantments they tell us in the legend of Amadis, on account of the great towers and [temples] and buildings rising from the water, and all built of masonry. And some of our soldiers even asked whether the things we saw were not a dream.[4]

The Mexica wondered at the hundreds of Spanish soldiers as they marched down the wide causeway into the city. They noticed the enormous bull mastiffs and greyhounds that went first followed by men on horseback, completely covered in gleaming steel armor. The horses neighed loudly, prancing with bells and pounding holes into the ground with their powerful hoofs. The conquistadors marched with their crossbows and arquebuses. Behind them, perhaps more threateningly, marched their Native American allies, led by the Tlaxcalans. They were fully outfitted for war, shouting and hitting their mouths with their hands.

Moctezuma, the great emperor of Mexico, met them on the causeway with a magnificent retinue of uniformed princes. He wore an impressive headdress of green feathers, and golden sandals inlaid with precious jewels. Members of his entourage brought rare and colorful flowers, including those of the cacao, corn, and tobacco plants, and placed them in arrangements on the ground in front of them. The flowers were tied into wreaths and necklaces to adorn the Spanish. Cortés dismounted from his horse, while Moctezuma descended from his litter. The captain offered his hand and even tried to embrace the Mexican emperor, but was prevented by the princes who accompanied him. By custom, his subjects could not even look at his face, much less touch him. Nevertheless, Moctezuma bowed deeply to show his respect. The conquistador gave him a necklace of crystals and pearls, while Moctezuma offered a necklace with dangling gold crustaceans.

Cortés spoke first, asking, "Is it you, Moctezuma?" To which the emperor replied, "Yes, it is I." The two men exchanged polite greetings, translated by Malinche. Then Moctezuma said to Cortés:

> Oh our lord, you are very welcome. You have reached your land, your settlement, your home Mexico. You have come to sit on your throne and seat, which I have possessed for some days in your name . . . You have undergone great travails in coming such a long way; rest now in your home and your palaces[5].

Did this strange greeting indicate that Moctezuma believed that Cortés was really Quetzalcoatl coming to take back his empire? Or did these words simply mean that the captain should make himself at home? Not even the Spanish could be sure of their meaning, or know whether the pleasant words were spoken sincerely or used to ensnare the visitors in an elaborate trap.

Moctezuma housed Cortés and his soldiers in the opulent palace of his father. The next day, Cortés visited Moctezuma at his palace. At 52 years of age, he had a slim build and stately bearing. He sported cropped hair and a short, but wellgroomed beard. Described by the Spanish as intelligent with a good sense of humor, the emperor had "fine" eyes able to express serious gravity as well as tenderness. Compared to his Spanish guests, he seemed meticulously clean, bathing every day and changing into clean clothes regularly.

Seated next to Moctezuma on a couch in his palace, the captain explained his religious faith, professing his belief in one God who had created the world and died on the cross to save souls, and that all people were brothers and sisters. The emperor replied that the Mexica worshipped their own gods who had been good to them throughout all time, and then he changed the subject. He explained that when the ambassadors first described the Spanish as angry gods, he dismissed the story as a silly fantasy. Cortés, the emperor said, impressed him more as a human being than as a false god. Moctezuma continued, saying that he imagined that the Tlaxcalans had described himself as some kind of god living in a house made of gold and jewels. "But look," he said laughing, "my body is flesh and bone like yours, my houses of stone and wood and lime." He said that surely Cortés would treat such nonsense as a joke, just as he himself had treated tales of guns as magical sticks producing thunder and lightning. The conquistador laughed and said that enemies always say false and evil things about each other, but that he was happy to find such a magnificent prince. The conversation had been civil, even friendly, an amazing exchange between two men, both potential predators, both potential prey.

The emperor's dinner consisted of at least thirty separate dishes, kept warm in braziers, and served on white tablecloths. The Mexicans did not have beef, pork, or chicken, but a multitude of birds, rabbits, venison, and fish as well as reptiles and insects. Servants brought water bowls for Moctezuma to wash his hands before and after dinner. At the end of the meal, dozens of beautiful women brought jugs of frothy hot chocolate, believed by the Aztecs to be an aphrodisiac. The Spanish observers noticed that he also enjoyed a long tube filled with herbs and a leaf called tobacco, which was lighted and smoked. Dancers, court jesters, and musicians entertained him after the meal, at the end of which he fell asleep.

The palaces of the Mexica ruler also held magnificent gardens with an endless variety of flowers, trees, and bushes, that grew along elegant rectangular pools of chiseled white concrete. Moctezuma astounded his Spanish guests with the collection of animals he kept in cages. Having never seen a zoo, Europeans thought it extraordinary that he would keep a staff of around three hundred people to do nothing but feed and clean the cages of a multitude of birds, snakes, jaguars, wolves, and carnivores of all kinds. They watched in horror as servants fed animals on human torso remains left over from the sacrifices. Also unsettling to the Spanish were cages containing human captives such as hunchbacks and albinos. They, too, were treated like animals.

After four days, Moctezuma escorted Cortés and a few others to see the grand temple of Huizilopochtli in the center of the city. The Spanish marveled at the marketplace of Tlatelolco with its booths selling every product one could want from pottery and delicate pastries to slaves and canoes of human excrement. There were more people and a greater variety of products than any of the soldiers had seen on their voyages to Istanbul and Rome. Government inspectors, customs officials, and law courts kept the city in good order.

Wonder gave way to horror, however, as the Spaniards made their way up the 114 steps that led to the top of the main temple. There they found the sacred rooms that held the statues of Huizilopochtli and his brother Texcat plastered with precious stones. Human blood, hardened and black, splattered the walls. Near the precious idols, chaffing dishes contained the burning hearts of the three victims who had died that day. The blood and smoke caused an unbearable stench. Cortés showed neither fear nor disgust. Almost amused, he asked Moctezuma, through Malinche, how a prince as wise as he could believe in such devils. Cortés then asked if he could set up a cross and a statue of the Virgin Mary in the temple. Clearly offended, Moctezuma replied that these gods had been good to them; they had brought victory, health, and rain. The captain begged his pardon and descended the steps. The emperor remained to worship and conduct purification ceremonies to cleanse the sacred space from the defilement caused by the Spanish disrespect. Up to that time, the Spanish and the Mexica enjoyed good relations. Unfortunately, the visit to the temple caused a falling out between them.

Meanwhile, in the region around Vera Cruz, tensions erupted between the Aztecs and Spanish. The Spanish soldiers had aided a local rebellion against the Mexica Empire. Although the Aztec army defeated the uprising, they killed many

Spanish soldiers in the process. Cortés demanded that Moctezuma execute his subjects for the offense, but the emperor refused. The captain used the occasion as a pretense to put Moctezuma under house arrest. He remained a captive for almost six months. As a captive, he continued to serve as a puppet ruler.

According to Spanish accounts, Moctezuma enjoyed a gentle captivity. Nevertheless, tensions flared as the people of Tenochtitlan grew restless. At this time, the Spanish went searching for everything of value in the imperial storehouses. They gathered necklaces and armbands, feather headdresses, diadems and nose plugs. Wherever they found gold, they detached it from well-crafted royal treasures, which they carelessly destroyed and threw away. They then put all of the gold into a vat and melted it into gold bricks.

Trouble erupted again in Vera Cruz as a Spanish army of over a thousand landed from Cuba in April of 1520. They had been sent by the governor, Diego Velásquez, to apprehend Cortés and bring him to trial for his illegal expedition. The captain left Tenochtitlan and headed for the coast. He placed the city under the command of Pedro de Alvarado, an outgoing and energetic, but mentally unstable nobleman. Although greatly outnumbered, Cortés easily overpowered the Spanish army. He then told the defeated soldiers about the gold and riches that awaited them in Tenochtitlan if they joined his army. When they agreed, the conquistador gained 1,400 additional soldiers.

While events in Vera Cruz kept Cortés from Tenochtitlan, Alvarado made a fateful decision with horrifying consequences. Mexica leaders had asked Alvarado permission to hold their most important festival, the celebration of Huizilopochtli. They wanted to show the Spanish the beauty of their religious ceremonies. In the central plaza beneath the two great pyramids, priests who had fasted for a whole year constructed Huizilopochtli in human form, adorning him with feathers and precious stones. The Nahua sources described the dancing and singing that followed as "the noise of waves breaking against the rocks."

At the height of this festival, Alvarado ordered his soldiers to block the entryways to the plaza, and when "song was linked to song," the Spanish unsheathed their swords. What began as a festival ended as a bloody massacre. A Spanish soldier severed the hands of a drummer as he beat his drum, and struck his neck so quickly that his head landed far from his body. Everywhere the conquistadors split skulls, disemboweled, dismembered, and hacked the unarmed and defenseless celebrants to death. According to one account, "The blood of the warriors ran like water; the ground was almost slippery with blood, and the stench of it rose, and the entrails were lying dragged out."

At this point an Aztec priest cried out, "Mexica! Who said we are not at war? Who said we could trust them?" As the warriors rose up with arrows and spears they shouted war cries and beat their hands against their lips. The Spanish sought refuge in the royal palace. When Cortés returned to the city with his new recruits, he found it in the midst of an uprising. The warriors of Tenochtitlan had attacked with javelins, arrows, spears, and rocks. The Spanish made the royal palace complex into a fortress and kept Moctezuma there in chains.

To pacify the rebels, the Spanish sent out Lord Itzcuauhtzin, a close relative of Moctezuma, to give a message to the people from the emperor. He shouted from the roof:

> We must not fight them. We are not their equals in battle. Put down your shields and arrows . . . it is the aged who will suffer most . . . the humblest classes will also suffer, and so will the innocent children who still sleep in their cradles.[6]

And then he added, "They have put your king in chains; his feet are bound with chains." But the uprising had become a revolution against a puppet emperor. The common people shouted insults at him and yelled, "Who is Moctezuma to give us orders? We are no longer his slaves."

What happened next is clouded in controversy. In the Spanish account, Moctezuma himself tried to calm the crowd from a parapet of the wall, but the people of Tenochtitlan called him a coward and a traitor. They threw stones at him, and three struck his head, arm, and leg. Badly wounded he collapsed and the Spanish brought him into the palace. They tried to dress his wounds and make him eat food, but the emperor refused any treatment. Four days later he died. Dìaz described the scene of his death: "Cortés wept for him, and all of us Captains and soldiers, and there was no man among us who knew him and was intimate with him, who did not bemoan him as though he were our father, and it is not to be wondered at, considering how good he was." In the soldier's account, the Spanish tried to save a king who had been killed by his own people.

The Nahua sources provide a much different account of Moctezuma's death. According to this version of the history, the Spanish soldiers opened a door of the palace in the dead of night and dumped out the bodies of Moctezuma and Itzcuauhtzin. Moctezuma had been stabbed to death by the Spanish, not the people of Tenochtitlan. The Mexica collected the bodies and built two funeral pyres. When Moctezuma's body burned, it emitted clouds of black smoke and a foul smell. Some took their anger out at the burning corpse by shouting, "He made the whole world fear him, in the whole world he was dreaded, in the whole world he inspired respect and fright. If someone offended him only in some small way, he immediately disposed of him. He punished many for imagined things." They moaned and shook their heads. They felt betrayed by their leader.

The conquest after Moctezuma

Without a puppet ruler to calm the people, the Spanish found themselves in a difficult position. The great council of Mexico elected a new emperor, Cuitlahuac, the younger brother of Moctezuma, who continued the rebellion against the Spanish. For days Cortés and his soldiers remained besieged in the palace devising a strategy of escape. The layout of Tenochtitlan presented unusual obstacles to the conquistadors. As an island crisscrossed with canals, few areas provided room for open combat. The deep water between the houses made horses worthless, and the soldiers had no way to go from one house to another. Each house had a drawbridge linking it to the next house, but these were retractable in case of attack. Constructed of adobe cement rather than wood, the detached houses did not burn easily. Finally, the native warriors of Tenochtitlan knew how to disable the causeways that led out of the city, essentially trapping the Spanish soldiers. Understanding these logistical problems, Cortés and his men constructed a wooden bridge inside the palace. Seven days after their confinement, they made an escape attempt in the middle of the night. The Spanish and Tlaxcalans took their swords and whatever small amount of gold and jewels they could carry, leaving their guns and crossbows at the palace.

A woman fetching water saw the soldiers and sounded the alarm. Hearing her, another person at the top of the temple of Huitzilopochtli shouted, "O warriors, O Mexica, your enemies are coming out, let everyone hasten with the war boats and on the roads!" The night was dark and rainy. Cortés had the bridge placed abroad the Tolteca canal. He and dozens of others managed to cross it before it collapsed or sank. From then on, assaulted on all sides by Mexica in war boats and from the rooftops, the train of Spanish soldiers, their allies, their women, and their horses, simply slipped into the deep water and drowned. Their dead bodies formed another bridge, however, which others used to escape. The Spanish called this terrible episode *La Noche Triste*, the sad night. Dìaz recounted that in this scene of death, "How happy I was to see Doña Marina still alive." Malinche nursed and comforted the wounded as they found shelter in a nearby town.

A year passed before the Spanish tried to reenter the city of Tenochtitlan. They spent this time sheltered by local allies constructing a fleet of ships in order to launch naval warfare against the Mexica. They built thirteen 40-foot ships, outfitted with the cannon from the ships Cortés had beached off the coast of Vera Cruz.

The Spanish had fled Tenochtitlan, but left behind their most destructive and effective weapon: the diseases they brought with them from Europe. The most devastating was smallpox, to which the Americans had no resistance. According to a Nahua account, "The pustules that covered people caused great desolation; very many people died of them, and many just starved to death; starvation reigned, and no one took care of others any longer." The Mexica could not count on fresh water brought to the city by their aqueducts, which the Spanish had destroyed. With only dirty, salty, water to drink, many died of dysentery.

In 1521 Cortés returned with his fleet of ships to take the city. For three months, fierce battles took the lives of many Mexica and Spanish soldiers. The Aztecs captured just as many soldiers as they killed to use as sacrifices. The Spanish watched in horror as the priests held their friends across the stone, extracted their hearts while still beating, and tossed their torsos down the bloody steps of the pyramid. On the grisly skull rack, the priests placed their heads right above the severed heads of their horses.

The warriors of Tenochtitlan rallied the troops shouting, "Who are these barbarians, these little back landers?" But the Spanish learned to fight through the canals by carrying portable bridges with them, and the ships they built were more powerful than the Mexica war canoes. Eventually, Cortés decided to destroy the houses of the city to prevent the citizens from throwing stones and darts from the rooftops. This required the leveling of Tenochtitlan, the merciless destruction of a beautiful city for which he later expressed regret. Finally, after months of starvation, disease, homelessness, and war, the Aztec leaders surrendered. In a massive exodus from the ashes of the city, the Mexica left by way of the bridges while some waded through water. The Spanish subjected the defeated migrants, both women and men, to humiliating cavity searches in their search for gold. Because the Spanish picked off the most beautiful women as slaves, many had rubbed their faces with mud, and wore tattered and torn garments.

The Nahua recorded the day of the final surrender of the Mexica to the Spanish: day "One Serpent" of the year "Three House." For the Spanish, it was 13 August, 1521. Leo X was the Pope and Charles V was the King of Spain. After the defeat, the Mexica wrote poetry to cope with the tragedy and loss. One of the most celebrated begins with the following verse:

> Nothing but flowers and songs of sorrow
> Are left in Mexico and Tlatelolco,
> Where once we saw warriors and wise men.[7]

From "The Broken Spears" by Miguel Leon-Portilla Copyright © 1962, 1990 by Miguel Leon-Portilla Expanded and Updated Edition © 1992 by Miguel Leon-Portilla Reprinted by permission of Beacon Press, Boston.

Much more than flowers and songs survived the conquest of Mexico. A new civilization, a blend of Mexica and Spanish cultures, grew and rebuilt itself on firm foundations. Malinche gave birth to a son by Cortés, Martin, who symbolically represented the first *mestizo*, or person of mixed European and Amerindian descent. After the conquest, she married a Spanish nobleman and raised her children in the new colonial society. Moctezuma did not survive the conquest, but his first and most beloved child, Tecuichpo, married first Cuitlahuac and then Cuauhtemoc, the last two Mexica emperors. As the last empress of Mexico, she converted to Christianity and took the name Doña Isabel in 1525. She married three more times, each time to Spanish noblemen, and her descendants became the ancestors of noble houses of Moctezuma that survive to this day.

Cortés, returned to Spain where he faced a number of law suits concerning the legality of his actions. The Spanish government ruled his conquest legitimate and granted him a noble title, Marquis of the Valley of Oaxaca. However, the king appointed a viceroy to rule Mexico as the head of a new royal administration. Although he continued to explore and fight in both the old world and the new, Cortés grew increasingly bitter. He felt unappreciated by a court that considered him a rogue and a potential liability.

The Mexica people converted to the Catholic faith, but they did so on their own terms. Ten years after the conquest, a miracle was reported on Tepeyac mountain, near Mexico City, which the Spanish had built on the ruins of Tenochtitlan. Before the conquest, the mountain contained a shrine to the Aztec mother goddess, Tonantzin. While wandering on the mountain, a Mexican peasant named Juan Diego saw a vision of the Virgin Mary. Although frightened at first, he reported that Mary calmed and comforted him with the words, "*No estoy yo aquí que soy tu madre*" (Am I not here who am your mother?). She instructed Juan Diego to collect the roses that grew on the hill and hold them in his Mexican *tilma*, or cloak. When he took the cloak to the archbishop in the city to show him evidence of the vision, the flowers fell to the ground, but an image of the Virgin remained. The cloak with a portrait of a young woman enrobed with a mantle of blue stars remains in the

FIGURE 4.4 Virgin of Guadalupe. One of the most famous images in the world, this depiction of the Virgin Mary contains religious symbolism associated with both Catholicism and traditional Mexica religion. The sunburst-like rays behind her, the crescent moon below her, and the stars that adorn her mantle all proclaim her standing in the cosmos.

Source: Wikimedia, Katsam

cathedral of the Virgin of Guadalupe that currently stands on the site. It is the most visited Catholic pilgrimage destination in the Catholic faith, and the image remains one of the most recognizable symbols of Mexico today.

Chronology

1466   Birth of Moctezuma II.
1492   Columbus lands in the New World.
1502   Moctezuma II becomes emperor of Mexico.
1519   Hernán Cortés lands on the mainland of Mexico. Spanish found city of Vera Cruz. Cortés and allies enter Tenochtitlan.
1520   Death of Moctezuma II. Uprising of Tenochtitlan causing Spanish defeat in *La Noche Triste*.
1521   Siege and defeat of Tenochtitlan. Fall of Mexican Empire.

Sources for further reading about Moctezuma II

Sources for Moctezuma II and the conquest of Mexico are plentiful in English. A recent book that looks at Moctezuma from a variety of perspectives, especially art, is Colin McEwan and Leonardo López Luján, eds., *Moctezuma: Aztec Ruler* (London: British Museum Press, 2009). An older biography intended as a popular history with a lively narrative is C. A. Burland, *Montezuma* (New York: Putnam, 1973). The classic work on the cosmography of the Nahua is Miguel León-Portilla, *The Aztec Image of Self and Society* (Salt Lake City, UT: University of Utah Press, 1992). Also see Inga Clendennen, *The Aztecs* (Cambridge: Cambridge University Press, 1991). Important works that look at the relationship between religion and empire building are Geoffrey Conrad and Arthur Demarist, *Religion and Empire: The Dynamics of Aztec and Inca Expansion* (Cambridge: Cambridge University Press, 1984) and Ross Hassig, *Time History and Belief in Aztec and Colonial Mexico* (Austin, TX: University of Texas Press, 2013). Also from Hassig, see *Aztec Warfare: Imperial Expansion and Political Control* (Norman, OK: University of Oklahoma Press, 1988). Interesting information can also be found in Ethelia Ruiz Medrano, *Mexico's Indigenous Communities, Their Lands and Histories 1500–2010* (Boulder, CO: University Press of Colorado, 2010). An essential primary source for information about all aspects of Aztec culture is a thirteen volume work written in Nahua and Spanish by a Spanish friar in the sixteenth century shortly after the conquest. He collected the information from the Nahua people, and volume thirteen contains an Aztec account of the conquest. The English translation appears in Bernardino di Sahaguìn, *The Florentine Codex*, trans. Arthur Anderson and Charles Dibble (13 volumes; Salt Lake City, UT: University of Utah Press, 1970). A shorter book that juxtaposes Aztec and Spanish accounts of the conquest is Stuart Schwartz, ed., *Victors and Vanquished: Spanish and Nahua Views of the Conquest of Mexico* (New York: Bedford St. Martins, 2000). Other good sources for the Aztec accounts of the conquest are James Lockhart, *We People Here: Nahuatl Accounts of the Conquest of Mexico* (Los

Angeles, CA: University of California Press, 1993), and Miguel León Portilla, *The Broken Spears: The Aztec Account of the Conquest of Mexico*, 2nd edition (Boston, MA: Beacon Press, 1992). There are many Spanish accounts from eyewitnesses. These include Bernal Díaz del Castillo, *The True History of the Conquest of New Spain*, ed. A. P. Maudslay (London: Hakluyt Society, 1908) and Anthony Pagden, trans. and ed., *Hernán Cortés: Letters from Mexico* (New York: Orion Press, 1971). A lively and thorough account of the conquest is Hugh Thomas, *Conquest: Montezuma, Cortés, and the fall of Old Mexico* (New York: Simon & Schuster, 1993). The figure of Malinche and her role in the conquest are covered in Rolando Romero and Amanda Nolacea Harris, *Feminism, Nation, and Myth: La Malinche* (Houston, TX: Arte Público Press, 2005). A fun discussion of Malinche that doubles as a travel memoir is Anna Lanyon, *Malinche's Conquest* (Crow's Nest, NSW: Allen & Unwin, 1999).

Comparison between Pope Clement VII and Moctezuma II

Historians in Italy and Mexico who wrote at the time of the Spanish conquest had the sense that they were witnessing the destruction of their own civilizations. Life continued, of course, and society carried on as before, but in radically altered forms, and under the direction of foreign influence. There was no attempt by any contemporary to portray the defeat as a victory.

Despite the cultural, religious, and technological differences that distinguished the Americans and the Italians, the Spanish used similar strategies of conquest for each. Both operations were part of an expansion directed from the same central power, the court of Charles V. The predatory and expansionist policy of the Spanish kings originated in the *Reconquista*, the effort begun in the eighth century to free the Iberian peninsula from Muslim rule. After 1492, when Spanish rulers had successfully retaken the peninsula, justifications for conquest expanded to include the regions of North Africa, Europe, the Holy Land, and eventually the world. This was the vision of Charles V's main advisor and grand chancellor, Mercurino di Gattinara, who claimed that God had ordained Spain to bring the entire globe under one monarch, so that all could live in peace as "one flock" with "one shepherd." In his view, Charles V had inherited the Roman Empire, which had given him dominion over the whole world. Spanish writers engaged in a massive propaganda campaign that used biblical passages and prophecies to defend this right. Brute military force and skillful diplomatic negotiations supported this imperial ideology. The empire sought allies among the enemies of their prey, while relying on the collaboration of local elites who believed they had more to gain from the new Spanish overlords than from local governments.

The fact that both regions were characterized by independent city-states that distrusted each other made these conquests much easier for Spain. In both Italy and Mexico, agents who represented Spain looked for allies to mount a resistance to the central power. In Italy, the Spanish enlisted German musketeers (*landsknechts*) with promises that Charles V would support evangelical interpretations of Christianity. As Protestants, they had their own reasons for fighting the Roman Catholic Church. In America, Cortés enlisted the support of Tlaxcala, an independent republic which had an interest in defeating their oppressive neighbor, the empire of Mexico. Although the Americans were astonished and awed by firepower, it would have been impossible for a thousand soldiers with guns to defeat hundreds of thousands of Mexica warriors. The Spanish conquered with the aid of local allies who fought with spears and arrows. Without this support, Spanish domination would not have been possible. Ultimately, disease played a larger role in killing their enemies than guns.

In both cases, Spain managed to entice support from members of the local elite. The Medici family used Spanish armies to defeat the republican government of Florence and establish a hereditary monarchy there. Although sources are unclear about what motives led Moctezuma to avoid resisting Spanish rule, his family members allied and intermarried with the Spanish to establish themselves as a ruling aristocracy in New Spain. The end result was the same in both Italy and Mexico: a very rigid social hierarchy with a noble caste at its top. Merchants, artisans, and farmers remained at the bottom of society with much fewer opportunities for social mobility. In this new regime the descendants of Moctezuma and Clement VII flourished.

When historians discussed the conquest in past centuries, they emphasized both the technical superiority and "more rational" mindset of the Europeans, but there is also no reason to suppose that one culture was more "superstitious" or irrational than the other. Clearly, the two societies shared a sense of fatalism. Interestingly, both Rome and Tenochtitlan had been built on ruins of past civilizations. Physical reminders that mighty empires rise and fall could have contributed to an acceptance of their fate. Some people, they may have believed, had the misfortune of living during a time in which invaders were destined to destroy them, as their ancestors had destroyed previous civilizations. Both believed the conquests were foretold by omens and prophecies. Although they differed on specific points, Renaissance Florentines and Aztec priests agreed that the alignments of the moon, sun, and planets impacted events on earth. They studied the calendars to predict the future or understand the present, and one side did not feel the heavy weight of fate more than the other, significantly, Cortés used the wheel of fortune as his device. He simply believed he was going up rather than going down. For the historians of both societies, the fall had little to do with technological or social superiority of their conquerors; both the Italians and the Mexica referred to the Spanish invaders as barbarians.

Perhaps the strangest correspondence between the Mexica and Italians concerns the role of human sacrifice in religion and culture. For the Mexica, gods required human sacrifice to replenish the energy of the world. The spilling of blood enabled physical, moral, and spiritual regeneration. Although Christianity did not call for human blood in its rituals, the sacrificial act lay at the heart of its theology. The language of blood and regeneration permeates the language of Christianity. In the book of John, Jesus presents himself as a sacrifice for the whole world; he dies in order to put humans in harmony with God. In the Christian calendar, rebirth has both a physical and spiritual meaning, as Christians commemorate the crucifixion of Jesus in the spring, when new crops emerge from the soil.

The idea of human sacrifice as a sustaining social force might have encouraged a greater acceptance of war. Based on readings of literature, one might argue that Aztecs and Florentines shared an obsession with moral corruption that could only be cured with martial valor. Aztec poetry linked the sacrifice of warriors to moral regeneration, while Machiavelli looked to military service as a foundation for republican virtues. Such coincidences lead one to ask to what extent beliefs about war in any age are connected to a primordial urge to preserve the moral order with human sacrifice.

The emphasis on moral failure permeated Nahua and Florentine historians in the wake of the conquests. Both saw the conquests as a result of disunity. As the

Nahua account explained, "People no longer took care of one another." Guic-ciardini's history gave a sorry enumeration of betrayals and acts of selfishness. More than anything, contemporary historians blamed their leaders. Clement VII and Moctezuma, although both devout and conscientious, showed constant indecision and cowardice. They failed to rally troops or put up a sufficient defense against the invaders as they sought to protect their families at the expense of their states. At least this is how they appeared in the histories. Whether such characterizations represent truthful accounts of personality, or simply reflect the desire for the historians to make the leaders scapegoats for the defeat cannot be determined. Curiously, in both accounts, there seemed to be a hesitation to blame the actual perpetrators for the conquest. Rather, the victims blamed themselves for their failure to put up a united front. In this way, Guicciardini and the Nahua historians described the fall of their civilizations not as a crime, but as an act of suicide. Perhaps that is the most distressing aspect of these conquest narratives. Not only did the victims have to endure the physical suffering caused by destruction and the senseless loss of life, they also had to bear a great psychological burden. Five hundred years later, not all wounds have fully healed.

Questions to consider

1   What might Clement VII or Moctezuma have done differently to save the inhabitants of Rome and Tenochtitlan from misfortune? Why was Elizabeth better able to defend England against a Spanish attack?

2   Florence and Tlaxcala were the only republican states discussed in this book. By 1530, both had surrendered to imperial rule. What made republics different from kingdoms and empires? Why do you think republics were so rare in the sixteenth-century world? Why were they unable to defend themselves from a larger imperial power?

3   In what ways might Clement VII be considered a success?

4   In 1527 the Roman Catholic Church as an institution had faced a serious threat to its existence. How and why did it survive and even grow? What role do you think Africa and the Americas played in strengthening it as an institution?

5   Both Spain and the Ottoman Empire defined themselves as crusader states in the sixteenth century. What other similarities existed between the two?

6   Both the Mexica and Japanese used the metaphor of the flower to refer to fallen warriors. How would you explain this metaphor?

7   Both Moctezuma and Afonso encountered invaders from a world that was totally new to them. How and why did Afonso keep his kingdom, and why did Moctezuma lose his?

8   Were Moctezuma and Clement truly trapped by their circumstances? To what extent did their actions contribute to their defeat?

9   Imagine a diagram linking all the major figures profiled in this work. What would it look like?

Notes

1 Christopher Hare, *Charles de Bourbon: High Constable of France "The Great Condottier"* (New York: John Lane, 1911), p 30.
2 Benvenuto Cellini, *The Autobiography of Benvenuto Cellini*, trans. George Bull (New York: Penguin, 1977), p. 71.
3 Stuart B. Schwartz, ed. *Victors and Vanquished. Spanish and Nahua Views of the Conquest of Mexico*, (Boston: Bedford/St. Martin's, 2000), p. 110.
4 Bernal Díaz del Castillo, *The True History of the Conquest of New Spain*, volume 2, ed. A. P. Maudslay (London: Hakluyt Society, 1908), p. 37.
5 James Lockhart, trans. and ed. *We People Here: Nahuatl accounts of the conquest of Mexico.* (Los Angeles: University of California Press, 1993), p. 117.
6 Stuart B. Schwartz, ed. *Victors and Vanquished*, p. 165.
7 Miguel León Portilla, *The Broken Spears: The Aztec Account of the Conquest of Mexico*, 2nd edition (Boston, MA: Beacon Press, 1992), p. 149.

CONCLUSION

Toward the seventeenth century

The preceding eight biographies have sought to provide a view of history from the standpoint of the individual. This conclusion hopes to give the reader a larger perspective on sixteenth-century society and the developments that will influence culture, society, and politics in the seventeenth century. Although they differed greatly in terms of culture, all eight regions in this book shared a number of qualities characteristic of traditional agricultural societies. These commonalities include a rigid social hierarchy, pre-scientific mindset, and a personal conception of political power.

From Mexico to Kongo to China, each society had a hereditary aristocracy that enjoyed social and/or legal privileges. The members of this elite wore easily recognizable clothes, and laws often dictated what fabrics and colors could be worn by each social group. For example, in much of Europe, sumptuary laws limited the right to wear silk to the nobility. In China, members of the gentry wore black gowns with insignia that announced their rank in society. At all social levels, people wore certain colors, dress, and hairstyles to announce their life stage or occupation. For example, in early modern Germany, the color of the cap worn over a woman's hair bun indicated whether she was single, married, or widowed. In this way, one's position in society would have been readily apparent to all members of the community. Adherence to social norms tended to matter more than individual fulfillment. Generally speaking, a person was more likely to identify as member of a family than as a unique person with independent interests.

A concern with supernatural forces and their impact on life permeated these traditional societies. Magic and divination (or the use of nature to predict the future) as well as omens and portents played a much larger role in daily life than it does in the modern world. Without an accepted definition of science as a form of reasoning, people made little distinction between natural and supernatural forces. All eight regions had words describing evil spirits and witchcraft. Although elites often differed from the common people in terms of how much of their life would be dominated by what is now commonly called superstition, it is fair to say that such thinking played a larger role in sixteenth-century life than it would after the acceptance of scientific reasoning in the late seventeenth century. Similarly, religion infused every aspect of life in each society, and none could conceive of a political regime disconnected from divine favor. There was no concept of the separation of church and state.

Finally, most of the societies described in this book adhered to the idea that political power was a personal possession. In accordance with this idea, peasants owed allegiance to the feudal warlord who ruled over their domains and clients owed loyalty to patrons. Everyone was subjected to the ruler. Although his or her authority might be limited by custom or laws, the monarch did not have to answer to anyone under heaven, except perhaps, his mother. In every case, people showed a sense of duty to an individual, rather than to an institution or set of laws. Personal rule, though the most traditional form of power, had a number of disadvantages. In dynasties where rulers determined the life or death of individuals, advisors often feared expressing opinions, no matter how rational, productive, or prudent. This made problems of policy very difficult to solve. Personal rule also created more incentives for the head of state to engage in warfare. Avenging attacks against the honor and reputation of the ruler took precedent over considerations of the well-being of subjects.

New technologies, customs, and ideas about the state transformed ideas about government. War played a large role in this. Firearms and printing both brought more people, especially common people, into armies throughout the sixteenth century, and the revival of ancient learning led to better military organization. In order to fund massive war efforts, rulers needed greater revenues. Tax collection and finance necessitated the creation of bureaucracies. In addition, more sophisticated military engagements required experts and specialists to develop new technologies and determine strategy. The proliferation of offices gave rise to the idea that the state was the collection of governmental functions, rather than the person of the ruler or his family. In this new administrative state, the sense of duty to a government replaced the sense of loyalty to a lord.

The transformations required a new set of cultural incentives for the elite, who in many cases increasingly defined themselves outside of a purely military role. In Japan, decades of brutal war ended when Hideyoshi established hegemony and gave the samurai nobility control over their domains in exchange for loyalty. Although he engaged soldiers in a disastrous foreign war, he established domestic peace. Moreover, during his regime and well after, a variety of social distinctions and entertainments occupied what had previously been a warrior nobility. Loyalty to the Japanese Empire served as a new source of honor. The situation in France was similar. After decades of religious conflict, Henry IV established hegemony over a feudal nobility. He created a court and a capital city to attract the aristocrats away from their domains. A sense of French national identity, related also to the pleasures of leisure and social distinction, helped to keep the nobility pacified. Both states elaborated administrative tax systems that paid government officials handsome sala-ries. When the government promised these elites such lucrative and prestigious offices, they supported the state.

For both the Spanish and Ottoman empires the primary thrust for hundreds of years had been conquest and expansion. Spain began as the effort of Christian kings to retake Iberia from the Moors from the eighth to the fifteenth centuries. The Ottomans began their wars of conquest for Islam in the thirteenth cen-tury. Both began as semi-nomadic tribes but became crusading societies led by warrior kings in the Middle Ages. This was still the case in the early sixteenth century when Cortés expanded the conquest into Mexico, and Suleiman laid siege to Vienna. However, the end of the sixteenth century brought an age of retrenchment, when both empires sought to keep what they had rather than con-quer new lands. This, like the nation state, required a sophisticated tax-collecting bureaucracy and legal system. Once again, societies built on conquest transformed into administrative states. Some contemporaries portrayed this as decline, even effeminate decadence. Jurists countered this argument by reviving the imperial ideals of classical antiquity to defend the idea of duty to the empire. This, as well as the promise of social distinction and legal privileges, provided the elite with new sources of honor apart from conquest and crusade. In the national model, the state sought to create a unified culture and sense of belonging. Ruling over a variety of ethnic, linguistic, and religious groups, empires could not secure loyalty to a particular culture. Rather, devotion to the rule of law and a civilizing mission purportedly beneficial to the interests of the ruled replaced the cultural homoge-neity at work in France and Japan. In either model, the shift toward loyalty to an administrative state rather than to an individual led to greater peace and stability in much of the world.

Finally, England's model of growth took a different path. It developed as a com-mercial empire according to the smaller-scale model that emerged in medieval Italy. Much like the Italian city-states such as Florence and Venice, the English government sought profit from capital enterprise. Dominated not by a landed elite or crusading aristocracy but by a prosperous merchant class, the English, Italians, and eventually the Dutch, looked toward constitutional structures guaranteeing economic freedom and the rule of law. The personal authority of an absolute ruler made little sense in these contexts, as arbitrary rule threatened the integrity of con-tracts and banking systems that rely on credit, which is essentially a form of trust. Commercial activity required strong institutions of government, which led to the transfer of state power from a personal dynasty to an administrative apparatus in which the ruler was only one part of a complex system.

The rise of administrative states and ever increasing global trade led to significant changes in traditional societies. By the middle of the eighteenth century, education and more plentiful economic opportunities fostered a greater sense of individual freedom. The development of royal academies of science as well as the proliferation of universities, libraries, and research institutions, promoted a more rational view of the world. For many, this offered a sense of control over misfortunes that replaced fears of supernatural forces that had dominated previous centuries. The Industrial Revolution continued these trends.

The half millennium that separates us from the world of this book is both long and short, and the painstaking work of building loyalties to abstract ideas and institutions undertaken over the course of centuries might be undone in an instant. Societies seeking strong leadership might see personal authority as more sound than laws and bureaucratic structures. In that case, the world is likely to return to the rule of warlords and dynasties. It was a world of intrigue, drama, and romance, but also endemic violence. The vast majority of the population experienced a misery that modern students can hardly imagine. Whether or not we go forward or back is up to the students of today to decide.

APPENDIX

Genealogical charts

Selected genealogy of the house of Oda in the Sengoku and early Tokugawa eras (simplified)

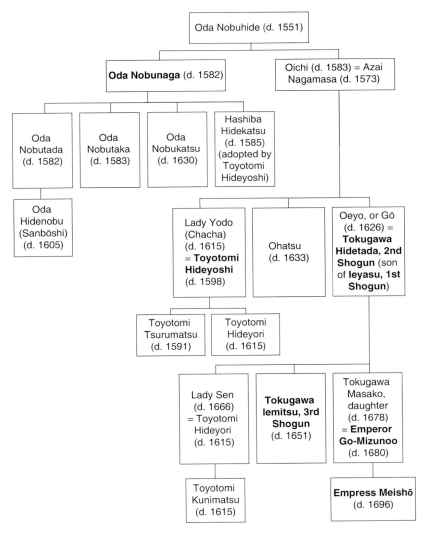

The author would like to thank Yasuko Sato for her help in constructing this genealogy.

Genealogy of the Valois dynasty of France in the sixteenth century (simplified)

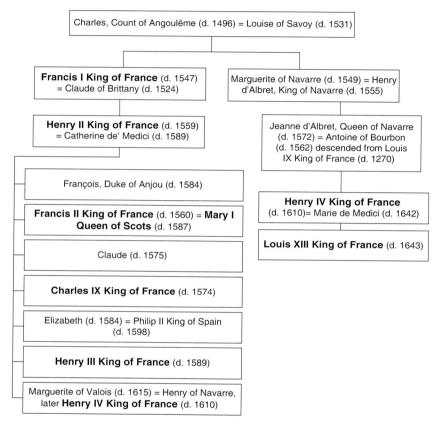

Charles, Count of Angoulême (d. 1496) = Louise of Savoy (d. 1531)

Francis I King of France (d. 1547)
= Claude of Brittany (d. 1524)

Marguerite of Navarre (d. 1549) = Henry
d'Albret, King of Navarre (d. 1555)

Henry II King of France (d. 1559)
= Catherine de' Medici (d. 1589)

Jeanne d'Albret, Queen of Navarre
(d. 1572) = Antoine of Bourbon
(d. 1562) descended from Louis
IX King of France (d. 1270)

François, Duke of Anjou (d. 1584)

Henry IV King of France
(d. 1610)= Marie de Medici (d. 1642)

Francis II King of France (d. 1560) = **Mary I
Queen of Scots** (d. 1587)

Louis XIII King of France (d. 1643)

Claude (d. 1575)

Charles IX King of France (d. 1574)

Elizabeth (d. 1584) = Philip II King of Spain
(d. 1598)

Henry III King of France (d. 1589)

Marguerite of Valois (d. 1615) = Henry of Navarre,
later **Henry IV King of France** (d. 1610)

Adapted from R. J. Knecht, *The Rise and Fall of Renaissance France 1483–1610* (Oxford: Blackwell Publishers, 2001), p. 537.

Genealogy of the Ottoman dynasty in the sixteenth century (simplified)

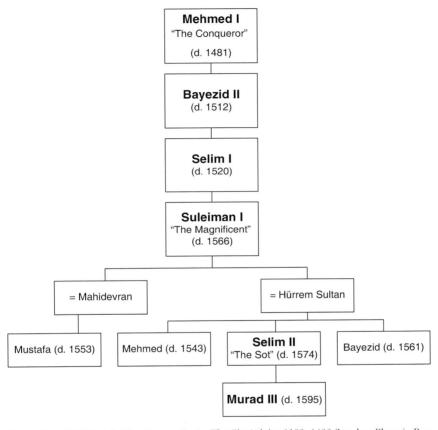

Adapted from Halil Inalcik, *The Ottoman Empire: The Classical Age 1300–1600* (London: Phoenix Press, 1973), p. 204.

Genealogy of the Ming dynasty in the sixteenth century (simplified)

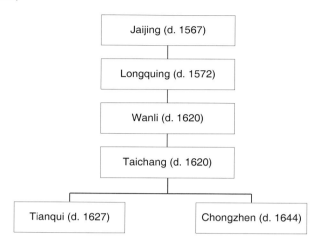

Genealogy of the kingdom of Kongo in the sixteenth century (simplified)

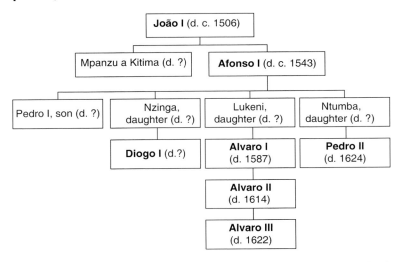

Adapted from Anne Hilton, *The Kingdom of Kongo* (London: Oxford University Press, 1985), p. 86.

Genealogy of the Tudor dynasty of England in the sixteenth century (simplified)

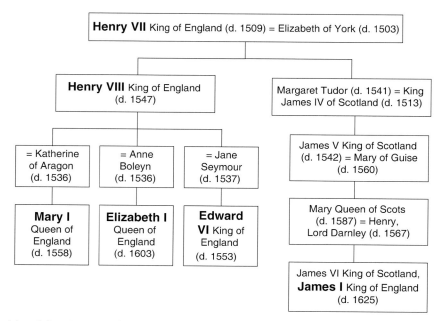

Adapted from Susan Brigden, *New Worlds, Lost Worlds: The Rule of the Tudors 1485–1603* (New York: Viking, 2000), p. 8.

Genealogy of the House of Medici (simplified)

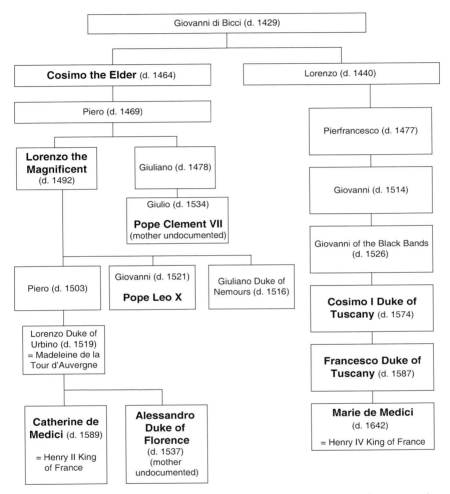

Adapted from J. R. Hale, *Florence and the Medici: The Pattern of Control* (London: Thames & Hudson, 1977), p. 10.

Genealogy of the Mexica emperors (simplified)

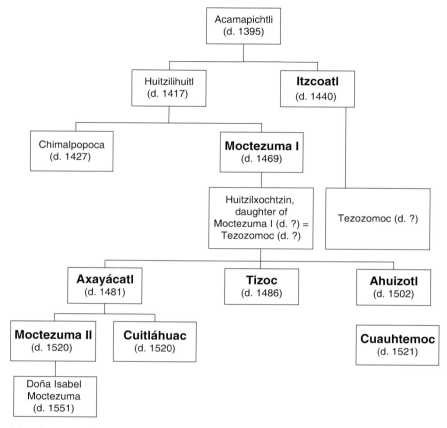

Adapted from Hugh Thomas, *Conquest: Montezuma, Cortés, and the Fall of Old Mexico* (New York: Simon & Schuster, 1993), p. 624.

BIBLIOGRAPHY

Primary sources

Alberi, Eugenio, ed. *Relazioni degli ambasciatori veneti al senato durante il XVI secolo, serie 3*. 3 volumes. Florence: Società editrice Fiorentina, 1842–1855.

Boscaro, Adriana, ed. and trans. *101 Letters of Hideyoshi: The Private Correspondence of Toyotomi Hideyoshi*. Tokyo: Sophia University, 1975.

Brasio, Antonio, ed., *Monumenta Missionaria Africana*. 1st series, 15 volumes. Lisbon: Agencia Geral do Ultramar, 1952–1988.

Cellini, Benvenuto. *The Autobiography of Benvenuto Cellini*. Translated by George Bull. New York: Penguin, 1977.

Cortés, Hernán. *Hernán Cortés: Letters from Mexico*. Translated by Anthony Pagden. New York: Orion Press, 1971.

Díaz del Castillo, Bernal. *The True History of the Conquest of New Spain*. Edited by A. P. Maudslay. London: Hakluyt Society, 1908.

Forster, Edward Seymour, ed. *The Turkish Letters of Ogier Ghiselin de Busbecq: Imperial Ambassador at Constantinople. 1554–1562*. Baton Rouge, LA: Louisiana State University Press, 2005.

Gallagher, Louis, ed. and trans. *China in the Sixteenth Century: The Journals of Matthew Ricci, 1583–1610*. New York: Random House, 1967.

Gattinara, Mercurino de. *Il Sacco di Roma: Relazione del commissario imp. Mercurino Gattinara*. Edited by D. Camillo Trasmondo-Frangipani. Geneva: G. G. Fick, 1866.

Giovio, Paolo. *Notable Men and Women of Our Time*. Edited and translated by Kenneth Gouwens. Cambridge, MA: Harvard University Press, 2013.

Jadin, Louis, ed. *Correspondance de Dom Afonso, roi du Congo 1506–1543*. Translated by Mireille Dicorato. Brussels: Académie royal des Sciences d'Outre-Mer, 1974.

Lau, D. C., ed. and trans. *Confucius: The Analects (Lun yü)*. New York: Penguin, 1979.

León Portilla, Miguel. *The Broken Spears: The Aztec Account of the Conquest of Mexico*. 2nd edition. Boston, MA: Beacon Press, 1992.

Lockhart, James. *We People Here: Nahuatl Accounts of the Conquest of Mexico*. Los Angeles, CA: University of California Press, 1993.

Machiavelli, Niccolò. *The Portable Machiavelli*. Edited and translated by Peter Bondanella and Mark Musa. New York: Penguin, 1979.

Mahdi, Muhsin, ed. *The Arabian Nights*. Translated by Hussain Haddawy. New York: Norton, 1990.

Plutarch. *Roman Lives: A Selection of Eight Roman Lives*. Translated by Robin Waterfield. Introduction and notes by Philip A. Stadter. Oxford: Oxford University Press, 2008.

Roy, David Todd, ed. *The Plum in the Golden Vase, or Chin P'ing Mei*. Princeton, NJ: Princeton University Press, 1993.

Sahaguìn, Bernardino di. *The Florentine Codex*. 13 volumes. Translated by Arthur Anderson and Charles Dibbles. Salt Lake City, UT: University of Utah Press, 1970.

Schwartz, Stuart, ed. *Victors and Vanquished: Spanish and Nahua Views of the Conquest of Mexico*. New York: Bedford St. Martins, 2000.

Seyssel, Claude de. *La Monarchie de France et deux autres fragments politiques*. Edited and translated by Jacques Poujol. Paris: Librairie d'Argences, 1960.

Vasari, Giorgio. *Lives of the Artists*. Volume I. Translated by George Bull. New York: Penguin, 1965.

Wiesner-Hanks, Merry, ed. *Religious Transformations in the Early Modern World: A Brief History with Documents*. Boston, MA: Bedford St. Martins, 2009.

Secondary sources

Anghie, Antony. *Imperialism, Sovereignty and the Making of International Law*. Cambridge: Cambridge University Press, 2004.

Asante, Molefi Kete, and Ama Mazama, eds. *The Encyclopedia of African Religion*. Los Angeles, CA: Sage, 2009.

Balandier, George. *Daily Life in the Kingdom of Kongo from the Sixteenth Century to the Eighteenth Century*. Translated by Helen Weaver. New York: Pantheon Books, 1968.

Baron, Hans. *The Crisis of the Early Italian Renaissance: Civic Humanism and Republican Liberty in an Age of Classicism and Tyranny*. Princeton, NJ: Princeton University Press, 1966.

Bentley, Jerry, and Herbert Ziegler. *Traditions and Encounters: A Global Perspective on the Past*. 5th edition. New York: McGraw-Hill, 2011.

Bergin, Joseph. *The Politics of Religion in Early Modern France*. New Haven, CT: Yale University Press, 2014.

Berry, Mary Elizabeth. *Hideyoshi*. Cambridge, MA: Harvard University Press, 1982.

Boone, Rebecca Ard. *War, Domination, and the Monarchy of France: Claude de Seyssel and the Language of Politics in the Renaissance*. Leiden: Brill, 2007.

Boone, Rebecca Ard. *Mercurino di Gattinara and the Creation of the Spanish Empire*. London: Pickering & Chatto, 2014.

Braudel, Fernand, *The Mediterranean and the Mediterranean World in the Age of Philip II*. Volume I. Translated by Siân Reynolds. New York: Harper Colophon, 1966.

Breton, Guy. *La Reine Margot avait deux amants: Les amours à la cour du Vert-Galant*. Paris: Editions Omnibus, 2014.

Brigden, Susan. *New Worlds, Lost Worlds*. New York: Penguin, 2000.

Brooks, Timothy. *The Confusions of Pleasure: Commerce and Culture in Ming China*. Berkeley, CA: University of California Press, 1999.

Brooks, Timothy. *Vermeer's Hat: The Seventeenth Century and the Dawn of the Global World*. New York: Bloomsbury Press, 2008.

Buisseret, David. *Henry IV King of France*. Boston, MA: G. Allen & Unwin, 1984.

Bullard, Melissa. *Lorenzo Il Magnifico: Image and Anxiety, Politics and Finance*. Florence: Leo S. Olschki, 1994.

Burland, C. A. *Montezuma.* New York: Putnam, 1973.

Caizhong, Wang, and Shu Aixiang. "Zheng Guifei." In *Notable Women of China: Shang Dynasty to the Early Twentieth Century*, edited by Barbara Bennett Peterson, pp. 303–306. New York: M. E. Sharp, 2000.

Chastel, André *The Sack of Rome, 1527.* Translated by Beth Archer. Princeton, NJ: Princeton University Press, 1983.

Clendennen, Inga. *The Aztecs.* Cambridge: Cambridge University Press, 1991.

Collins, James B. *From Tribes to Nation: The Making of France 500–1799.* Toronto: Wadsworth, 2002.

Collinson, Patrick. "Elizabeth I." In *Dictionary of National Biography*, volume 18, edited by H. C. G. Matthew and Brian Harrison, pp. 95–130. Oxford: Oxford University Press, 2004.

Conrad, Geoffrey, and Arthur Demarist. *Religion and Empire: The Dynamics of Aztec and Inca Expansion.* Cambridge: Cambridge University Press, 1984.

Croutier, Alev Lytle. *Harem: The World Behind the Veil.* New York: Abeville Press, 1989.

Curtain, Philip D. *Cross Cultural Trade in World History.* Cambridge: Cambridge University Press, 1984.

Dardess, John. *Blood and History in China: The Donglin Faction and its Repression, 1620–1627.* Honolulu, HI: University of Hawaii Press, 2002.

Dardess, John. *Ming China 1368–1644: A Concise History of a Resilient Empire.* Lanham, MD: Rowman & Littlefield, 2012.

Dening, Walter. *The Life of Toyotomi Hideyoshi.* New York: AMS Press, 1971.

Dewald, Jonathan. *The European Nobility, 1400–1800.* Cambridge: Cambridge University Press, 1996.

Dewald, Jonathan. ed. *Europe 1450–1789: Encyclopedia of the Early Modern World.* 6 volumes. New York: Thomson Gale, 2004.

Disney, A. R. *A History of Portugal and the Portuguese Empire.* Cambridge: Cambridge University Press, 2007.

Doran, Susan, and Norman Jones, eds. *The Elizabethan World.* London: Routledge, 2011.

Durant, Will. *The Story of Civilization, Vol. 5: The Renaissance. A History of Civilization in Italy from 1304–1576 AD.* New York: Simon & Schuster, 1953.

Ehret, Christopher. *The Civilizations of Africa: A History to 1800.* Charlottesville, VA: University of Virginia Press, 2002.

Elison, George, and Bardwell Smith, eds. *Warlords, Artists, and Commoners: Japan in the Sixteenth Century.* Honolulu, HI: University of Hawaii Press, 1981.

Fang, Chaoying. "Cheng Kui-Fei." In *Dictionary of Ming Biography*, edited by L. Carrington Goodrich and Chaoying Fang, vol. II, pp. 208–211. New York: Columbia University Press, 1976.

Farinha, António Lourenço. *D. Afonso I Rei Do Congo.* Lisbon: Agência-Geral do Ultramar, 1969.

Faroqhi, Suraiya N., and Kate Fleet, eds. *The Cambridge History of Turkey. Vol II: The Ottoman Empire as a World Power 1453–1603.* Cambridge: Cambridge University Press, 2012.

Fletcher, Catherine. *The Black Prince of Florence: The Spectaculary Life and Treacherous World of Alessandro de Medici.* Oxford: Oxford University Press, 2016.

Fromont, Cecil. *The Art of Conversion: Christian Visual Culture in the Kingdom of Kongo.* Chapel Hill, NC: University of North Carolina Press, 2014

Gallo, Max. *Henri IV: Un roi français.* Paris: XO Éditions, 2016.

Getz, Trevor R., ed. *African Voices of the Global Past: 1500 to the Present.* Philadelphia, PA: Westview Press, 2014.

Gouwens, Kenneth. *Remembering the Renaissance: Humanist Narratives on the Sack of Rome.* Leiden: Brill, 1998.

Grafton, Anthony. "Humanism and Political Theory." In *Humanism and the Renaissance*, edited by Zachary S. Schiffman, pp. 157–167. Boston, MA: Houghton Mifflin Company, 2002.

Guy, John, ed. *The Reign of Elizabeth I: Court and Culture in the Last Decade*. Cambridge: Cambridge University Press, 1995.

Haigh, Christopher. *The Reign of Elizabeth I*. London: Macmillan Press, 1984.

Hale, J. R. *Florence and the Medici: The Pattern of Control*. London: Thames & Hudson, 1977.

Hall, John Whitney, ed. *The Cambridge History of Japan, Vol. 4: Early Modern Japan*. Cambridge: Cambridge University Press, 1991.

Hall, John Whitney, Keiji Nagahara, and Kozo Yamamura, eds. *Japan Before Tokugawa: Political Consolidation and Economic Growth, 1500–1650*. Princeton, NJ: Princeton University Press, 1981.

Hare, Christopher, *Charles de Bourbon: High Constable of France "The Great Condottiere"* (New York: John Lane, 1911).

Hassig, Ross. *Aztec Warfare: Imperial Expansion and Political Control*. Norman, OK: University of Oklahoma Press, 1988.

Hassig, Ross. *Time History and Belief in Aztec and Colonial Mexico*. Austin, TX: University of Texas Press, 2013.

Headley, John. "Rhetoric and Reality: Messianic, Humanist, and Civilian Themes in the Imperial Ethos of Gattinara." In *Prophetic Rome in the High Renaissance Period*, edited by Marjorie Reeves, pp. 241–269. Oxford: Clarendon Press, 1992.

Heller, Henry. *Iron and Blood: Civil Wars in Sixteenth-Century France*. Montreal: McGill-Queen's University Press, 1991.

Hibbert, Christopher. *The House of Medici: Its Rise and Fall*. New York: William Morrow & Company, 1975.

Hilton, Anne, *The Kingdom of Kongo*. Oxford: Oxford University Press, 1985.

Hoetzsch, Otto. *The Evolution of Russia*. London: Thames & Hudson, 1966.

Holt, Mack P. *The French Wars of Religion 1562–1629*. Cambridge: Cambridge University Press, 1995.

Hook, Judith. *The Sack of Rome 1527*. New York: Palgrave Macmillan, 2004.

Huang, Ray. *1587 A Year of No Significance: The Ming Dynasty in Decline*. New Haven, CT: Yale University Press, 1981.

Inalcik, Halil. *The Ottoman Empire: The Classical Age 1300–1600*. London: Phoenix Press, 1988.

Kafadar, Cemal. *Between Two Worlds: The Construction of the Ottoman State*. Berkeley, CA: University of California Press, 1995.

King, Margaret. *Venetian Humanism in an Age of Patrician Dominance*. Princeton, NJ: Princeton University Press, 1986.

Kingdon, Robert. *Myths about the St. Bartholomew's Day Massacres 1572–1576*. Cambridge, MA: Harvard University Press, 1988.

Klieman, Kairn A. *"The Pygmies Were Our Compass": Bantu and Batwa in the History of West Central Africa, Early Times to c. 1900*. Portsmouth, NH: Heinemann, 2003.

Knecht, R. J. *The Rise and Fall of Renaissance France*. Oxford: Blackwell Publishers, 2001.

Kunt, Metin, and Christine Woodhead, eds. *Suleyman the Magnificent and His Age: The Ottoman Empire in the Early Modern World*. London: Longman, 1995.

LaGamma, Alisa, *Kongo: Power and Majesty*. New York: Metropolitan Museum of Art, 2015.

Lanyon, Anna. *Malinche's Conquest*. Crow's Nest, NSW: Allen & Unwin, 1999.

Lanza, Rosalba, et al. *I papi da Pietro a Franceso*. Rome: Istituto della Enciclopedia Italiana, 2014.

Lazzarini, Isabella. *Communication and Conflict: Italian Diplomacy in the Early Renaissance, 1350–1520*. Oxford: Oxford University Press, 2015.

León-Portilla, Miguel. *The Aztec Image of Self and Society.* Salt Lake City, UT: University of Utah Press, 1992.

Levack, Brian P. *The Witch Hunt in Early Modern Europe.* 4th edition. London: Routledge, 2016.

Madar, Heather. "Before the Odalisque: Renaissance Representations of Elite Ottoman Women." *Early Modern Women: An Interdisciplinary Journal* 6 (2011), pp. 1–41.

Major, J. Russel. *From Renaissance Monarchy to Absolute Monarchy: French Kings, Nobles, and Estates.* Baltimore, MD: Johns Hopkins University Press, 1994.

Mallett, Michael. *Mercenaries and their Masters: Warfare in Renaissance Italy.* Totowa, NJ: Rowman & Littlefield, 1974.

Martines, Lauro. *April Blood: Florence and the Plot against the Medici.* Oxford: Oxford University Press, 2003.

Matsumori, Natsuko. "The School of Salamanca in the Affair of the Indies: Toward an Alternative Theory of the Modern State." *International Relations—Comparative Cultural Studies* 10(1) (2011), pp. 27–48.

Mattingly, Garrett. *Renaissance Diplomacy.* Baltimore, MD: Penguin, 1955.

Mattingly, Garrett. *The Armada.* Boston, MA: Houghton Mifflin, 1959.

McEwan, Colin, and Leonardo López Luján, eds. *Moctezuma Aztec Ruler.* London: British Museum Press, 2009.

McMahon, Keith. "The Potent Eunuch: The Story of Wei Zhongxian." *Journal of Chinese Literature and Culture* 1(1–2) (2014), pp. 1–28.

McMahon, Keith. *Celestial Women: Imperial Wives and Concubines in China from Song to Qing.* Lanham, MD: Rowman & Littlefield, 2016.

Medrano, Ethelia Ruiz. *Mexico's Indigenous Communities, Their Lands and Histories 1500–2010.* Boulder, CO: University Press of Colorado, 2010.

Mortimer, Ian. *A Time Traveler's Guide to Elizabethan England.* New York: Penguin, 2014.

Mote, Frederick W., and Denis Twitchett, eds. *Cambridge History of China, Vols VII and VIII: The Ming Dynasty 1368–1644, Parts I and II.* Cambridge: Cambridge University Press, 1988, 1998.

Mousnier, Roland. *The Assassination of Henry IV: The Tyrannicide Problem and the Consolidation of the French Absolute Monarchy in the Early Seventeenth Century.* New York: Charles Scribner's Sons, 1973.

Murdoch, James, and Isoh Yamagata. *A History of Japan, Vol. II: During the Century of Early Foreign Intercourse 1542–1651.* Kobe, Japan: Office of the "Chronicle," 1903.

Naohiro, Asao. "The Sixteenth-Century Unification." In *The Cambridge History of Japan, Vol. 4: Early Modern Japan*, edited by John Whitney Hall, translated by Bernard Susser, pp. 40–95. Cambridge: Cambridge University Press, 1991.

Neale, J. E. *The Age of Catherine de Medici.* London: Jonathan Cape, 1943.

Neuschel, Kristen. *Word of Honor: Interpreting Noble Culture in Sixteenth Century France.* Ithaca, NY: Cornell University Press, 1989.

Northrup, David. *Africa's Discovery of Europe 1450–1850.* Oxford: Oxford University Press, 2014.

Pagden, Anthony. *Lords of All the World: Ideologies of Empire in Spain, Britain and France c. 1500–c. 1800.* New Haven, CT: Yale University Press, 1995.

Parker, Geoffrey. *The Military Revolution: Military Innovation and the Rise of the West 1500–1800.* Cambridge: Cambridge University Press, 1988.

Parry, J. H. *The Age of Reconaissance.* New York: Mentor Books, 1963.

Pastor, Ludwig. *A History of the Popes from the Close of the Middle Ages.* Translated by Ralph Kerr. London: Kegan Paul, Trench, Trübner & Co., 1910.

Pierce, Leslie. *The Imperial Harem: Women and Sovereignty in the Ottoman Empire.* Oxford: Oxford University Press, 1993.

Pirenne, Henri. *Early Democracies in the Low Countries: Urban Society and Political Conflict in the Middle Ages and the Renaissance.* New York: W. W. Norton, 1963.

Pitts, Vincent J. *Henri IV of France. His Reign and Age.* Baltimore, MD: Johns Hopkins University Press, 2009.

Reeves, Marjorie. *The Influence of Prophecy in the Later Middle Ages: A Study in Joachimism.* Notre Dame, IN: University of Notre Dame Press, 1969.

Riess, Sheryl, and Kenneth Gouwens, eds. *The Pontificate of Clement VII: History, Politics, Culture.* London: Routledge, 2005.

Ringrose, David R. *Expansion and Global Interaction, 1200–1700.* New York: Longman, 2001.

Romero, Rolando, and Amanda Nolacea Harris. *Feminism, Nation, and Myth: La Malinche.* Houston, TX: Arte Público Press, 2005.

Ruggles, D. Fairchild. *Women, Patronage, and Self-Representation in Islamic Societies.* New York: SUNY Press, 2000.

Russell, P. E. *Portugal, Spain and the African Atlantic, 1343–1490: Chivalry and Crusade from John of Gaunt to Henry the Navigator* . Brookfield, VT: Variorum 1995.

Salmon, J. H. M. *Society in Crisis: France in the Sixteenth Century.* London: Routledge, 1979.

Salmon, J. H. M. "Sovereignty, Theory of." In *Europe 1450–1789: Encyclopedia of the Early Modern World*, edited by Jonathan Dewald, pp. 447–450. New York: Thompson Gale, 2004.

Sansom, George. *A History of Japan 1334–1615.* Stanford, CA: Stanford University Press, 1961.

Schalk, Ellery. *From Valor to Pedigree: Ideas of Nobility in France in the Sixteenth and Seventeenth Centuries.* Princeton, NJ: Princeton University Press, 1986.

Schama, Simon. *A History of Britain: At the Edge of the World? 3000 BC–AD 1603.* New York: Hyperion, 2000.

Schevil, Ferdinand. *The Medici.* New York: Harper, 1949.

Schlesinger, Roger. *In the Wake of Columbus: The Impact of the New World on Europe, 1492–1650.* Wheeling, IL: Harlan Davidson, 1996, 2007.

Simonetta, Marcello. *The Montefeltro Conspiracy.* New York: Doubleday, 2008.

Skinner, Quentin. *The Foundations of Modern Political Thought, Vol I: The Renaissance.* Cambridge, Cambridge University Press, 1978.

Smith, Mark M., ed. *Stono: Documenting and Interpreting a Southern Slave Revolt.* Columbia, SC: University of South Carolina Press, 2005.

Soll, Jacob. *Publishing the Prince.* Ann Arbor, MI: University of Michigan Press, 1995.

Stone, Lawrence. *The Causes of the English Revolution 1529–1642.* New York: Harper Torchbooks, 1972.

Thomas, Hugh. *Conquest. Montezuma, Cortés, and the fall of Old Mexico.* New York: Simon & Schuster, 1993.

Thornton, John. "Early Kongo-Portuguese Relations: A New Interpretation." *History in Africa* 8 (1981), pp. 183–204.

Thornton, John. *The Kingdom of Kongo: Civil War and Transition, 1641–1718.* Madison, WI: University of Wisconsin Press, 1983.

Thornton, John. *Africa and Africans in the Making of the Atlantic World, 1400–1800.* Cambridge: Cambridge University Press, 1998.

Thornton, John. *The Kongolese Saint Anthony: Dona Beatriz Kimpa Vita and the Antonian Movement, 1684–1706.* Cambridge: Cambridge University Press, 1998, 2009.

Thornton, John. "Afro-Christian Syncretism in the Kingdom of Kongo." *Journal of African History*, 54 (2013), pp. 53–77.

Totman, Conrad. *Early Modern Japan*. Berkeley, CA: University of California Press, 1993.

Turnbull, Stephen. *Toyotomi Hideyoshi: Leadership, Strategy, Conflict*. Oxford: Osprey, 2010.

Vries, Jan de. *The Economy of Europe in an Age of Crisis, 1600–1750*. Cambridge: Cambridge University Press, 1989.

Wagner, John A. *Historical Dictionary of the Elizabethan World: Britain, Ireland, Europe, and America*. Chicago, IL: Fitzroy Dearborn Publishers, 1999.

Wagner, John A., and Susan Walters Schmid. *Encyclopedia of Tudor England*. 3 vols. Santa Barbara, CA: ABC-CLIO, 2012.

Walthall, Anne, ed. *Servants of the Dynasty: Palace Women in World History*. Berkeley, CA: University of California Press, 2008.

Warner, Jayne L., ed. *Rapture and Revolution: Essays on Turkish Literature by Talat S. Halman*. Syracuse, NY: Syracuse University Press, 2007.

Wernham, R. B. *Before the Armada: The Emergence of the English Nation, 1485–1588*. New York: Norton, 1966.

Wiesner-Hanks, Merry E., ed. *Religious Transformations in the Early Modern World: A Brief History with Documents*. Boston, MA: Bedford St. Martins, 2009.

Yanqing, Lin. "Zheng Consort of the Wanli Emperor Shenzon of Ming." In *Biographical Dictionary of Chinese Women, Vol. II: From Tang to Ming 618–1644*, edited by Lily Xiao Hong and Sue Wiles, pp. 618–619. London: Routledge, 2015.

Yermolenko, Galina. *Roxolana in European Literature, History and Culture*. London: Routledge, 2010.

Yoshikawa, Eiji. *Taiko: An Epic Novel of War and Glory in Feudal Japan*. Tokyo: Kodansha International, 1992.

Zilfi, Madeline. *Women and Slavery in the Late Ottoman Empire: The Design of Difference*. Cambridge: Cambridge University Press, 2010.

Zurndorfer, Harriet. "Wanli China versus Hideyoshi's Japan: Rethinking China's Involvement in the Imjin Waeran." In *The East Asian War 1592–1598: International Relations, Violence, and Memory*, edited by James B. Lewis, pp. 197–235. London: Routledge, 2014.

INDEX